WRITING IN THE DISCIPLINES: BUILDING SUPPORTIVE CULTURES FOR STUDENT WRITING IN UK HIGHER EDUCATION

EDITED BY

LISA CLUGHEN
Nottingham Trent University, UK

CHRISTINE HARDY
Nottingham Trent University, UK

United Kingdom – North America – Japan
India – Malaysia – China

Emerald Group Publishing Limited
Howard House, Wagon Lane, Bingley BD16 1WA, UK

First edition 2012

British Library Cataloguing in Publication Data
A catalogue record for this book is available from the British Library

ISBN: 978-1-78052-546-4

ISOQAR certified
Management Systems,
awarded to Emerald for
adherence to Quality
and Environmental
standards ISO 9001:2008
and 14001:2004,
respectively

Certificate Number 1985
ISO 9001
ISO 14001

INVESTOR IN PEOPLE

WRITING IN THE DISCIPLINES: BUILDING SUPPORTIVE CULTURES FOR STUDENT WRITING IN UK HIGHER EDUCATION

Acknowledgements

The editors would like to acknowledge and thank the following for their considerable support, encouragement and patience in the preparation of this book.

All of the book's authors, who offered great support and editing suggestions throughout; Frank Webb; Margaret and David Clughen; Mary Deane; Lisa Ganobscik-Williams; David Jeckells; Linda Taylor; Alan Tuckman; Liz Morrish and all of the students who participated in the research or who commented on different sections.

Contents

Preface

Academic Writing is a growing field for teaching and research in the United Kingdom and internationally. While 'writing centers', 'writing programs' and 'Composition and Rhetoric' scholarship have been a fundamental part of US higher education for many decades, universities in the United Kingdom, Europe and around the world have begun more recently to consider that writing in the academy needs to be taught explicitly. With higher education agendas focusing increasingly on the student experience, university managers, academics and support staff are becoming interested in writing development and are seeking to enhance students' growth as scholarly writers by developing institutional strategies to promote the teaching and learning of writing.

Writing in the Disciplines: Building Supportive Cultures for Student Writing in UK Higher Education brings a fresh perspective to existing debates on Academic Writing research and pedagogy. The book argues that writing is a sociocultural practice, and provides examples of different ways in which lecturers in the disciplines and writing support practitioners are responding to this idea. What is particularly stimulating about the collection is that it focuses on students, and in doing so prompts subject academics and those working in the field of writing development to recognise the full extent to which student-writers are 'embodied' individuals who bring their own histories, preferences, strengths, anxieties and differing levels of experience to their writing.

The book also demonstrates how the field of Academic Writing is growing and maturing. In the general introduction and chapters that follow, Lisa Clughen, Christine Hardy and colleagues make use of current historiographical, corpus-based and Academic Literacies writing scholarship, but they also critique and challenge some of the central tenets of established UK writing theory. In addition, they offer new pedagogical theories and models, including an emphasis on the importance of socialization in student writing, a 'dialogic lecture analysis' technique for teaching writing as a social practice, a 'guided discovery' approach to teaching writing conventions and a 'social writing' model. Drawing on sources such as Kafka and Merleau-Ponty to situate student-writers as sociocultural beings, and on discussions of new technologies and the teaching of writing, alternative writing genres, and the application to student writing of insights gained from working with academics on their scholarly writing, the book demonstrates how academics can learn to teach relevant writing genres explicitly and how writing can become a process that students can learn to control and even enjoy.

Writing in the Disciplines: Building Supportive Cultures for Student Writing in UK Higher Education looks at the teaching of disciplinary writing conventions as well as at how writing genres, exercises and processes developed in specific disciplinary contexts often can be used effectively with student-writers in other disciplines. The book underscores the student-focused nature of writing research, and provides an opportunity for writing teachers and scholars to showcase the practical pedagogies they employ in their own work with students and to theorise these pedagogies to enable a deeper understanding of writing development work.

Lisa Ganobcsik-Williams
Centre for Academic Writing,
Coventry University, UK

Introduction

> I was born from writing; before that there was only a reflection in a mirror. ... By writing, I existed, ... but I existed only to write and if I said: me — that meant the me who wrote.
>
> (Sartre, 1964, p. 97)

What does writing mean to you? It is likely that your answer ranges over a variety of areas that may include the functional (it means I can do my job), the relational (it means I can keep in contact with my friends) and the profoundly personal, as in the quotation from Sartre above (it means I exist). You may have responded in emotional terms 'pain!', 'pleasure!', 'power!'. It might even be that you have not given this question much thought.

If you are studying at university, however, writing is likely to be at the forefront of your mind as you prepare for assignments or examinations. You may also be anxious about your writing, wondering whether it is at the right level, whether it follows the conventions of your discipline or even whether it meets the expectations of your tutor. All of these are frequent concerns for many students within UK Higher Education (HE).

This book addresses such concerns by examining some of the writing cultures that students encounter during the course of their education and offering practical activities to support them with their writing. It is intended for all involved in designing and delivering academic programmes within HE and is primarily aimed at mainstream academic and professional services staff. Wider audiences, such as UK HE policymakers, the National Union of Students and teachers working with those pupils who intend to go to university might also find this book useful as it offers contextualised, practical approaches to aid students with transition in writing from pre-university educational establishments to HE.

Our aim, then, is to offer insights into issues surrounding academic writing encountered both by UK university students and those supporting them. We do not claim universality here and would note that different universities and individuals frame writing and its support in different ways. We are concentrating on the United Kingdom in order to give examples of very specific contexts which frame our thinking about writing and writing support, but this does not mean that the issues presented are purely local concerns. Indeed, much of the research drawn on in the book is from international literacy scholarship and, as we have derived great inspiration from it as we have reflected on our own contexts and practices, we also hope our reflections might be useful to people across the globe whose aim is to support writing.

The introduction takes an overview of the current debates around literacy (which we term reading and writing) and how it is developed within UK universities. It begins with an exploration of the importance of literacy for the individual and continues this theme with reference to academic writing within HE. The ways in which different perspectives of literacy impact on the approaches taken to writing support are discussed and critiqued in the subsequent section which culminates in an exploration of embedding writing in the disciplines. Finally, there is a description of the aims and organisation of the book.

In general, the book takes the perspective that academic writing is a social and cultural act, something which is both culturally located and which, as an act of knowledge production, is socially constructed. Using insights derived from both research and experience, the contributors examine and explore the creation of different writing cultures. The intention is to enable academic tutors to have a greater understanding of different cultures of writing in order that they practise culturally aware approaches to writing development. Alongside the unravelling of the specificities of a disciplinary writing culture, we also believe that an essential aspect of writing development is an awareness of the person who writes, the student-writers themselves, and so we argue for approaches that seek to nurture student-writers' confidence and self-belief in order that they might own, identify with and be proud of their writing. This book, then, is not just about writing practices, but also about the individuals who engage with them: it is therefore about being as much as it is about the practicalities of writing.

THE ROLE AND IMPORTANCE OF LITERACY AND ACADEMIC WRITING FOR THE INDIVIDUAL

The importance of writing in an individual's life is not to be underestimated. Indeed, it has been argued, in no uncertain terms, that 'literacy changes lives' (Dugdale & Clark, 2008). The importance ascribed to literacy is, of course, ideologically framed and changes in accordance with who is discussing it, their particular interests in literacy and the sociohistorical conditions in which it is discussed (Rassool, 2002, p. 37). The benefits derived from literacy are spoken about variously with different interest groups emphasising different outcomes, from its contribution to individual development and empowerment, social development and/or transformation, economic development and/or advantage, to the furtherance of moral values, democratic or human rights (see Rassool, 2002, pp. 19–39). Rassool's key claim here is that definitions and meanings of literacy are shaped by the material and political conditions in which they are produced and, as we shall see later in this introduction, an awareness of such sociopolitical determinants is crucial to an understanding of the importance and framings given to academic writing within the institutional context of the academy of HE in the United Kingdom.

As they emphasise the benefits of literacy, commentators also count the social costs if literacy is not seen as a priority area by national policymakers. The National Literacy Trust, for example, argues that literacy shapes the most important aspects of human life, including economic well-being, aspirations, family life, health (physical and mental) and civic and cultural engagement (Dugdale & Clark, 2008). Given its reach, it argues, the consequences of low levels of literacy can be disastrous for both the individual and for society: 'low literacy levels are a barrier to social justice. They produce social, economic and cultural exclusion that scars communities and undermines social cohesion' (Dugdale & Clark, 2008, p. 4).

Rather than literacy in general, the focus of this book is on academic writing in UK universities. In this regard, however, the aforementioned claims for the role and importance of literacy in general certainly resonate. The effects of positive or negative relationships with literacy on students' lives are inestimable. Obviously, their abilities to read and write appropriately at university level constitute success or failure in their degrees. Thus, at the most basic level, literacy has the potential to change students' relationships with the academy and so its supported development whilst at university can be truly life changing for them at this particular stage in their lives. Student participation in university, in other words, their ability to enter into academic conversations with their social groupings, is largely mediated by their relationships with their reading and writing, given that the written word is the dominant mode of communication in all university subjects. As people who have for many years supported students as they strive to develop their writing in HE, we are starkly aware of the ways in which the development of writing is entwined with personal issues. These include student engagement and participation or alienation and withdrawal (Bowstead, 2009; Haggis, 2006; Leathwood & O'Connell, 2003;

Mann, 2001), with feelings of belonging to or exclusion from communities of practice (Read, Archer, & Leathwood, 2003, p. 271), with health issues, especially the poor mental health that can issue from distressful relationships with one's reading and writing (Bowstead, 2009) and with the building of self-esteem and personal aspirations or the crushing of one's self-belief and personal efficacy (see also Ahmad & McMahon, 2006, pp. 5–6; Bowstead, 2009; Mann, 2001). Building supportive environments for writing, we argue, is fundamental if we are to work towards the positive, enriching student experience that is the goal of all UK universities.

THE CONTEXT OF ACADEMIC WRITING IN UK HIGHER EDUCATION

The fluctuating attention given to writing support and the approaches taken towards it in UK universities come in response to the contexts in which they are situated (Ivanic & Lea, 2006). In recent years, calls to teach writing have been heard everywhere both without and within UK universities. The former Labour government's education policy following Dearing (NCIHE, 1997) situated literacy development high on the agenda and university staff have demonstrated a high level of support for writing instruction (Ganobcsik-Williams, 2006, p. xxii). The urgency to deal head-on with writing development will, perhaps, be exacerbated in response to the educational reform programme recently embarked on by the current government in the United Kingdom. Since its inception in 2010, the government has further entrenched the market values within HE that have been evident since the conservative government of Margaret Thatcher (Pennell & West, 2005, p. 128). Key to its strategy to marketise HE is the policy to increase student fees to a maximum of £9000 proposed by the Browne review of funding in HE (2010b). Promoting the 'student as consumer' model (Maringe, 2010), the review further encourages a commodified approach to a university education and an increase in student expectations and demands as costs rise, suggesting that 'HEIs must persuade students that they should "pay more" in order to "get more"' (Department for Business, Innovation and Skills, 2010b, p. 4).

Debates rage over the effects of the government's educational reforms with many commentators, both students and staff, forecasting cataclysmic consequences for HE such as irreconcilable tensions between students and staff (Beer, 2011) or the potential destruction of some university areas entirely — Sir Andrew Motion, for example, talks about 'the Bonfire of the

Humanities' (2011). Although at the time of writing we cannot predict how students will respond to this latest rise in fees, one potential outcome of an increasing, more strident adoption of a consumer mentality towards their university studies, and one that is mobilised by the rhetoric of the Browne review (2010b), is an appreciation of a university degree in terms of its 'value for money'. It is likely, we suggest, that student-consumers will largely define this through their results (the end product) and, especially if the results are not of the value they expected, the support they have received to succeed in their studies. Success with writing will therefore be of central concern for students who adopt a consumer approach towards education as, in many subjects across the university, it is largely the feedback they receive on their writing in the form of the end result that sets a context for student satisfaction with their studies.

Some commentators forecast an unprecedented hike in student demands as a direct consequence of the increase in student fees. The sociologist David Beer (2011), for example, warns of 'expectation inflation' and urges universities to put structures in place to respond to this where possible:

> All this will create new tensions and challenges that we must anticipate and plan for. We are about to see an escalation in student expectation ramped up to a magnitude that is almost impossible to imagine or comprehend, a magnitude far beyond that which might already have created challenges for us to resolve.

The 'unbearable demands' a market orientation had already placed on HE (Molesworth, Nixon, & Scullion, 2009, pp. 278–279) may only increase.

We do not wish to homogenise the space of the school or the university and would emphasise that individuals respond to the same social structures in very different ways — not all students will adopt the 'student as consumer' identity, for instance. If we do follow the logic of the Browne review (2010b), however, and anticipate that student-consumers will expect more as they pay more, then foregrounding writing support within university policy-making should be an essential part of a university's plans to meet consumer demands. It is anticipated that future students will be comparing their previous educational experiences with their university experiences. Taking into account that a great deal of writing support is provided for students at school, as Hardy and Boulton's chapter in this book describes, it is likely that this 'escalation in student expectation' will include more personalised and explicit support for writing, as it is configured at school.

The foregoing is not to condone, but to set the context for the urgency to bring academic writing support to the forefront of decision-making in HE structures. We would argue that we have to find ways of being both critical of the context in which HE institutions must operate and of working within it. For instance, it may be possible to foreground writing support in HE in response to market drivers and still heed critical comments about the pedagogic constraints wrought by marketisation (Molesworth et al., 2009, p. 278). Molesworth, Nixon and Scullion argue, for instance, that perceiving education as a product where students seek to "*have* a degree" rather than "*be* learners" (2009, p. 278) works against university goals to promote deep learning, critical thinking and self-transformation. Mobilising Erich Fromm's distinction between the 'having mode of living' and 'the being mode', they argue against seeing education as a possession, something you are 'given', and for the idea that it is an experience, a place where 'beings' can develop (Molesworth et al., 2009, pp. 279–280). The 'having' mode, they argue, impoverishes the university experience, and we would add that it is not conducive to active, self-reliant employees post university either:

> A desire to *have* reduces the individual's experience to a desire for something external — a commodity. In doing so, self-knowledge and a satisfaction in one's own practice is disallowed. The *being* mode foregrounds understanding the self and the practice of skills may be hard gained (see Fromm, 1993). It is educationally pertinent that a *having* mode indulges the belief that gain may comes (sic) without endeavour, "people are convinced that everything, even the most difficult tasks, should be mastered without or with only little effort" (Fromm, 1993, p. 25). Yet such an approach in education (and Fromm explicitly uses education as an example) results in *having* a qualification without the satisfaction derived from mastering skills or the associated potential for personal change.

This offers a salutary note when applied to academic writing. We argue that it would mean viewing with caution 'skills' approaches to writing if they progress in such a way that academic writing is disbanded and taught only in terms of 'the discrete parts that make up an essay'. Successful academic writing is a labour, a process of discovery and potential transformation as the authors move towards greater clarity over their own position on their subject. It demands that the author's own voice comes through her/his script, and it is usually obvious in the writing if student-writers just repeat ideas that have been given to them, rather than interrogate and articulate ideas for their own purposes. Instead, of 'skills' sessions that are often appended to programmes, we might offer spaces where students can go through and explore the experience of writing. Such spaces would offer them regular opportunities to enter into respectful, supportive and compassionate dialogues with others about their writing so it becomes meaningful and unique to them, and so that they can, through their interactions with others, realise that their writing has distinctive value rather than simply being a standardised product that is 'acquired'.

Yet, however phrased, whether as a part of good pedagogic practice, as an ethical, political or philosophical drive to include students into the life-changing experience that is university study, or as an appropriate anticipatory response to the rise in student fees and other moves to commercialise HE, we argue that writing support needs to be foregrounded by all involved — by university policymakers and managers, subject tutors and support staff. It ought to be seen as a prime motor of a successful university experience, rather than as a mere adjunct. Writing is not a separate area of concern, an appendage to the current agendas of HE decision makers — it is at the core of discussions about widening participation, student transitions to and within the different levels in university, the student experience, retention, employability, graduateness, global citizenship and lifelong learning (to name but a few areas of current concern). The importance of providing supportive environments for writing thus cuts through the different ideological conceptions of writing we describe above.

PERSPECTIVES ON AND APPROACHES TO WRITING SUPPORT IN UK HE

Writing support is usually offered in different arenas in UK universities. There may be specialist services, usually centrally located, that focus on support for students with special needs such as dyslexia or for students whose first language is not English. Some universities provide additional writing support aimed at all students and this is either offered in centrally located units, services within the faculties and/or embedded within the subject areas themselves. Some may have a combination of all of these. In this book, when talking about writing support, we are referring to the support that is offered across the board to all students, as opposed to those students with particular needs.

As with the definitions of what it means to be literate, the forms writing support might take are also subject to intense debate and change according to the optic through which language (Lillis, 2006, p. 31) and literacy itself is viewed (Rassool, 2002, p. 27). Whether consciously theorised or not, writing support is always underpinned by an idea of the nature of literacy itself, and when constructing one's strategies for it, the potential benefits and limits of one's general concepts of literacy should be taken into account. How we should support writing is not 'common sense', and it is important that those in HE who are not aware of or involved in the long-standing debates in writing support scholarship become familiar with the established critiques of conceptions of writing and writing support within global literacy scholarship. Academic writing pedagogy is a contested area (Lea & Street, 1998; Street, 2003, pp. 77–78) — the different meanings ascribed to it should be recognised as the products of different ideologies, and each framing risks limiting rather than opening up academic writing to the wider range of possibilities that can be afforded to the student.

These different perspectives on and approaches to writing development in UK HE have been well summarised in literacy scholarship (Dysthe, 2001; Ivanic, 2006; Ivanic & Lea, 2006; Lea & Street, 1998; Lillis, 2006, pp. 31–32) and fall largely into two main categories. Firstly, literacy is often conceived of as 'autonomous', in other words, as a technical skill that can be learned in a decontextualised fashion and transferred to other contexts, and, secondly, as a social practice (see Street, 1984), in other words, as never neutral, but inherently defined by its social context and imbued with the dynamic of the social (such as its specific ways of thinking, its power relations, its problems with communication). Thus, there may indeed be common principles to academic writing (as autonomous perspectives highlight), for example that writing in the academy is either the presentation of, or a route to critical thought, but as sociocultural theorists of academic writing point out (Barton & Hamilton, 1998; Clark & Ivanic, 1997; Street, 1984), there are also contextual issues that govern the act of academic writing. Alongside (and for some scholars, rather than) teaching students to 'write academically', then, we need to realise the limits of the generalist approach to writing and teach them to write, for example as literary theorists, lawyers or biologists. If we accept the notion that writing is a sociocultural practice, we also need to recognise that social communication as one person enters into social relationships with another is replete with interpersonal and personal concerns.

Models of literacy, as Rassool says (2002, p. 27), do not instantiate automatic, concrete writing pedagogies. As we shall see in this book, how one responds to the notions of writing as a skill or social practice is a matter of active interpretation. Perspectives on writing that might be loosely grouped under the term 'sociocultural' will have different epistemological approaches to those that view literacy as 'autonomous'. Thus, tutors will variously emphasise different features in the pedagogies they construct (see Lillis, 2006, p. 31). A consideration of the social aspects of writing might therefore generate pedagogies that aim to socialise students into academic writing cultures, and writing in the disciplines (WiD) methodologies are good examples of this (see below). Alternatively, they might stimulate challenges to the top-down nature of socialisation approaches and produce pedagogies that seek to construct entirely different writing cultures, originating from the starting point of the student-writers themselves and arguing that they should also shape, rather than fit into fixed writing cultures. Theorists who adopt academic literacies perspectives on the sociocultural nature of writing are examples of this type of critical approach to writing cultures (see below).

The beauty of writing support, then, is its openness to interpretation. There are, however, some recognised approaches to writing support in UK HE and these, whilst they are rather crude and by no means exhaustive, are summarised in Table 1.

It is important to recognise that the above approaches are not necessarily mutually exclusive or in opposition to each other (Lea & Street, 1998, p. 158). For example, it is not inconsistent with an academic literacies approach to discuss general rules for sentence construction or paragraphing. As we have mentioned above, what is essential to discussions over how we might construct genuinely supportive environments for writing is an awareness of the limitations and restrictions of each approach, so we shall now allude briefly to some of the key critiques of each.

Separating writing from the disciplines, as the autonomous approach does, is problematic as it ignores the nature of writing as an act of knowledge construction (Wingate, 2006, p. 458). As an exercise in thought, writing must, to be fully fit for purpose, be undertaken in relation to the construction of knowledge and ways of presenting it within a specific writing domain. For example, students might know how to construct a paragraph, but if they have no appropriate content with which to populate their paragraphs, this knowledge is inert. Constructing writing support in response to the skills paradigm, then, gives little, if any, attention to how or indeed whether what can be said generally about writing can be inflected locally or how writing is related to thinking. Further, such segregationist approaches can also skew students' attitudes to writing itself so that it is seen as unimportant, or at least as peripheral rather than fundamental to their academic practices (Wingate, 2006). If universities wish to promote the view that writing is important to personal and social development, then this situation is untenable. Finally, skills approaches to writing are not always helpful to students in that they find it difficult to transfer the knowledge they gain, for example about critical analysis, to their own particular writing needs.

Table 1. Perspectives on literacy and approaches to writing support.

Perspective on literacy	Definition	Approaches to writing support
Literacy as autonomous (see Street, 1984)	Literacy is a discrete, technical skill which, once learned, can be transferred to other contexts. Literacy as a 'neutral technology that can be detached from specific social contexts' (Street, 1984, p. 1).	'The skills approach'. This is largely a text-based approach to writing development where typical features of written text are taught through a series of writing exercises. This normally occurs outside the curriculum and is often provided by centralised writing support services and/or with recourse to online writing materials.
Sociocultural Perspectives (SCP) on Literacy:	Literacy is fundamentally social. It is defined by and experienced within the different social contexts in which it is used.	
SCP 1: Functional	Literacy is fundamental for social development. 'One who can engage in all those activities in which literacy is required for the effective functioning of his or her group and community and also for enabling him or her to continue to use reading, writing, and calculation for his or her own and the community's development' (UNESCO, 2004, p. 12)	Activities are geared towards the skills and knowledges required to function in a particular social setting such as the workplace. In UK universities, this may be embraced through an emphasis on 'real world' writing tasks.
SCP 2: Writing Across the Curriculum (WAC)	WAC scholars argue for the use of writing for cognitive development as well as communication. It offers a selection of tools to develop writing that can be applied to any course (see Bean, 2001; WAC Clearinghouse, 1997–2012). 'A simple definition of WAC is that students use written language to develop and communicate knowledge in every discipline and across disciplines' (Young, 2011, p. 3).	As WAC stresses the way in which writing can assist thinking, it argues for the increased use of writing within the classroom. Techniques from WAC approaches in the US, especially writing-to-learn and peer review, have also influenced writing support practitioners, but, unlike the US, there are no fully-fledged WAC programmes as yet in the UK.

Table 1. (*Continued*)

Perspective on literacy	Definition	Approaches to writing support
SCP3: Writing in the Disciplines (WiD)	This is a branch of WAC that encourages writing competence in an epistemological, subject-related way (see Deane & O'Neill, 2011, pp. 3–7). It focuses on 'how academic writing shapes and is determined by disciplinary knowledge, and on helping students come to terms with disciplinary writing conventions' (Deane & O'Neill, 2011, p. 7).	British literacy development has been influenced by WiD approaches in the US as calls to embed writing within a disciplinary context are almost standard amongst literacy scholars and practitioners. WiD activities ask students to do writing that will engage them with their course and/or build up to the writing they will have to do for it. Examples are: writing on a specific theory learned; describing the context of a topic; writing out the process of an experiment.
Academic literacies	'The ways in which people address reading and writing are themselves rooted in conceptions of knowledge, identity and being. It is also always embedded in social practices, such as those of a particular job market or a particular educational context and the effects of learning that particular literacy will be dependent on those particular contexts. ... engaging with literacy is always a social act even from the outset' (Street, 2003, pp. 77–78)	This constitutes a dynamic response to the social nature of writing and considers the 'hidden features' of writing (Street, 2009) such as matters of epistemology, power and authority, identity and the self in writing. It seeks to open up writing cultures for wider participation. This approach is not fully embedded into HE curricula.

Viewing literacy as an autonomous entity does not, then, capture its full complexity. For one thing, it overlooks the sociocultural context in which literacy develops. Scholars who have emphasised the relationship between text and context largely operate within two main frameworks: the first stems from systemic functional linguistics (SFL) and the second from post-structuralist cultural and social theory (Christie & Misson, 2002, p. 54). Both approaches focus on the workings of the text. The first emphasises the functional nature of the text and the choice of language to make meaning in different contexts, and the second focuses on the ideological workings of texts and considers how they seek to reproduce and naturalise features of the ideological context.

SFL approaches to literacy, developed by writers such as Halliday, Hasan, Martin and Matthiesson (see Christie & Misson, 2002, p. 54), teach how in different contexts, different genres of writing will be prominent (e.g. shopping lists might be regular features in the home, essays in education and reports at work) and consider how people will make different language choices to respond to such different purposes. To 'function in society', it is important that a writer realises that language is used in different ways for different purposes and is conversant with the specific features and language choices used in different genres. Such language awareness will allow her/him to succeed in different contexts and to move freely from one context to another.

Following the publication of the 2011 UK white paper *Higher Education: Students at the Heart of the System* (June 2011) which issued from other reports such as 2010 *Skills for Jobs: Today and Tomorrow* (2010) and *Skills for Sustainable Growth* (2010a), this focus on the purposive, functional nature of literacy is on the ascendancy in current debates on literacy in HE. These firmly construct the discourse on skills around economic advancement, with skills improvement being linked to employment and earnings, economic growth and the ability to compete globally. The implication is clear: one of the functions of HE is preparation for the world of work (2011, p. 4), with students developing enterprise skills to meet the needs of employers and engaging in more university–industry collaborations, incorporating industrial involvement with the development of the curriculum.

Of course the ways in which universities address this vary and we do not suggest that there is a uniform response to the call to address employability in HE. Yet a professionalised framing of literacy is in many cases impacting on university curricula and staff are increasingly encouraged to embed 'real world' tasks to ensure that students are prepared for the workplace. This emphasis on working towards graduate jobs is useful in many respects, as writing tasks become real for the students and the importance of writing development becomes more immediate as the benefits of taking writing seriously become more obvious to them. However, there are limitations if this ethos becomes the guiding function, rather than one of many, of university writing cultures. Only using and teaching writing for limited functional purposes (e.g. to write a business report) risks systematising and limiting writing if this approach is applied in such a way that students are only invited to follow regimented patterns to fit into a specific professional culture, and are taught only one or two genres, rather than many. Some writing scholars critique the functional approach on the basis that it represents a minimal approach to literacy that ignores the ways in which writing can be used for other purposes, such as the writer's own, as a 'functionally literate person can at best *cope* with their world. (...) It is, then, a negative state – avoiding failure to cope – rather than any optimal achievement, or a *positive* achievement of human capacities. It is, moreover, passive functional literacy equips the person to respond to outside demands and standards, to understand and follow' (Lankshear & Lawler, 1987, p. 64).

Whilst we are mindful of the above and other caveats over socialisation approaches (Lillis, 2006, p. 32), we believe that recognising and being able to adapt to the contextual nature of writing is important for students to succeed in HE. We therefore draw on insights from scholars, for example of genre-based literacy to offer ways in which they might do this (see, e.g. Lisa Clughen & Matt Connell, Chapter 6). A recurring theme throughout this book is that, to support writing effectively, it is important to consider how context shapes writing and how disciplines configure writing in different ways. In doing so, however, we also follow the work of other sociocultural theorists who take the sociocultural awareness of the contingency of writing (and reading) into a critical and political direction and argue for it on the basis that they are 'complex human activities, inseparable from both people and the places involved' (Barton & Hamilton, 1998, p. xii). Writing, as it is constructed and used by different people in different places for very different purposes, is far from innocent or neutral, but is already saturated with cultural difference.

This political turn for sociocultural theorists of literacy (Clark & Ivanic, 1997; Lillis, 2003; Street, 1984) has been influenced by the entrance into debates of critiques from social and cultural theorists such as Freire, Geertz, Foucault, Bhaktin and Levi-Strauss. Such critics examine the political, power-laden negotiations that occur during the complex human activity of writing (as Barton and Hamilton put it). Bringing to the fore what Street (2009) calls the 'hidden features of writing', critics of socialisation models of writing pedagogy argue that such models assume the neutrality of the act of writing and work to expose the ideological, exclusionary force of writing practices (Clark & Ivanic, 1997; Lillis, 1997, 1999, 2001, 2003; Street, 1984, pp. 2–3). For such theorists, academic writing is not a neutral activity, but a socially constructed discursive practice that serves the communicative purposes of a specific culture — the academy. Ignoring the ways in which academic writing is constructed to establish the identities and promote the values of this culture is also to ignore the ways in which it might exclude those who do not necessarily share a similar cultural positioning (with its specific values, its ways of thinking, speaking or acting). Issues of identity are of prime concern to such theorists as they consider how academic writing practices might be, for example class, gender and race specific, rendering them potentially exclusive and discriminatory against those who do not share these cultural practices or the authority bestowed by knowledge and familiarity with these practices.

Taking the above into account, we argue that genuinely supportive environments recognise that literacy is 'essentially social' (Barton & Hamilton, 1998). Our task is to engage students as social beings and to invite them to participate fully in university literacy cultures, and to recognise impediments to this. We strive to do this by offering literacy development that is 'culturally relevant' (Barton, Hamilton, & Ivanic, 2000, p. xvi), by recognising and countenancing the problems writers may face as they negotiate the social relations governing the social exchange of writing (Lea & Street, 1998) and by mobilising the potential joys in writing for the people who write that are to be derived from this 'inexhaustible source of true pleasure and lifelong learning' (Ahmad & MacMahon, 2006, p. 6). The task of writing development, then, is not just about socialising students into a particular writing culture, but also about opening opportunities for them to enter into dialogue about and even shape the cultural conventions of writing so that their individual contexts are recognised as being central to the culture in which they are participating.

The following insights taken from different sociocultural critics underpin the embedded approach to writing development offered in this book:

1. Writing is contextual: it varies over time and place.
2. Writing is an exercise in thinking and its development is linked to clarity in conceptual knowledge.[1]
3. Writing development demands an awareness of disciplinary epistemologies, practices and discourses.
4. Writing is linked to identity construction and requires dialogue with the self and others.
5. As knowledge production is a social construction, discussions over knowledge are best done within groups.

---

1. The link between writing and thinking is, of course, advanced by many scholars from different strands of literacy theory and practice. It also connects, for example with 'writing-to-learn' theories developed by US composition scholars who emphasise how writing assists cognitive development (see Bazerman et al., 2005, pp. 57–65; Bean, 2001, pp. 1–53; Britton, Burgess, Martin, McLeod, & Rosen, 1975; Emig, 1977; Young, 2011, pp. 9–11).

UNIVERSITIES AND WRITING AS SPACES FOR GROWTH

Before we detail the ways in which the chapters aim to respond to the issues mentioned above, we will return to the theme with which we opened this book: the idea that writing can be meaningful for people in many different ways. We argue that creating supportive environments for writing means helping students to find the ways in which writing is meaningful for them and that this is done by constructing social environments that engage them helpfully with their writing through its many iterations, rather than alienate them from it as described by the educational literature we cited.

At university, students have to grapple with writing for their disciplines or writing for their potential employers, both of which are important acts that do indeed give meaning to writing. To help them find positive meaning in these different types of writing, we argue that we need to help students to understand the conventions for writing for different environments, and this book offers ways in which this might be done.

Yet academic writing also contains within it a guard against prescriptiveness in writing. Despite its conventional nature, there is within it a certain freedom that can allow the writer to speak through the writing. As it asks students to explore ideas critically, academic writing also promotes individual growth and development. Fromm's (1976) point that education is an experience and his privileging of 'the being mode' where education is seen as a place of growth and of self-transformation is also a useful way of thinking about academic writing. For academic writing is itself an experience — you engage in it, go through its stages and experience its highs and lows. The experience writers go through is the active enterprise of production: the production of knowledge (you gain and create knowledge as you write) and of the self (you grow and may even be transformed through your new knowledge). You can therefore learn things from the experience of writing — enter new arenas that you knew nothing about or come to understandings that you might not have had before writing.

Writing, then, is something whose meaning can lie beyond the purely instrumental. We began this chapter by foregrounding the existential meaning Sartre finds in writing as we would like to highlight, retain and foster this potentiality of writing. As Sartre indicates, writing is not just an act of constructing the text, but also of constructing the self (*By writing, I existed*). To write is to generate one's own sense of identity. The way into this idea of writing as an experience is for writers to inhabit their writing — the dialogues we have with writing are also dialogues we have with ourselves as we grapple with knowledge and try to fit it together to a greater understanding. The deeper rewards and challenges of writing often come out of these dialogues.

Sustaining and supporting writing in its potential to foster self-growth is a challenge in the current climate of academia, where funding structures change and direct government funding of universities decreases (Putting Students at the Heart of the System, 2011, p. 15) and where the purpose of the university is being rewritten through the eyes of the market. A decrease in government funding for universities should, as we have argued, lead to an increase in support for writing so we can ensure we are enabling students to succeed and grow during their educational experience. The emphasis on universities as spaces of growth and the ways in which writing is an institutional practice which, in view of its relationship with thinking and being, provokes and supports this growth is an important one. Research conducted for this book demonstrates that students often speak of the ways in which they have grown through their writing. They speak passionately about the personal meanings beyond the purely instrumental that they have found in writing, of the personal satisfactions they derive from social exchanges over writing and from writing itself as it challenges them to think differently and then gives them a space to engage with and contribute to their worlds. They speak of their joy in writing, of the self-pride and self-confidence that can issue from their engagements with it. And sometimes, they even say that, despite all of the difficulties they have with writing, they actually love it. It is these kinds of affordances of writing that we wish to recall in this book as we present some of the ways in which we have strived to create environments that will stimulate them. To stay with the life-affirming contribution that writing can make to a student's time at university, we end this section with the students' own words for they herald and lead us into the main concern of this book — to place the experience of student-writers at the heart of our writing support:

> I loved the sessions where we talked about our writing. (...) When you discuss your ideas within a small group, you get other people's perspectives, which can lead you to think of things in a completely different way.

> (Student 1) If I've got an idea, as soon as I start writing, I start remembering things and bringing in other things. I'm like, 'Yeah! Go me!' It's great, and I get really excited.
> (Student 2) I do; I do!
> (Student 1) Yeah, I do. I know it sounds ridiculous, but I do. I'm writing and I'm thinking 'yeah, this sounds great. Brilliant!'. And I get really excited about it.
> (Student 3) It's like what you just said. Sometimes you'll click on something you've read and you think 'Oh, wow, it just goes there! Put it in', and you're excited to blend it in.

Yeah, it's growing something. It's building something that's all yours and ... I love reading it and afterwards going, 'Did I write this?'
(Student 2) (laughs) Yeah.

Also with an essay I want to show that I am aware of what I'm saying ... not just, 'oh, you know, blah, blah said, and this is matched with this, and then he ... ' I want to put some of me in it. That's what I like about writing. (...). I like to put me in there a little, but sometimes sneakily 'cos you know, you might not really need that. I have to put a little of me in, and it just makes it your own.

Oh, words, words, words (laughs)! I love words. (...) I just love words. I love the way you can just write something down and it can make an emotional impact. I love that.

AIMS AND ORGANISATION OF THE BOOK

Writing is, therefore, a sociocultural practice and this book contributes to debates over the implications of viewing writing in this way. It starts from the assumption that, to be genuinely supportive, writing development must take into account what it actually means, from the perspectives of students and subject staff, to write within the disciplines. Presenting empirical research that offers student and staff accounts on writing, it elucidates some of the contexts in which writing is practised. Certain nuances of the disciplines under discussion are described in several chapters and in some cases practical exercises or descriptions of types of writing that can be used to broaden students' writing practices are presented. Finally, it offers practical activities that tutors have used to engage dialogically with students about their understandings of writing within the disciplines.

Deliberately seeking to capture a flavour of the different epistemologies and styles of writing of the disciplines in HE, we specifically chose authors from different academic subjects and/or specialisms and have preserved the differences in style and approaches to writing that this might invoke. The authors therefore bring insights into academic writing that originate from their own disciplinary locatedness. Of course, not all of the disciplines are represented in this text, but they do face similar challenges regarding academic writing, so we hope to generate further debate about disciplinary similarities and differences and about how best to support all students to address these in an inclusive way.

Herein lies one of the greatest challenges facing anybody who wants to help students with their writing and one that this book is attempting to address: how might we identify and speak about the specifics of a writing culture in ways that would move beyond generic abstractions about writing and how might we engender positive social relationships over writing that would assist this process? The book is structured around these two questions with all chapters offering specific responses to them, though some focus more on the construction of student writing cultures and others on the practicalities of addressing the sociocultural nature of writing.

The formal teaching of literacy starts at school and this influences students' relationships with writing. They thus come to university with certain knowledges and expectations about how writing is taught, how it is assessed, how adept they are at writing and what it means to write. School writing cultures contrast established cultures of writing at university, so some understanding of how writing is configured within the school system will allow university tutors to understand the questions students ask about writing, the confusions they might face and the expectations they might have regarding writing support. In chapter 1, therefore, Christine Hardy and Helen Boulton consider the construction of writing cultures at school. Situating writing within the current political and educational contexts which structure the experience of students entering university, they draw on empirical evidence from research with pre-university students to describe both their experiences and expectations of writing.

Chapter 2 moves into the university setting to continue the exploration of participants' framings of writing. Here, Christine Hardy and Lisa Clughen draw on empirical research to identify, compare, contrast and discuss both student and staff expectations and experiences of writing at university and the support offered. The research demonstrated that student writing was a concern for staff and students alike and that there was a mismatch of understandings of and expectations around writing between students and staff. The authors therefore conclude that writing support should aim to align student and staff expectations through dialogue with subject specialists.

An important part of the process of alignment of student/staff expectations around writing is the identification of local writing require-ments. This is the subject of Chapter 3 where Hilary Nesi describes her extensive work on genre research to identify different forms of writing used across the disciplines and the different epistemologies and discourses with which students must be conversant if they are to succeed. Taken together, then, these first three chapters point to the increasing complexity of writing as a child/student progresses through the educational system.

Complexity is a defining feature of writing. Not only do the varying demands of educational contexts contribute to this, but considerations of the writer who writes will further complicate the matter and raise new insights for thinking about writing as a social practice. Patrick O'Connor and Melanie Petch use Merleau Ponty's philosophies, in Chapter 4, to construct and hold onto notions of the writing subject as 'embodied' and argue that supportive environments for writing need to embrace this notion. Ways in which the embodied nature of the writer might be welcomed within physical spaces for writing support are then offered as they discuss writing groups for postgraduate students.

Bringing the social into writing need not only be done in physical space, however. Today's students spend much of their time in virtual space, particularly socialising through writing on social networks. In Chapter 5, Helen Boulton and Alison Hramiak move us into the virtual environment to examine student relationships with Web 2.0 and mobile technologies and the impact of these on student writing in HE. Taking into account student relationships with digital writing cultures, the authors discuss how these might be woven into university cultures to produce environments that are congruent with student lives.

The virtual environment may produce thriving writing communities in itself, but in HE they are often initiated and sustained by face-to-face contact. Chapter 6 moves us into physical space and discusses the construction of an environment that nurtures a thriving, socially supportive writing community. Here, the focus is on the difficult issues of helping students to identify and to deploy the conventional and discursive practices of the different learning communities to which they belong and of assisting staff to engage in this identification in dialogue with them. Using case studies from the English subject area, Lisa Clughen and Matt Connell argue for dialogic lecture analysis as a simple but new method for subject acculturation and its concomitant writing development. They conclude by providing practical exercises that can be used across the disciplines to discuss with students how the lecture can be used to for the purposes of writing within their learning community.

The theme of the dialogic ways in which students can be integrated into their writing communities continues in Chapter 7, where Sarah Haas discusses the use of story cards as a way into scientific writing. The story cards are based on a problem-solution textual pattern found in many genres of science writing. The exercises are based on 'guided discovery' pedagogy, aiming to lead users to realisations about scientific writing and aiming to facilitate reflective thought on, and dialogue about, writing in participants' specific contexts.

In Chapter 8, Erik Borg details how various non-traditional writing genres are used in the discipline of Art and Design to engage students whilst enabling them to demonstrate knowledge and understanding of their subject and contextualise their practice. Offering a historical account of the relationship of the disciplines of Art and Design to writing, he discusses forms of writing that issue from the creative context. These forms include reflective writing, visual essays and patchwork writing, and all of them can be used across the disciplines to engage students with writing, especially when they might struggle to find personal meanings in traditional institutional forms of writing such as the academic essay.

The final chapter provides a specific take on the ways in which opportunities for social exchange can be brought into writing pedagogy. Here, Rowena Murray describes different forms of social writing which range from interventionist to writer-determined approaches to writing development. The chapter moves from tutor-led, formal writing interventions through to less formal, tutor-led interventions, before considering, finally, students' own ways of working together on their writing.

Lisa Clughen
Christine Hardy

REFERENCES

Ahmad, R., & McMahon, K. (2006). The benefits of good writing: Or why does it matter that students write well. In S. Davies, D. Swinburne & G. Williams (Eds.), *Writing matters. The royal literary fund report on student writing in higher education* (pp. 1–6). London: The Royal Literary Fund.

Barton, D., & Hamilton, M. (1998). *Local literacies: Reading and writing in one community.* London: Routledge.

Barton, D., Hamilton, M., & Ivanic, R. (2000). *Situated literacies: Reading and writing in context.* London: Routledge.

Bazerman, C., Little, J., Bethel, L., Chavkin, T., Fouquette, D., & Garufis, J. (2005). *Reference guide to writing across the curriculum.* Lafayette, IN: Parlor Press. (Retrieved from http://wac.colostate.edu/books/bazerman_wac/wac.pdf

Bean, J. (2001). *Engaging ideas: The professor's guide to integrating writing, critical thinking, and active learning in the classroom.* San Francisco, CA: Jossey Bass.

Beer, D. (2011, January 20). Expectation inflation: As demands rise, ability to meet them declines. *Times Higher Education.* Retrieved from http://www.timeshighereducation.co.uk/story.asp?storycode = 414893

Bowstead, H. (2009, February). Teaching English as a foreign language — A personal exploration of language, alienation and academic literacy. *UK Journal of Learning Development in Higher Education,* (1). Retrieved from http://www.aldinhe.ac.uk/ojs/index.php?journal = jldhe&page = article&op = viewFile&path%5B%5D = 14&path%5B%5D = 10

Britton, J., Burgess, T., Martin, N., McLeod, A., & Rosen, H. (1975). *The development of writing abilities* (pp. 11–18). London: Macmillan.

Christie, F., & Misson, R. (2002). Framing issues in literacy education. In G. Reid, J. Soler & J. Wearmouth (Eds.), *Contextualising difficulties in literacy development: Exploring politics, culture, ethnicity, and ethics* (pp. 47–58). London: Routledge.

Clark, R., & Ivanic, R. (1997). *The politics of writing*. London: Routledge.

Deane, M., & O'Neill, M. (2011). *Writing in the disciplines*. Houndmills, UK: Palgrave MacMillan.

Department for Business, Innovation and Skills. (2010a). *Skills for sustainable growth*. Retrieved from http://www.bis.gov.uk/assets/biscore/further-education-skills/docs/s/10-1274-skills-for-sustainable-growth-strategy.pdf

Department for Business, Innovation and Skills. (2010b). Independent review of higher education funding & student finance (Browne Review). Retrieved from http://webarchive.nationalarchives.gov.uk/+/hereview.independent.gov.uk/hereview/report/

Department for Business, Innovation and Skills. (2011). *Higher education: Students at the heart of the system*. Education white paper. Retrieved from http://c561635.r35.cf2.rackcdn.com/11-944-WP-students-at-heart.pdf

Dugdale, G., & Clark, C. (2008). *Literacy changes lives: An advocacy resource*. London: National Literacy Trust. http://www.literacytrust.org.uk/assets/0000/0401/Literacy_changes_lives_2008.pdf

Dysthe, O. (2001, June 18). 'The mutual challenge of writing research and the teaching of writing' Keynote address. The European Association for the Teaching of Academic Writing (EATAW) & The European Writing Centre Associaltion (EWCA). University of Groeningen, Netherlands. Retrieved from http://www.uib.no/filearchive/keynote_eataw18-1-.pdf

Emig, J. (1977, May). Writing as a mode of learning. *College Composition and Communication*, *28*(2), 122–128. National Council of Teachers of English. Retrieved from http://api.ning.com/files/dyd9zNIe01SZCip1A*laTe8YCSSs3*cbfGntdo*3ytB9EZwOTyj430RvsQMEemRnQuZ4xeLab1IyZWizRYiNuR2f2Yh7ZfPB/WritingasaModeofLearning.pdf

Fromm, E. (1976). *To have or to be?* London: Continuum.

Ganobcsik-Williams, L. (Ed.) (2006). *Teaching academic writing in UK higher education*. Hampshire, UK: Palgrave MacMillan.

Haggis, T. (2006). Pedagogies for diversity: Retaining critical challenge amidst fears of 'dumbing down'. *Studies in Higher Education*, *31*(5), 521–535.

Ivanic, R. (2006, May 11–12). The fifth 'P': Writing as participation. *Writing Development in Higher Education (WDHE) Conference: Challenging Institutional Priorities*, Open University, Milton Keynes.

Ivanic, R., & Lea, M. R. (2006). New contexts, new challenges: The teaching of writing in UK higher education. In L. Ganobcsik-Williams (Ed.), *Teaching academic writing in UK higher education: Theories, practices and models* (pp. 6–15). London: Palgrave Macmillan.

Lankshear, C., & Lawler, M. (1987). *Literacy, schooling and revolution*. Lewes, UK: The Falmer Press.

Lea, M., & Street, B. V. (1998). Student writing in higher education: An academic literacies approach. *Studies in Higher Education*, *23*(2), 157–172.

Leathwood, C., & O'Connell, P. (2003). 'It's a struggle': The construction of the 'new student' in higher education. *Journal of Education Policy*, *18*(6), 597–615.

Lillis, T. (1997). New voices in academia? The regulative nature of academic writing conventions. *Language and Education, 11*(3), 182–199.

Lillis, T. (1999). Whose "common sense"? Essayist literacy and the institutional practice of mystery. In C. Jones, J. Turner & B. V. Street (Eds.), *Students writing in the university: Cultural and epistemological issues* (pp. 127–147). Amsterdam: John Benjamins.

Lillis, T. (2001). *Student writing: Access, regulation, desire.* London: Routledge.

Lillis, T. (2003). Student writing as 'Academic literacies': Drawing on Bakhtin to move from critique to design. *Language and Education, 17*(3), 192–207.

Lillis, T. (2006). Moving towards an academic literacies pedagogy: Dialogues of participation. In L. Ganobcsik-Williams (Ed.), *Teaching academic writing in UK higher education; theories, practices and models* (pp. 30–45). Basingstoke, UK: Palgrave MacMillan.

Mann, S. (2001). Alternative perspectives on the student experience: Alienation and engagement. *Studies in Higher Education, 26*(1), 1–19.

Maringe, F. (2010). The student as consumer: Affordances and constraints in a transforming higher education environment. In M. Molesworth, R. Scullion & E. Nixon (Eds.), *The marketisation of UK higher education: The student as consumer* (pp. 142–154). London: Routledge.

Molesworth, M., Nixon, E., & Scullion, R. (2009). Having, being and higher education: The marketisation of the university and the transformation of the student into consumer. *Teaching in Higher Education, 14*(3), 277–287.

Motion, A. (2011, June 2). *The bonfire of the humanities.* Romanes Lecture, University of Oxford. Retrieved from http://www.ox.ac.uk/media/news_stories/2011/110206_1.html

The National Committee of Inquiry into Higher Education (NCIHE). (1997). *Higher education in the learning society: Report of the National Committee of inquiry into higher education.* The Dearing Report, HMSO, London.

Pennell, H., & West, A. (2005). The impact of increased fees on participation in higher education. *Higher Education Quarterly, 59*(2), 127–137.

Rassool, N. (2002). Literacy: In search of a paradigm. In G. Reid, J. Soler & J. Wearmouth (Eds.), *Contextualising difficulties in literacy development: Exploring politics, culture, ethnicity and ethics* (pp. 17–46). London: Routledge.

Read, B., Archer, L., & Leathwood, C. (2003). Challenging cultures? Student conceptions of 'belonging' and 'isolation' at a post-1992 university. *Studies in Higher Education, 28*(3), 261–277.

Sartre, J. P. (1964). *Words* (I. Clephane, Trans.). Middlesex, UK: Penguin.

Street, B. (2003). What's "new" in new literacy studies? Critical approaches to literacy in theory and practice. *Current Issues in Comparative Education, 5*(2), 77–91 Retrieved from http://www.tc.columbia.edu/crce/Archives/5.2/52Street.pdf

Street, B. (2009). *'Hidden' features of academic paper writing.* Working Papers in Educational Linguistics, University of Pennsylvania. Retrieved from http://www.thinkingwriting.qmul.ac.uk/documents/Street%20Hidden%20features%20of%20AW%20Aclits%202009.doc

Street, B. V. (1984). *Literacy in theory and practice.* New York, NY: Cambridge University.

UK Commission for Employment and Skills. (2010). *Skills for jobs: Today and tomorrow.* The national strategic skills audit for England, Volume 2: The evidence report. Retrieved from http://www.ukces.org.uk/assets/bispartners/ukces/docs/publications/national-strategic-skills-audit-for-england-2010-volume-2-the-evidence-report.pdf

UNESCO. (2004). *The plurality of literacy and its implications for policies and programmes* (Retrieved from http://unesdoc.unesco.org/images/0013/001362/136246e.pdf). Paris: UNESCO.

WAC Clearinghouse. (1997–2012). Colorado State University. Retrieved from http://wac.colostate.edu/

Wingate, U. (2006). Doing away with 'study skills' in teaching. *Higher Education, 11*(4), 457–469.

Young, A. (2011). *Teaching writing across the curriculum* (4th ed.). WAC Clearinghouse Landmark Publications in Writing Studies. Originally Published in Print, 2006, by Pearson Education, Upper Saddle River, NJ. Retrieved from http://wac.colostate.edu/books/young_teaching/

Chapter 1

Writing at School

Christine Hardy and Helen Boulton

Literacy has always been contested within the United Kingdom (UK) education system-content, delivery and assessment. One area of contestation is the many government initiatives that have impacted on the teaching and outcomes of literacy in schools, which have affected pupils' attitudes and behaviours towards reading and writing, and ultimately their abilities. It is important that those working in higher education have an appreciation of the school context in which literacy is taught so they can gain a greater understanding of students' prior experiences and hence facilitate their writing. This chapter, therefore, will give a brief overview and context of the teaching and assessment of literacy (reading and writing) within schools in the UK, then focus on the current situation, and discuss the experiences of students transitioning to higher education.

The responsibility for teaching literacy in schools was first enshrined in the 1870 Elementary Education Act for England and Wales, and in Scotland in the Education (Scotland) Act 1872. These acts made provision for the elementary education of all children aged 5–13, which provided for mass education and state intervention. State intervention was via school boards who oversaw the network of schools and brought them all under some form of supervision. The main subjects taught were reading, writing and arithmetic, and schools were paid for students who passed examinations in these subjects.

> ... [the] Act fulfils general expectation by securing a larger and more effective diffusion of knowledge among the people ... that the taxpayers of the country should know according to

Writing in the Disciplines: Building Supportive Cultures for Student Writing in UK Higher Education
ISBN: 978-1-78052-546-4

what methods and under what guarantees this portion of the
national income is expended ... to which the Government
Inspector has access at all times for the purposes of
examination in any subject except religious knowledge ... Six
shillings per scholar is paid on the average attendance in the
year, and a variable sum for every scholar present at the
Inspector's examination ... Children between four and seven
years old are counted as "infants" and paid at the rate of 8s a
head, or 10s if taught in a separate department. Pupils above
seven years are subject to examination in reading, writing, and
arithmetic, and, if passed, are paid for at the rate of 4s. a head
in each of the three subjects. (*Times*, 1871, p. 9)

Pupils were examined according to one of six standards, roughly
corresponding to ages 7–12 (see Table 1.1), which restricted the curriculum.
In addition, schools 'pursued other, less clearly defined, aims including
social-disciplinary objectives (acceptance of the teacher's authority, the need
for punctuality, obedience, conformity etc.)' (Gillard, 2011, online). By the
end of the 19th century, there was a national system of elementary education,
which was free with compulsory attendance (Elementary Education Act of
1881 and 1880) and a new government department to oversee it (Board of
Education Act, 1899).

According to Gillard (2011), there was a lot of opposition to this
system, with teachers objecting to the methods of testing and to the
principle of 'payment by results' because 'it linked money for schools with
the criterion of a minimum standard', therefore 'it was becoming difficult
to dissociate reading and writing from qualification and examination.
Teaers had to be trained; pupils had to achieve rigidly defined standards'
(Vincent, 1989, p. 68).

Furthermore, the standards themselves were defective because
they were based not on an experimental enquiry into what
children of a given age actually knew, but on an a priori
notion of what they ought to know. They largely ignored the
wide range of individual capacity, and the detailed formula-
tions for the several ages were not always precise or
appropriate. (Gillard, 2011)

The standards gradually fell into disuse and were abandoned around the
turn of the century and the curriculum was expanded with the obligatory
subjects of reading, writing and arithmetic (and needlework for girls) and
optional subjects; payment by results who also abandoned. In 1902 (Education Act), the local education authorities were established with the authority

Table 1.1: The six standards of education contained in the revised code of regulations, 1872.

	Reading	**Writing**
Standard I (age 7)	Read a narrative that comes after monosyllables in an elementary reading book used in the school	Copy in handwriting a line of print, and write from dictation a few common words
Standard II (age 8)	Read a short paragraph from an elementary reading book	Write a sentence, slowly read once, and then dictated in single words, from the same book
Standard III (age 9)	Read a short paragraph from a more advanced reading book	From the same book, write a sentence slowly dictated once a few words at a time
Standard IV (age 10)	At the choice of the inspector, read a few lines of poetry or prose	From a reading book, such as is used in the first class of the school, write a sentence that is slowly dictated once, a few words at a time
Standard V (age 11)	From a newspaper, or other modern narrative, read a short ordinary paragraph	From another newspaper, or other modern narrative, write a short ordinary paragraph that has been slowly dictated once a few words at a time
Standard VI (age 12)	Read with fluency and expression	Write a short theme or letter, or an easy paraphrase

Source: Adapted from The Standards of Education in schools in England from 1972.

to support teacher training colleges, and the basis for a national system of secondary education was established. With the implementation of mass education, literacy rates continued to increase, and in the last full year of peace, following the First World War, the official literacy level in the UK first peaked at 99% (Vincent, 1989, p. 4), measured by the number of children completing the first three or five grades of schooling (Street, 1995, p. 23).

The period between the wars was one of consolidation in education and preparation for the Education Act of 1944. The school leaving age was raised from 12 to 14 in 1921 and to 15 in 1935. Government policy from

1928 was for pupils to transfer from primary to secondary schools at the age of 11, although according to Gillard (2011) the secondary schools 'continued to provide a curriculum based on the arid drill methods of the elementary schools'.

The importance of the 1944 Education Act cannot be overemphasised. It replaced almost all previous education legislation and set the framework for the post-war education system in England and Wales. There were similar Education Acts for Scotland (1945) and Northern Ireland (1947) (Gillard, 2011).

> The Act divided responsibility for education between central government, which was to set national policies and allocate resources; the local education authorities (LEAs), which were to set local policies and allocate resources to schools; and the schools themselves, whose head teachers and governing bodies would set school policies and manage the resources. (Gillard, 2011)

The Act therefore not only strengthened the role of central government in education but also encouraged decentralisation, with no '… stipulations about curriculum and pedagogy, teachers had considerable capacities to initiate school-level change …' (Jones, 2003, p. 20 cited in Gillard, 2011). Although the Act did not specify a tripartite system of secondary education, one was soon established with grammar schools for the most able being selected on the basis of the 'eleven plus' examination (tests of intelligence and attainment in English and arithmetic), secondary modern schools for the majority (those who 'failed' the 'eleven plus') and secondary technical schools for those with a technical or scientific aptitude (Gillard, 2011). This system had a damaging effect on primary schools, as success of the schools was judged on the success of those pupils in the 'eleven plus' examination. 'Once again, the fate of the junior school and its educational role depended on developments at the upper levels' (Galton, Simon, & Croll, 1980, p. 38 in Gillard, 2011), meaning that the primary schools had to continue with a teaching approach emphasising basic literacy and numeracy, 'In fact the tradition derived from 1870 was still dominant' (Galton, Simon, & Croll, 1980, p. 36 in Gillard, 2011). It was not until 1967 and *The Plowden Report* that the individual child was put at the heart of the educational process, and children were encouraged to learn for themselves rather than by 'drill methods', but this pedagogy was not to last. In 1976, the then Prime Minister James Callaghan gave a speech at Ruskin College, Oxford, calling for a return to a 'core curriculum' and a 'national standard of performance' that is inspected (Callaghan, 1976).

At the same time (during the 1970s), there was a move from the field of 'reading', which was mainly 'grounded in psychology and associated with time-honoured methods of instruction for teaching new entrants into school how to decode printed text and, secondarily, how to encode text' (Lankshear & Knobel, 2005, p. 3), which is what the 'drill method' entailed to a formal educational discourse of literacy studies and development. Lankshear and Knobel (2005) identified a number of reasons why the change from reading to literacy occurred:

1. A rise to prominence of Paulo Freire's work, who suggested that learning to read and write was an integral part of learning to understand how the world works socially and culturally, which produces unequal opportunities and outcomes for different groups of people (*ibid.*, p. 6);
2. The increasing development and popularity of a *socio-cultural* (their italics) perspective within studies of language and the social sciences, using anthropological and ethnographic approaches to study literacy. Literacies are bound up with social, institutional and cultural relationships and can only be understood when they are situated within their social, cultural and historical contexts (*op. cit.*, p. 8); and
3. The discovery of widespread illiteracy (what Lankshear and Knobel call 'the invention of illiteracy') among adults in the United States (US) during the 1970s, which then spread to other Western nations, including the UK. Lankshear and Knobel infer that this 'literacy crisis' coincided with early awareness of profound structural change in the economy, as the US moved towards becoming a post-industrial society, which entailed a restructuring of the labour market and employment, and changes in the institutions of daily life. Governments responded to this 'literacy crisis' by intervening in the school curriculum, making changes to ensure that all learners became literate enough to live effectively under contemporary conditions (*op. cit.*, p. 6).

Today, statistics are collected regularly on literacy levels internationally by the Organisation for Economic Co-operation and Development (OECD) for children and adults.[1] This is a continuation of the gathering of systematic statistics on literacy by governments and international agencies that began in the 1950s, as concern about the levels of literacy in the general population grew (St. John Hunter & Harman, 1979, pp. 9–12).

The testing of literacy among both adults and children is based on a functional view of literacy, which became prominent with governments

---

1. Programme for International Student Assessment (PISA) measures literacy levels of 15-year olds on a 3-year cyclical basis and began in the late 1990s. International Adult Literacy Survey (IALS) measures literacy levels of 16–65-year olds on a cyclical basis and began in 1994. Both are organised by the OECD.

and United Nations Economic, Social and Cultural Organisation (UNESCO) in the 1960s. Functional literacy is promoted as a response to economic demand, with a focus on the reading and writing skills required to increase productivity of the individual and hence the nation (UNESCO, 2003, pp. 8–9).

Based upon the results of testing in the 1970s, the government concluded that large numbers of individuals have not got the necessary literacy skills and so established literacy programmes for both adults and children. In the UK, the first national agency for improving adult literacy was set up in 1975, becoming the Basic Skills Agency. Originally it was only concerned with adult literacy programmes, but in 1995 their work was extended to work with schools and children. The Basic Skills Agency was merged with the National Institute for Adult Continuing Education (NIACE) in 2007, and responsibility for literacy for under 16 was given to the Department for Education and Skills, who had established the National Literacy Strategy in 1997. The strategy was developed to increase literacy standards among primary schoolchildren and came to an end in June 2011; so far has not been replaced.

One outcome of the 'literacy crisis' and criticisms of education in the 1970s and early 1980s was the Education Reform Act (1988). It was the most important Act since 1944, making provision for a National Curriculum to be introduced in all maintained schools which set the groundwork for what subjects should be taught and attainment targets. English became a core subject, with mathematics and science, and children were tested in these subjects at the ages of 6/7, 10/11 and 13/14. The National Curriculum in England was revised in 2000, and continues to be revised periodically.

1.1. The National Curriculum

The National Curriculum applies to pupils of compulsory school age in state maintained schools and provides a framework for what pupils should be taught. Each subject is underpinned by a Programme of Study: 'The programmes of study, in relation to a Key Stage, are the matters, skills, and processes which are required to be taught to pupils of different abilities and maturities by the end of that Key Stage. In short, they set out what pupils should be taught in each National Curriculum subject at each Key Stage' (Department for Education, 2012). It is organised on the basis of four Key Stages.

Primary education
Key Stage 1: Ages 5–7 (years 1–2)
Key Stage 2: Ages 7–11 (years 3–6)

Secondary education
Key Stage 3: Ages 11–14 (years 7–9)
Key Stage 4: Ages 14–16 (years 10–11). This incorporates GCSEs and
  vocational qualifications such as GNVQ and BTEC.

Post-16 qualifications include A levels and vocational qualifications such
as GNVQ and BTEC, but are not part of the National Curriculum.

Each Key Stage in all subject areas has attainment targets: the
knowledge, skills and understanding which pupils of different abilities and
maturities are expected to have by the end of that Key Stage. There are
currently eight-level descriptions of increasing difficulty plus a description
for exceptional performance above level 8, which provide the basis for
making judgements about pupils' performance and are the main means of
assessing attainment in National Curriculum subjects.

The level descriptions provide the basis for making judgements about
pupils' performance at the end of Key Stages 1, 2 and 3. At Key Stage 4,
national qualifications are the main means of assessing attainment in
National Curriculum subjects (Department for Education, 2012). English is
a statutory subject at each of the four Key Stages and will be the focus for
discussion within this chapter as it is where most literacy teaching occurs.
While brief information on the current National Curriculum focussing on
English is provided here, it is important to note that at the time of going to
print the government has announced a review of the National Curriculum
with a new curriculum for all subjects from 2014.

The 2000 framework, in addition to core subjects, introduced key skills:
communication, numeracy, information and communications technology
(ICT), problem solving, working with others, improving own learning and
performance. These were compulsory for those working at levels 1, 2 and
3 of the new National Qualifications Framework. The intention was that
whether students remained in full-time education or took other routes
such as apprenticeships, they would continue to develop these key areas.
External tests were established for the first three subjects, with moderated
coursework for the other subjects. UCAS points were attached to level 2
(equivalent to GCSE) 10 points and level 3 (equivalent to A2) 20 points,
although it was the decision of universities whether they accepted them.
Additional funding for further education colleges was attached to the
successful completion of key skills. Over the last decade, these key skills
have lost prominence and have been replaced by functional skills designed
by the Qualifications and Curriculum Development Agency (QCDA) as
found in diplomas, apprenticeship frameworks and in some elements
within GCSE English Examination Board specifications, for example,
AQA.

1.2.   Literacy Within the National Curriculum (English)

On the Department for Education website, it is clear that English is for pupils to 'develop skills in speaking, listening, reading and writing that they will need to participate in society and employment. Pupils learn to express themselves creatively and imaginatively and to communicate with others confidently and effectively' (2012). Currently, the English Programme of Study, at all levels, has three key areas: speaking and listening, reading, and writing. The skills and processes that students should learn for level 4 English are shown in Table 1.2.

English, Key Stage 4, in common with all subjects in the National Curriculum, has a consolidated set of eight-level descriptors (plus exceptional performance) against which students are judged for each of the skills and processes. This can mitigate against 'holistic marking' whereby students can do well on some of the skills and processes, and badly on others: as one English teacher in a secondary school recently said to us 'pupils can get a grade 5 on summarising and taking notes, but grade 2 on the use of punctuation marks'. Generally speaking, those students who have achieved GCSE grade C (the minimum entry qualification for English to higher education) are performing at level 5 overall, but there will be variation in the levels of the individual skills and processes achieved. The descriptors are shown in Table 1.3.

Within the National Curriculum, therefore, there is a focus on assessment, the results being used for school 'league tables'. This focus, particularly in the use of reading materials, has been criticised by many, Bell (2005) in particular:

> Too often we see teaching of reading, the shared consideration of texts, that stops short of discussing issues of meaning and content. Some teachers see all texts as a means of teaching about writing. So, a poem is mined for use of adjectives, metaphors and contrasting short and long sentences without attempting to engage pupils' personal response to the ideas and feelings in the poem. The text becomes a type of manual rather than a personal response to lived experience. (Bell, 2005)

Bell asserts that reading instruction in schools, and the pursuit of high test results, is mitigating against children deriving pleasure from reading, and making reading 'functional'. Text, in some schools, is not used to encourage children to gain pleasure from reading but instead is used for learning about writing. This leads to less engagement and involvement in the text and so reading is a less pleasurable experience. As Resnick and Resnick

Table 1.2: Skills and processes for level four English in the national curriculum.

Reading — Students should be able to:	Writing — Students should be able to:
Reading for meaning	**Composition**
a. Analyse and evaluate information, events and ideas from texts	a. Write imaginatively, creatively and thoughtfully, producing texts that interest, engage and challenge the reader
b. Understand how meaning is constructed within sentences and across texts as a whole in media, moving image and multimodal texts	b. Write fluently, adapting style and language to a wide range of forms, contexts and purposes
c. Recognise subtlety, ambiguity and allusion within sentences and across texts as a whole	c. Present information and ideas on complex subjects concisely, logically and persuasively
d. Develop and sustain independent interpretations of what they read, supporting them with detailed textual reference	d. Establish and sustain a consistent point of view in fiction and non-fiction writing
e. Select, compare, summarise and synthesise information from different texts and use it to form their own ideas, arguments and opinions	e. Use a range of ways to structure whole texts to give clarity and emphasis
f. Reflect on the origin and purpose of texts and assess their usefulness, recognising bias, opinion, implicit meaning and abuse of evidence	f. Use clearly demarcated paragraphs to develop and organise meaning
g. Relate texts to their social and historical contexts and to the literary traditions of which they are a part	g. Use a wide variety of sentence structures to support the purpose of the task, giving clarity and emphasis and creating specific effects, and to extend, link and develop ideas
h. Recognise and evaluate the ways in which texts may be interpreted differently according to the perspective of the reader	h. Support and strengthen their own views by incorporating different kinds of evidence from a range of sources
i. Analyse and evaluate the impact of combining words, images and sounds	i. Select appropriate persuasive techniques and rhetorical devices
	j. Draw on their reading and knowledge of linguistic and literary forms when composing their writing

Table 1.2: (*Continued*)

Reading — Students should be able to:	Writing — Students should be able to:
Reading for meaning	**Composition**
The author's craft j. Analyse and evaluate writers' use of language in a range of texts, commenting precisely on how texts are crafted to shape meaning and produce particular effects k. Identify the purposes of texts, analysing and evaluating how writers structure and organise ideas to shape meaning for particular audiences and readers l. Analyse and evaluate how form, layout and presentation contribute to effect m. Compare texts, looking at style, theme and language and exploring connections and contrasts n. Compare and analyse the connections between texts from different cultures and traditions	k. Summarise and take notes l. Use planning, drafting, editing, proofreading and self-evaluation to revise and craft their writing for maximum impact *Technical accuracy* m. Use the grammatical features of written standard English accurately to structure a wide range of sentence types for particular purposes and effect n. Use the full range of punctuation marks accurately and for deliberate effect o. Spell correctly, including words that do not conform to regular patterns and words that are sometimes confused in use

Source: Table compiled by authors from information contained in the Department for Education (2011c).

said in 1989 'A test, as in school literature courses, for example, can change the context for even the best of literary texts, from pleasure giving literacy to functional literacy' (p. 188).

In 1999 Gallik found, in common with other studies, that recreational reading habits are acquired early in an individual's school life, probably in elementary school, and that if a student is to have good reading skills and positive attitudes towards reading these must be developed during the elementary years. In their research, Cox and Guthrie (2001) concluded that although the cognitive and motivation variables showed simple associations with the amount of reading for enjoyment, only motivation accounted for a

Table 1.3: Level five descriptors for English Key Stage 4.

Reading	Writing
Pupils show understanding of a range of texts, selecting essential points and using inference and deduction where appropriate. In their responses, they identify key features, themes and characters and select sentences, phrases and relevant information to support their views. They understand that texts fit into historical and literary traditions. They retrieve and collate information from a range of sources.	Pupils' writing is varied and interesting, conveying meaning clearly in a range of forms for different readers, using a more formal style where appropriate. Vocabulary choices are imaginative and words are used precisely. Sentences, including complex ones and paragraphs are coherent, clear and well developed. Words with complex regular patterns are usually spelt correctly. A range of punctuation, including commas, apostrophes and inverted commas, is usually used accurately. Handwriting is joined, clear and fluent and, where appropriate, is adapted to a range of tasks.

Source: Table compiled by authors from information contained in the Department for Education (2011d, 2011e).

significant amount of variance in reading for enjoyment after all other factors were held constant statistically (Cox & Guthrie, 2001, p. 127).

With the review of the National Curriculum in 2000, and the subsequent revision, emphasis was put on the need to encourage positive attitudes towards reading as a major objective. In March 2005 David Bell, Her Majesty's Chief Inspector of Schools, in a speech to mark World Book Day, acknowledged that the National Literacy Strategy is 'having a positive effect on the quality of reading and writing' (p. 9) and that 'standards of reading have improved significantly in recent years' (p. 10), but that reading is not seen as a pleasurable activity for many children. When children are asked about why they think reading is important they gave pragmatic answers: it helps to get a job, helps to do well in tests and helps to do well at school by teaching good words to use or helping spelling (p. 3). He goes on to say that 'it is disappointing how few mention the joy of reading' and that they do not mention the wider benefits. He suggests that some schools have forgotten to instil into the pupils the pleasure of reading in their 'pursuit of higher test results that will improve their position in the league tables. You will find no pleasure in books if you cannot read, but it is equally possible to be able to read and derive little pleasure' (p. 3).

Over the last four decades, there has been a focus, within the UK government, on the development of reading, writing and communication skills, with the term 'literacy' being increasingly used within government discourse; but it is interesting to note that in more recent discourse the term is being superseded by communication (Wolf Report, 2011a).

In 2008 OfSTED (the inspectorate for standards in schools in England) drew together key inspection findings on the standards of English in schools from 2005 to 2008 in a report titled 'English at the Crossroads'. The title in itself provides the view that the English curriculum in schools needed review, due to a 'context of broadly static standards' (p. 1). The work argued that 'the most effective schools are those that have revised their English curriculum to meet changes in modern technology and pupils' developing literacy needs' (p. 4) and called for a review of the English curriculum in schools. The report was critical of the lack of clear school plans to develop independent reading (para. 44) and a need 'to reinvigorate the teaching of writing' (para. 48).

In 2009, the Rose Review was published which has had significant impact on the teaching of literacy in primary schools. This followed a previous report in 2005 by Rose which emphasised the importance of engaging young children in interesting reading through worthwhile pre-reading activities. This 2005 report indicated that the teaching of phonics was key to developing speaking, listening, reading and writing. The 2009 report followed a review of the primary curriculum making recommendations including a focus on literacy and development of training for teachers in the use of phonics. In 2010, changes were made at GCSE level in English with 'controlled assessments' under supervision replacing coursework.

In 2010, the Department for Education produced 'The Case for Change'. This document drew on the results of the latest PISA studies from across the world to provide evidence that English students came 17th in reading, behind countries such as Finland and Canada. Shepherd (2010) in the *Guardian* commented on the results as follows:

> It shows the UK's reputation as one of the world's best for education is at risk, and has tumbled several places since 2006. ... The UK is ranked 25th for reading, 28th for maths and 16th for science. In 2006, when 57 countries were included in the study, it was placed 17th, 24th and 14th respectively. Poland has stretched ahead of the UK in maths, while Norway is now ranked higher in reading and maths. Andreas Shleicher, head of the Pisa programme, said the picture for the UK was "stagnant at best". "Many other countries have seen quite significant improvement," he added. (Shepherd, 2010)

The report also drew on evidence of the need for a workforce with high levels of literacy to succeed in a global economy.

Most recently the 2011 guidance for OfSTED inspectors draws on the Wolf Report (2011a) to support the importance of all young people being able to communicate effectively. This guidance to OfSTED inspectors refers to literacy being different to English making reference to the National Curriculum programmes of study which 'are organised according to the skills of speaking and listening (attainment target AT1), reading (AT2) and writing (AT3)' (p. 10), stating that the

> actual programmes of study are set in a context of study which goes beyond 'the ability to read and write', taking in skills of analysis and response to literature and other texts, and exposure to the work of particular authors and poets. It is reasonable to suggest that literacy is a very important element within the English curriculum but that the two are not wholly the same. The curriculum and programmes of study for English extend far more widely than the acquisition of literacy skills. (p. 10)

If individuals develop positive attitudes towards reading in primary school, then it is important that children be encouraged to see books as giving pleasure, as well as a tool for learning. Indeed the OfSTED (2008) report referred to this and supported the view of an international reading survey (Twist, Schagen, & Hodgson, 2006) 'which showed that enjoyment among pupils in England was poor when compared with many other countries, and had declined since 2001'.

The next section of this chapter will consider the experience of students in their pre-university education regarding their learning, paying particular attention to literacy. To inform the discussion data was collected through two studies: student focus groups and an annual survey of a sample of students (data from three years) offered places at a large East Midlands University.

1.3. Literacy Experiences Prior to Attending University

Nine student focus groups (a total of 28 students) were run, four in Art and Design (A&D) and five in Arts and Humanities (A&H), across all taught levels of study (undergraduate years one, two and three and postgraduate) to explore students' reality of academic literacy. They were asked to discuss their experiences of reading and writing prior to attending university.

Table 1.4: Samples and response rates for the annual experience and expectations survey.

	Academic school A (hereafter called department A)			Academic school B (hereafter called department B)		
	No. of responses	Base	Response rate (%)	No. of responses	Base	Response rate (%)
2011	42	493	9	78	799	10
2010	183	1136	16	110	1345	8
2009	228	672	34	83	383	22

The data from both departments and across years were combined and averaged in the analysis, percentage frequencies being used. If there were any emergent trends over the three years, or differences between departments, these are commented upon.

The annual experience and expectations survey asks students questions about their choice of university and course; their current experience of education, based on their current behaviours in studying including time spent in various activities; their expectations of university, including expected behaviours, confidence and expected difficulty in aspects of studying and how prepared they are for university; and the importance of various university provision regarding learning and teaching. Questionnaires were sent out electronically to a sample of students who had been offered places within two schools in May/June in the years 2009, 2010 and 2011. The samples and response rates are shown in Table 1.4.

1.4.   Focus Groups

From the focus groups, it was clear that student reading and writing experiences prior to coming to university vary depending on where they were studying and the subjects that they were studying. Regarding reading, most students had 'directed reading' with set textbooks and '[got] information from their tutors in terms of the subject and the content' (final year A&H). Those who were studying English experienced 'group reading' where they were expected to read a chapter of a book prior to the class (although few did) and then it was analysed in class; rarely was the whole book read. Very few did reading outside of school hours, even if directed to do so. Even though students were not reading a lot, they were writing a substantial amount; doing more writing than reading. International students, in particular, reported that they did a lot of writing, both in English and their first language, writing articles and essays for homework and examinations, one student writing 'two or three times a week' (second year A&H) another 'every week … 2,000 words' (second year A&H). On access programmes, students also experienced a large amount of writing, essays of 2,000 words 'four or five for each subject over the year' (first year A&H), having three essays on the go at any one time with three essays each half term. With those students who did 'A2'[2] level, the amount of writing varied with the subjects studied, the examination board and the approach of the teacher.

Experience of writing is dependent on subject(s) chosen for AS/A2 study. For example, Students studying the sciences did not write many essays but had practical assessments and examinations where they had to write two or three paragraphs on a topic. Those studying arts, social sciences and humanities were expected to write many essays, sometimes with a focus on examinations, including having 'timed essays' in class every week or one for 'homework'. Students reported that the essays they wrote at school for some subjects were quite long, 2,500–3,000 words, and that they received a lot of support and formative feedback from teachers to develop their skills in writing:

> … you would write something and then … I remember for my coursework in History, I would hand it in, he would mark it and tell me what I needed to improve on, and I would get it back and I could do some more and then hand it in. So I think that was – it was 'spoonfed' to you I guess, you got a lot of support. It was the same for English. (final year A&H)

For those taking more practical subjects or vocational subjects, the amount of writing would not be as substantial. For example, for those taking ICT the examinations mainly consisted of fairly short-answer questions; coursework required more significant writing but was mainly associated with specific projects such as database creation. For those taking vocational courses such as BTEC, the writing appears again to be limited. For those on Art Foundation courses, the writing was minimal, the focus being on practical work 'I got away with doing the bare minimum of reading and writing … I did an Art Foundation, which is all practical … we did one essay throughout the whole of the year' (first year A&D). Consequently some students reported some 'anxiety' about reading and writing at university.

---

2. In the UK, students take AS in Year 12 (16–17 years) and A2 in Year 13 (17–18 years).

1.5. Questionnaires

Respondents answered questions about how much reading and writing, they currently did in their pre-university educational establishment. Regarding reading assigned books and other materials given by their pre-university establishment, across the whole sample only 22% did this a lot, 44% some, 21% very little and 12% none. For applicants to department A (an art and design department with mainly female respondents) reading these materials a lot increased from 2009 to 2011, but for the other department B (a design and built environment department with mainly male respondents) it decreased. When asked about reading recommended books, respondents indicated that they read recommended books less than they did those that were assigned: 14% reading them a lot, 48% some, 30% very little and 9% never; for applicants in department A the percentage reading other materials went down from 2009 to 2011, while in department B it increased slightly over the same period. Other materials, for example, journal articles, were read more regularly than other recommended texts: 22% reading them a lot, 48% some, 24% very little and 8% none; over time these figures were consistent, although in department A more students read these types of materials a lot than in department B. The most popular reading undertaken by all respondents was researching subjects on the Internet: 51% of respondents doing this a lot, 41% some, 6% very little and 1% none.

Applicants to both departments were asked about their current writing experiences, focusing on the length of their writing. For short essays or reports (5 or fewer pages), 31% of respondents did them a lot, 41% some, 18% very little and 9% none. In comparison when asked about longer pieces of writing (more than 5 pages), only 10% wrote longer pieces a lot, 26% some, 38% very little and 26% none.

Questions were asked about their current study behaviour and the following relate to reading and writing and teacher support. When asked whether they went to class without completing homework, coursework or reading, nearly half the respondents (43%) said never, 49% sometimes, 3.2% often and 1% never. There was consistency across both departments and an increase over time in those who never went to class without completing work. Regarding support from teachers, applicants were well supported: 19% discussing grades or coursework with their teacher very often, 48% often, 30% sometimes and 3% never. Applicants also asked their teacher for help with their coursework: 15% very often, 36% often, 45% sometimes and 5% never. This help extended to marking drafts of coursework; when asked about preparing two or more drafts of coursework before handing in 21% did that very often, 31% often, 36% sometimes and 12% never.

Applicants were then asked about their expectations of university. The majority of students thought that they would have to work on a project that requires integrating ideas or information from various sources very often (45%) or often (48%); only 0.1% felt that they would never have to do it. They also expected support from the tutors particularly discussing grades or assignments with them with 21% expecting to do this very often, 48% often, 30% sometimes and only 3% never; this expectation has increased slightly from 2009 to 2011. Regarding receiving prompt feedback from tutors, 28% expected this very often, 52% often, 19% sometimes and 0.9% never.

They were then asked about how confident they expected they would be to undertake certain tasks around reading and writing. When asked about finding additional information for course assignments when they did not understand the materials, they were confident that they would do that (36% very certain, 45% towards very certain on the Likert scale); however, they were less confident about reading recommended texts when they were not sure why they were reading them, although still confident, with 21% being very certain, 43.1% towards very certain and 27% neither certain or uncertain.

Students were then asked about how difficult they expected aspects of university to be and how prepared they felt to undertake aspects of reading and writing. They expected that getting help with academic work to be 'not that difficult', and interacting with tutors to be 'not that difficult'. Regarding understanding requirements and the rules, they felt that that too would be 'not that difficult'. Overall they felt prepared to write clearly and effectively, think critically and analytically, analyse problems and analyse written materials. An overwhelming majority felt that support to help them to succeed academically was 'important' or 'very important'.

In summary, students while at school did not do that much reading of assigned texts, recommended books or other materials, but they did read materials found on the Internet. The writing they undertook tended to be shorter (less than five pages) rather than longer pieces and they felt that they were well supported in their writing, with their tutors marking drafts. They prepared for their classes and felt well supported at school in their learning.

Their expectations for university tended to be based on their pre-university experiences. They expected to receive support in their studies and were confident that they could access this easily. They felt that support to help them to succeed was very important, and they expected to receive prompt feedback on their work. Overall they felt confident in their reading and writing behaviours and abilities going into university, and that they would understand assignment requirements and the 'rules of the game'.

1.6.   Feedback to School Pupils at School

At this point it is worth considering the feedback on developing literacy skills. This is often the focus of English staff in secondary schools. Prior to 2011, those applying to become teachers of subjects other than English were required to have GCSE English (or equivalent), and were required to take a text in English as part of their teaching qualification. Their standard of literacy is therefore at GCSE level (C grade). This may limit the level of support they can give to their students in terms of literacy. There is also rarely a policy or consistency in secondary schools giving all teachers a responsibility for developing literacy. Thus, students' experience prior to university, depending on the subject chosen for AS/A2 level, may not result in high levels of literacy, that is, not developed beyond GCSE level. The new Teaching Standards (2011b) includes a new standard, strengthening the development of literacy skills across all subject areas, but this will only impact on new trainee teachers from September 2012 when they will have to

> ... demonstrate an understanding of and take responsibility for promoting high standards of literacy and the correct use of standard English, whatever the teacher's specialist subject. (Part 1, point 3)

1.7.   Conclusion

Drawing together the key points from this chapter, it is clear that students arriving at university will have mixed experiences of reading and writing depending on the school/college they attended, the focus on developing writing skills within their pre-institution and the subjects they have taken post-16. Students entering higher education appear to believe that they are more prepared for the reading and writing they will encounter, than they actually are — they may fail to appreciate the 'step up' and getting beyond the 'false confidence'. Part of becoming an undergraduate is about becoming more independent, which could cause problems when they have experienced an 'assessment led' culture that has promoted dependency. Those coming from further education colleges may have greater independence than those coming from school sixth forms where they tend to experience smaller groups and greater individual support from teachers. Thus, many undergraduates need support in many aspects of literacy; we are considering literacy in the widest sense here, so include digital literacy (see Boulton & Hramiak, Chapter 5). The areas we are going to focus on here include finding sources of information and using them in their work, referencing, how to understand marking criteria and an introduction to aspects of academic writing which will be new to these students (see Hardy & Clughen, Chapter 2). We make recommendations of what to cover in this transition period and possible sources of help for the student.

Undergraduate students should be able to support an argument, but this will depend again on the subjects they have taken at AS/A2. Those who have taken subjects such as English, law and politics will have more experience, while those who have taken more practical subjects such as design, multimedia and ICT will need support in developing these skills. Students need to know that they will need to refer to several sources of information in their written work; that these sources need to be up-to-date (with the exception of some disciplines, such as history, or accessing key texts), varied so they can present an argument, and reliable. Reliability of resources tends to be left to the ICT programme of study within the National Curriculum where they will have been taught to find resources and know how to locate reliable sources, particularly via the Internet, in Year 7 (when they are 11). This does not focus again in the National Curriculum for ICT so much of their learning may have been forgotten by the time they arrive at university.

It is unlikely that undergraduates will have had experience of using more than one resource to inform an essay, and may not understand how to present an argument. Undergraduates may also need support in how to search for sources of information and how to recognise reliable sources; librarians can often provide support with this. It is likely that under-graduates will not have had access to journal articles prior to university, so it is essential that they are introduced to the key periodicals within the disciplines they are studying, and are shown how to search the journal databases. It is important undergraduates understand that journal articles have generally been peer reviewed so that they are reliable sources of information. Undergraduates need to be taught how to find articles that present different views and develop skills in how to structure an article/argument. Many undergraduates will lack experience of reading groups so tutors may want to create these so that students can support each other in reading and discuss some of the key texts for their course. Using some of the new technologies can help with this, such as community web blogs, discussion boards and wikis so that students can share key findings from the literature and start to share with other students how to carry out literature searches, and how to store useful information to refer back to later, as well as share reflections on readings in order to develop and co-construct meaning and understanding. It is important to remember that the education processes in England do not always encourage reading for pleasure (Bell, 2005), so establishing reading groups can have far-reaching benefits for undergraduates. In managing expectations of reading, some undergraduates may need help in organising their time and recognising the importance of setting aside time each week, outside of class contact time to engage with reading lists, taking notes from texts and becoming the independent learners that universities strive to develop.

Undergraduates will also need to know how to reference correctly the articles they are using. This is very likely to be a new skill for them to learn. There are online bibliographic databases such as Endnote and RefWorks which undergraduates will need introducing to which will simplify the process of referencing, but they need to understand the correct way, in their subject discipline, to reference a range of materials such as texts, articles, newspaper articles, interviews, websites and videos. It is also important while encouraging them to reference correctly and that students understand plagiarism and the penalties for this. Undergraduates may have been encouraged to work together in school and may not understand that at university collusion can have serious consequences.

Undergraduates will need to understand what may be new language in terms of assessment and marking criteria, for example, what does 'accurate, broad and deep' mean in criteria. Providing information with a brief explanation of key assessment terms such as 'we're looking for a wide appreciation of the issues that demonstrate real thought, not just a regurgitation of lecture materials or an online podcast' will help to reduce their anxieties. Also what does 'evaluate' mean for those aiming for higher marks, for example, it's not sufficient for them to simply quote from materials provided by tutors, instead undergraduates need to critically assess the validity of sources, see how they agree, or not, with other sources and establish what (if anything) they add to their argument. In school, students may well have had coaching in what the right answer needs to include, while at university, in becoming independent learners, they need to read a variety of materials that reflect a range of type and provide depth for their responses. They will need help in assembling their reading and drawing out the 'evidence' to support their argument which they will need to ensure is coherent and well structured. Undergraduates may, as part of their transition, need help with the overall structure and discipline requirements through tutor and peer feedback on aspects such as their plan, their literature search, their introduction and conclusion.

In terms of feedback, undergraduates, pre-university, will have received regular formative feedback, and often support in writing assignments on an almost one-to-one basis. There is therefore real anxiety in the transition into university when faced with being part of a large cohort. It is important to ensure undergraduates know where and how to access academic writing support, know and understand what feedback they will get and when. In higher education in the UK, there is a cultural shift to providing more formative feedback, but this is still rarely to the degree the undergraduates will have received at school or in college. They also need to know how to engage with targets and improve their marks.

In this chapter, we have provided a brief overview and context of the teaching and assessment of literacy (reading and writing) within schools in the UK. We have also provided an overview of the current situation and concluded with a discussion of the experiences of students transitioning to higher education and provided insight into the areas of writing that undergraduates may require additional support. The following chapter will consider the expectations and experiences of students when they arrive at university regarding literacy and academics' expectations for student literacy.

References

Bell, D. (2005). *A good read: Speech to mark World Book Day: 2 March 2005.* Retrieved from www.ofsted.gov.uk/publications/index.cfm?fuseaction = pubs. displayfile&id = 8848&type = doc. Accessed on 4 March 2005.

Callaghan, J. (1976). *A rational debate based on the facts.* Speech given at Ruskin College Oxford, 18 October 1976. Retrieved from http://www.educationengland. org.uk/documents/speeches/1976ruskin.html. Accessed on 21 January 2011.

Cox, K. E., & Guthrie, J. T. (2001). Motivational and cognitive contributions to students' amount of reading. *Contemporary Educational Psychology, 26*, 116–131.

Department for Education. (2010). *The case for change.* Retrieved from https:// www.education.gov.uk/publications/standard/publicationDetail/Page1/DFE-00564-2010. Accessed on 20 January 2012.

Department for Education. (2011a). *Review of vocational education — The Wolf Report* (00031-2011). Retrieved from www.education.gov.uk/publications/stan dard/publicationDetail/Page1/DFE-00031-2011. Accessed on 20 January 2012.

Department for Education. (2011b) *Teaching standards.* Retrieved from http:// media.education.gov.uk/assets/files/pdf/t/teachers%20standards.pdf. Accessed on 22 January 2012.

Department for Education. (2011c). *Key stage 4 English: Key processes.* Retrieved from http://www.education.gov.uk/schools/teachingandlearning/curriculum/ secondary/b00199101/english/ks4/programme

Department for Education. (2011d). *Key stage 4 English: Attainment target level descriptions. English: Reading.* Retrieved from http://www.education.gov.uk/ schools/teachingandlearning/curriculum/secondary/b00199101/english/ks4/attain ment/reading. Accessed on 22 January 2012.

Department for Education. (2011e). *Key stage 4 English: Attainment target level descriptions. English: Writing.* Retrieved from http://www.education.gov.uk/ schools/teachingandlearning/curriculum/secondary/b00199101/english/ks4/attain ment/writing. Accessed on 23 January 2012.

Department for Education. (2012). *About the school curriculum: Programmes of study.* Retrieved from http://www.education.gov.uk/schools/teachingandlearning/

curriculum/b00200366/about-the-school-curriculum/pos. Accessed on 22 January 2012.

Gallik, J. D. (1999). Do they read for pleasure? Recreational reading habits of college students. *Journal of Adolescent & Adult Literacy, 42*(6), 480–488.

Gillard, D. (2011). *Education in England: A brief history.* Retrieved from www.educationengland.org.uk/history. Accessed on 17 January 2012.

Lankshear, C., & Knobel, M. (2005). *New literacies. Changing knowledge and classroom learning.* Maidenhead, UK: Open University Press.

Office for Standards in Education (OfSTED). (2008). *English at the crossroads.* Retrieved from http://www.ofsted.gov.uk/publications. Accessed on 20 January 2012.

Office for Standards in Education (OfSTED). (2011). *Reading, writing and communication (literacy): Guidance and training for inspectors.* Retrieved from http://www.ofsted.gov.uk/publications. Accessed on 20 January 2012.

Resnick, D. P., & Resnick, L. B. (1989). Varieties of literacy. In A. E. Barnes & P. N. Stearns (Eds.), *Social history and issues in human consciousness: Some interdisciplinary connections* (pp. 171–196). New York, NY: New York University Press.

Rose, J. (2009). *Independent review of the primary curriculum: Final report.* Retrieved from http://www.literacytrust.org.uk/sitemap_overview. Accessed on 19 January 2012.

Shepherd, J. (2010). World education rankings: Which country does best at reading, maths and science? The OECD's comprehensive world education ranking report, PISA, is out. Find out how each country compares. *The Guardian* (online), Tuesday 7 December 2010. Retrieved from http://www.guardian.co.uk/news/datablog/2010/dec/07/world-education-rankings-maths-science-reading. Accessed on 21 January 2012.

St. John Hunter, C., & Harman, D. (1979). *Adult illiteracy in the United States: A report to the Ford Foundation.* New York, NY: McGraw-Hill Book Company.

Street, B. (1995). *Social literacies: Critical approaches to literacy in development, ethnography and education.* Harlow: Longman.

The Standards of Education in schools in England from 1972. Retrieved from *The Victorian School Website.* Retrieved from http://www.victorianschool.co.uk/school%20history%20lessons.html

Times. (1871). The Education Act of 1870 has of necessity [editorial]. *Times,* 27 February, p. 9. London: The Times Digital Archive. Retrieved from http://find.galegroup.com/ttda/infomark.do?&source=gale&prodId=TTDA&userGroupName=nottstrent&tabID=T003&docPage=article&searchType=BasicSearchForm&docId=CS151301211&type=multipage&contentSet=LTO&version=1.0. Accessed on 17 January 2012.

Twist, L., Schagen, I., & Hodgson, C. (2007). *Readers and reading: The National Report for England 2006* (PIRLS: Progress in International Reading Literacy Study). Slough: NFER. Retrieved from http://www.nfer.ac.uk/publications/otherpublications/downloadable-reports/pirls-2006.cfm. Accessed on 20 January 2012.

UNESCO. (2003). *Literacy, a UNESCO perspective* (online). Paris: UNESCO. Retrieved from http://unesdoc.unesco.org/images/0013/001318/131817eo.pdf. Accessed on 22 January 2012.

Vincent, D. (1989). *Literacy and popular culture: England 1750–1914*. Cambridge: CUP.

Chapter 2

Writing at University: Student and Staff Expectations and Experiences

Christine Hardy and Lisa Clughen

2.1. Introduction

Academics bemoan student writing at university; students bemoan academic writing at university (Lea & Street, 1998). While we must emphasise that this is not universally the case, the mismatch between student and tutor expectations around writing (see Hounsell, 1997; Lillis, 1999; Lillis & Turner, 2001) and the impact of this on student and staff experiences of student writing have long been reported (Davies, Swinburne, & Williams, 2006, *passim*; Ganobcsik-Williams, 2004; Haggis, 2006). This chapter will demonstrate that the 'communication failures' (Haggis, 2006, p. 521) over the task of academic writing and their associated confusions and frustrations for both students and staff are still to be found in contemporary higher education. It begins by contextualising the issues surrounding the disparities between student and staff expectations and experiences of academic writing and then presents research undertaken at a large East Midlands university in the United Kingdom around these issues.

That the academic transition to university is often challenging for students is of no surprise when one considers the extent of their task. They are expected to adapt to 'new ways of knowing: new ways of understanding, interpreting and organising knowledge' (Lea & Street, 1998, p. 158), to become independent in their learning and thinking; to reflect on their beliefs in order to form judgements (what Baxter Magolda, 2010, refers to as 'self-authorship')

Writing in the Disciplines: Building Supportive Cultures for Student Writing
in UK Higher Education
ISBN: 978-1-78052-546-4

and to demonstrate those judgements through appropriate academic discourse. The written work that students encounter at university often differs from the writing they have previously undertaken, both in terms of genres and writing conventions. Ganobcsik-Williams (2004, p. 14), points out, for example, that students are 'expected to possess or to acquire a working knowledge of a variety of written forms and writing conventions' and identifies 64 varieties of writing genres to which university students could be exposed. In addition, student-writers often struggle to understand the conventions of the institution (Lillis & Turner, 2001) and the ways in which they are shaped by both the various disciplines (Lea & Street, 1998) and the particular preferences of individual tutors (Adams, 2008; Lea & Street, 1998; Read, Francis, & Robson, 2001; Vardi, 2000). Yet, despite the very different inflections given to such conventions at a disciplinary and local level, they are often treated as if they were 'common sense' and communicated to the students through documents that are thought to be transparent and meaningful (Haggis, 2006; Lillis & Turner, 2001). This is often not the case and students end up not knowing what the 'rules of the game' are (Adams, 2008; Kember, 2001; Lea, 2004; Lillis, 1997; Read et al., 2001). These difficulties are particularly acute for students who study more than one discipline as there are often contradictory inter-disciplinary variations in accepted style; and by the organisation and delivery of large courses and modules (Adams, 2008, p. 6) whereby one member of the teaching staff 'may write the handbook and manage the teaching staff' and others teach on the module, each having their own 'unique expectations of the writing'. In her study on lecturer expectations for writing in assignments, Vardi (2000), for example, found that most lecturers will expect in-text and end-text referencing in first-year student essays (Vardi, 2000, p. 4), but that other requirements varied greatly depending on a different combination of factors, which she found to be

1. The reason for setting the essay, which can impact on the type of critical engagement expected, structure and content of the essay, and the types of sources that needed to be consulted;
2. The thinking of the discipline;
3. The lecturer's personal beliefs about 'good writing' in relation to teaching objectives and
4. The need to assess students' understanding.

As these factors vary, so too do lecturers' expectations of student writing, meaning that each task could result in a unique set of particular expectations. This makes it difficult for students to determine what is expected from them for each individual piece of writing:

> Every time a student sits down to write for us he or she has to
> invent the university for the occasion — invent the university,

that is, or a branch of it ... The student has to learn to speak our language, to speak as we do, to try on the particular ways of knowing, selecting, evaluating, reporting, concluding, and arguing that define the discourse of our community. Or perhaps I should say the various discourses of our community. (Bartholomae, 1985, p. 134)

This confusion about requirements can negatively impact on student performance, but in addition to this, there is much criticism about students' technical skills, particularly the basic ability to express themselves adequately in their writing (Ahmad & McMahon, 2006; Cabral & Tavares, 2002; Frean, Yobbo, & Duncan, 2007; Ganobcsik-Williams, 2004; Murray & Kirton, 2006; Winch & Wells, 1995).

Yet in stark contrast to the criticisms levelled at student writing, when they enter higher education, students themselves often feel adequately or well prepared for its demands in terms of reading and writing (Cook & Leckey, 1999; Lowe & Cook, 2003; Smith, 2005), and a large proportion of students do indeed leave school with well-developed writing skills (McMahon, 2004). However, as we indicate above, student perceptions of their preparedness for HE writing cultures are often at odds with the realities of the cultures themselves and, especially given with the increasing diversity of the student body, many reach university without the essential skills to make the most of their studies and find that their successful strategies for A level are now inappropriate (Lea & Street, 1998), so they can increasingly lose confidence once there (Ahmad & McMahon, 2006) as '[they] suddenly see their undergraduate essays marked more harshly than their school essays' (Murray & Kirton, 2006, p. 9).

These problems often occur due to students' epistemological beliefs about learning, as they often enter with reproductive conceptions of learning which are not compatible with study in higher education (Kember, 2001). In terms of their writing, these epistemological beliefs extend to their readiness to work with and contest the authoritative knowledge presented in texts (Lea & Street, 1998). Many commentators agree this to be the result of

... limited resources and over-stretched staff in schools. [and] ... the grade focused mentality of the secondary school system, and its (understandable) tendency to spoon-feed students rather than develop their critical abilities. (Husain & Waterfield, 2006, p. 28)

It has been argued that this grade-focused mentality is a result of an emphasis on league tables resulting in the temptation to teach to the syllabus and the assessment criteria, with a close reading of a narrow range of texts rather than wider readings (Smith, 2005, p. 19). In response to this, students can develop a set of study skills that persist at university, where they 'value a simple approach in which staff present classes with precise information which can be easily translated into examination answers and assignments' (Cook & Leckey, 1999, p. 163), and 'are more focused on the material delivered by staff than on the wider subject' (*ibid.* p. 164).

Because of the above experience of writing at school and the different literacy practices and expectations at university, students can experience difficulties with the reading and writing required at university. In a Flying Start project,[1] for example, it was found that students perceive academic writing to be 'writing involving analytical and critical thinking and presenting a clear argument supported by evidence' (Coffey, Merryweather, Itua, & Foxcroft, 2010) and the barriers to academic writing to be: referencing (the primary issue), academic jargon and difficulties in structuring academic work, finding academic reading boring and finding it hard to read academic texts. Lecturers, on the other hand, viewed the barriers to successful academic writing to include lack of time (pressures of jobs, budgeting time, work-study balance), lack of reading and understanding of (complex) texts, challenge/fear of 'open pieces of writing' and not understanding what is expected of students in respect of academic writing (Coffey et al., 2010).

For students to succeed in academic writing, they are required to read academic texts, which, as previously noted, they find difficult. One of the difficulties is due to the different types of text they are expected to read at university, their lack of previous knowledge of these text genres and their lack of familiarity with content. In a study with postgraduate students, Francis and Hallam (2000) suggested that adequate understanding of a text requires:

> ... sufficient prior subject knowledge, an approach charac-
> terised by the intention to understand (deep approach), ability
> to recognise and use the text genre concerned, and adequate
> time to reflect on apparent differences or contradictions ...
> Students had little difficulty with the kind of academic text
> typical of their first degree courses, but perceived more text

---

1. Flying Start is a collaborative project to help bridge the gap between further and higher education. It is a widening participation project taking a cross-sector approach to bridge the 'separate worlds' of writing and assessment at pre-university and undergraduate level and ease the transition between the two. It is funded by the Higher Education Academy National Teaching Fellowship Scheme Project Strand. Liverpool Hope University is the lead institution, and the collaborating partner institutions include the University of Derby, Edge Hill University, Queen Mary University London and Nottingham Trent University.

genre problems the nearer they got to being inducted into a
research community and into the practices of research and
research reporting which underpin the epistemology of their
academic subject. (*ibid.*, pp. 294–295)

They concluded that students underestimate the work needed to
understand texts which may lead to 'vastly overloaded schedules of required
course reading' leading to an 'unwitting pressure on students to try to cope
with their course by downplaying understanding and settling for what they
sense to be inadequate mental work' (*op. cit.*, p. 296), which impacts on their
writing. These difficulties in reading academic texts are often downplayed
by lecturers, who perceive the main difficulties for students' reading to be
associated with 'comprehension of questions, data and demonstrations' rather
than vocabulary, understanding connections between ideas and abstract
concepts (Cabral & Tavares, 2002, p. 295).

Expectations of academic writing by staff vary according to year of
study, but by the final year most academics agree that

> ... students should be able to structure and organise complex
> and cohesive arguments and ... demonstrate a command
> of language, or an understanding of how language works,
> ability to present work which is not in need of correction of
> basic grammar and punctuation and spelling ... write critically
> ...[exhibiting] a stronger point of view synthesising their
> reading and research with their own reasoned views and
> opinions. [There should be] a sense of audience, grasp of
> referencing/citation, understanding of content and [an] ability
> to utilise language and arguments appropriate to disciplinary
> conventions. (Ganobcsik-Williams, 2004, p. 13)

The development of 'voice' in their work often causes problems for
students. Many students know that they need to present their own voice to
achieve good grades (Read et al., 2001, p. 394), but frequently do this by
'responding to feedback and, modelling from the research articles assigned
on the course' (Adams, 2008, p. 3). This modelling or 'emulation' often leads
them to

> ... attempt to write at a higher academic register that that in
> which they feel comfortable: they imitate their tutors and/or
> the academic books and papers they read, and when this
> imitation happens without full comprehension, without the
> broad and deep knowledge of the subject which their models
> have attained, and without experience at writing, the result is

> ill-digested, pompous prose and a yawning gap between the
> standard the tutor expects and the work the student can offer.
> (Husain & Waterfield, 2006, pp. 27–28)

Even when they have acquired the 'ground rules' and skills, the expression
of voice can still be impeded by an awareness of the social situation of
writing which is shrouded by the 'unequal power relations between student
and lecturer'. Many students feel 'that their opinion is worthless and should
not therefore be articulated' and 'they do not trust that they will be assessed
objectively by the tutor ... as they feel they are not able to challenge the
opinions of "established academics"' (Read et al., 2001, p. 397) so they
determine which views are favoured and present them as 'their own voice'.

Yet student confusions about academic writing and calls from the critics
to make writing conventions explicit also come in a context in which much
has been done to rectify the situation. Academics, when interviewed, often
state that they explicitly teach academic writing orally within sessions by
'showing students' samples to model from and by clearly outlining expectations in course and module handbooks' (Adams, 2008, p. 3). In addition to
giving guidance at the beginning of the assignment, nearly half of academics
develop strategies to 'help their students with their assignments through
feedback instructions or direct instruction to promote their proficiency ... '
although the majority did not (Cabral & Tavares, 2002, no page no.). It is
widely recognised that feedback on student work is one of the major tools to
improve students' ability in academic writing, though this is not a widespread and institutionalised procedure. In many UK academic departments

> ... staff have agreed to a policy of not reading students' drafts,
> or of not reading more than a certain percentage of a draft,
> such as an introduction, a conclusion, or a set number of
> paragraphs. Such policies have apparently been set both to
> protect staff time and because there is widespread perception
> that reading or discussing student writing too closely will be
> seen as collaborating or 'spoonfeeding'. (Ganobcsik-Williams,
> 2004, p. 15)

Support for academic writing is a feature of UK higher education, although
its shape and extent do, of course, differ across institutions, university
departments and individual lecturers. Yet students still struggle with their
writing for a variety of reasons including their previous experiences being
incompatible with university requirements, understanding these requirements
and tutor expectations. To understand more fully the difficulties involved
with academic writing from both student and staff perspectives, research was

undertaken with students and academics into the experiences and expectations of academic writing at university.

2.2. The Research

The research was conducted from February to June 2011 at a large East Midlands university in the United Kingdom. It consisted of student focus groups, student questionnaires and staff questionnaires. Prior to the collection of data, the research was considered and agreed with the appropriate university ethics committee.

Nine student focus groups (a total of 28 students) were run, four in Art and Design (A&D) and five in Arts and Humanities (A&H), across all taught levels of study (undergraduate years one, two and three and postgraduate) to explore students' lived experiences of academic literacies. The areas for discussion were previous experiences of reading and writing prior to attending university, expectations of reading and writing at university and how they changed, practice of reading and writing at university, feelings about reading and writing and support required for reading and writing while at university.

Questionnaires were sent out electronically to a sample of all students within the university (8296) with an incentive offered to complete the questionnaire (entered into a prize draw to win shopping vouchers). Students were asked questions about their reading and writing at university, school and for leisure and their behaviours and feelings around this. In addition, they were asked questions on feedback they receive on their writing and support that they accessed. The response rate was 5.5%, giving a total of 455 responses. Two-thirds of the respondents were female, with 88% under the age of 25 years (62% were 18–21). The sample was representative of all the disciplines with 87% of respondents studying for their first degree, the rest studying for a master's qualification (11%) or a research degree (2%). There were slightly more students studying in first year than second year or three plus. English was the first language for most of the respondents (86%) and the majority of respondents' previous educational experience was either at sixth form school or college (59%) or college of further education (19%) which reflected the age and level of study for the sample. The data was analysed using percentage responses to questions and content analysis for the 'free questions', the sample was analysed as a whole.

Questionnaires were sent electronically to all academic staff (1507) with a response rate of 9%, giving 136 responses. The questions focused on expectations of students regarding reading and writing, types of written work set, support and feedback offered and the hurdles they thought students encountered with their reading and writing. Forty eight per cent of the respondents were male, with 23% working in higher education for less than

6 years, 22% for 6 to 10 years, 36% 11 to 20 years and 19% more than 20 years. All disciplines were represented, although only 4% of respondents were from Animal, Rural and Environmental Sciences. The largest percentage of respondents was from A&H (20%) and Social Sciences (16%). A large majority of respondents taught on undergraduate and postgraduate courses, with 46% involved with PhD supervision.

2.3. Student Expectations of Literacy at University

All students had expected literacy (reading and writing) at university to be harder than their previous experiences, either at school or college but were unclear about what this meant:

> Harder than it was before, as university is the next step and it seems like a bigger thing ... [harder] in a more professional way maybe, more challenging as it would be the next step in your education. (first-year A&D)
> I imagined it to be extremely difficult, as my whole perception of university was like the crème de la crème. ... I just thought it would be extremely hard. (first-year A&H)

Alongside their awareness of the increasing challenge of the reading, they all thought that they would be expected to do a lot more reading and 'be a lot more independent and find the evidence for yourself' (second-year A&H).

Some students felt that writing would be completely different, but were not clear about how 'I thought [the tutors] were expecting something completely different. I don't know what I expected ...' (final-year A&H). Many students felt anxious about what was required of their writing at university, particularly having to 'sound' academic.

> My expectations were really high when I came to university, how I was expected to write. I almost felt intimidated by what I was reading, which is what I thought I had to write so it was really 'scary' as you read something and think about how well they have written it and the quality of what you are saying. (final-year A&H)
> I thought things had to be elaborate and sound as if I knew what I was talking about and the words and the vocabulary had to be more complicated. (second-year A&H)

Other students felt that writing would be a continuation of what they did in their previous educational establishment and felt confident about writing at university, as they felt 'prepared'. 'To begin with [I was] not worried about it. I felt from school and college I knew enough about what to do' (second-year A&D). Some students were taught referencing and encouraged to read and others were 'schooled' — 'they're very much geared to make sure we do well at university, get into a good university' (second-year A&H). However, the majority of students were not prepared for the type of literacies they would encounter at university and were critical of the education system in the United Kingdom:

> ... it seems strange that it is a whole education system in one, but they are so different [school and university]. You would think there would be more of a gradual change to becoming more independent. (first-year A&D)

2.4. Academics' Expectations of Student Literacy at University

The majority of academic staff (76%) felt that first-year students were not prepared for university and stated that they had specific expectations about how the students' first assignment should be written. They expected first-year students to reference appropriately (58%), to structure a coherent argument (76%) and to follow the conventions of their discipline for presenting written work (87%). When it came to synthesis and criticality, they expected students to undertake synthesis of others' work, but the expectations of critical appraisal at this stage were less onerous.

Staff were asked in detail about their differing expectations of reading and writing at first year and third year of an undergraduate programme of study. The responses were very similar across the disciplines for these expectations.

Regarding reading, in the first year they expect it to be focused and narrow, reading for information, engaging with good quality textbooks and online materials. They expected students to read with understanding and to integrate the ideas they have read into their written work, with an ability to reflect but not necessarily to critique. By the final year, there was agreement that students should be much more independent in their studies, seeking out relevant information that was broader, having a context for their reading and relating texts to other texts and concepts. They should also increase their depth of reading, using peer-reviewed journals, academic textbooks and monographs and be reading them critically and evaluating them:

> Third year students go beyond synthesis or analysing a wide range of texts, artefacts etc. to being able to formulate an original argument or approach which they have arrived at

through close reading; analysing those texts rather than simply taking an idea from one or more of them and running with it.

There was a degree of consensus that writing was different in the first and final years of undergraduate study. In the first year, there was an expectation of some form of structured and coherent assemblage of facts to address the question, which is largely descriptive, but referenced. By the final year there should be evidence based, coherent argument or position that draws upon the research literature and follows the academic and disciplinary conventions, taking into account the audience, in forming a synthesised critical analysis. There should also be an integration of theory and practice when relevant and competent referencing, and the writing should be more 'sophisticated'. Finally, there was an expectation at all levels that students should be able to spell and have a good grasp of grammar and punctuation.

2.5. Types of Writing Undertaken at University

Academics were asked about specific written work for assessment, such as longer essays (over 1,000 words), reports, reflective writing, creative writing and group writing and all of these were used by a majority of respondents, with the exception of the longer essay where it was a significant minority.

In addition to the above, academics identified 47 forms of assessed writing that they used within the courses (Table 2.1). Although some of the types identified were a little vague, it is clear that the purpose, form and the audience of the writing were varied; students being expected to understand a variety of writing genres. These included traditional academic writing tasks, reflective writing, writing for and in the virtual environment, writing for employment, using visuals in their writing and group writing.

The majority of students (59%), when asked about the last piece of writing they had undertaken, had written an essay of over 1,000 words and 26% had written a report. Students identified a further 17 genres of writing which they had been asked to undertake (Table 2.2). The dissertation was the most common answer, probably due to the timing of the survey.

2.6. Student Experiences of Literacy at University

2.6.1. Reading

Students' experience of literacy at university depended on the course they were studying for and their attitude towards their studies. All students found the reading broader and less determined at university, whereas at school it

Table 2.1: Varieties of writing expected of students in higher education.

Laboratory notebooks	Opinions
Scientific papers	Draft documents
Examination	Field notebooks
Newspaper articles	Popular science articles
Literature surveys	Dissertation
Critique of ideas and/or each other's written critiques	Case studies
Projects	Research reports
Critical piece linked to a visual presentation	Numeric calculations exercises (sometime comprehensive and complicated, where each step should be explained clearly so that others can follow the work)
Patchwork texts	Short answers to explain mathematical derivations
Annotated bibliographies	Popular journal article writing
News and book summary	Analytical commentary featuring a portfolio of selected sources from a range of relevant academic, professional and popular literature
Film reviews	
Portfolios	Diary log assessment
Critical diaries (mixture of analysis and reflection)	Reviews of their progress
Assessed discussion boards	Wiki collaborations
E-portfolios	
CVs	Letters
Letter of application	Memoranda
Judgments and power point presentations	Written advice to clients
Specifications	Mooting
Heads of argument	Scripts for radio and TV
Technical communication (i.e. bills of quantity, risk assessments, technical drawings with notes/ annotations)	
Image and text (visual essays using quotes)	Posters where content rather than presentation techniques is assessed
Photo-essay	
A group qualitative database	A group presentation script

Table 2.2: Varieties of writing students experienced on their course.

Dissertation	Examination
Research and reporting	Short-form questions
Contextual statement	Literature review
Detailed plan and specification	Seminar paper
Research methods	Peer-reviewed article
Learning journal	
A wiki	
Opinion on the merits of a legal case	
Illustrated essay	Poster
Creative portfolio	
Group presentation materials	

was more directed and this caused problems of uncertainty for them. 'Here [you are] reading everything and not directly working on it, but keeping that knowledge until you may need it' (first-year A&D). Some students felt that as the reading was not directed '[it was] pointless 'cause you are not sure where you are reading or what you are doing with it' (first-year A&D).

In addition, all students found that there was a lot of reading that was expected of them and most could not keep up with it and so only read for relevance, although they found it difficult to determine what was relevant:

> [I] knew I would have a lot, especially reading. I just cannot keep up with it ... I am just about doing the basic reading for any assignment. I just can't keep up. ... trying to find the relevant stuff, I find that quite difficult sometimes. It is a lot of work. (first-year A&H)

The amount of expected reading was stressful for some students 'And Jesus; you can get really stressed over it. Really stressed' (second-year A&H), and developed coping strategies in response that included skim-reading books, checking the contents and the first paragraph of chapters for relevance. Because of the perceived amount of reading they were expected to undertake, many students only read when they had to prepare for seminars or an assignment:

> [the] only time I read for my course is if I am reading for an essay. I don't really have the time to read more widely, out of general interest. So I read to prepare essays. That is all I get time to do. (final-year A&H)

The amount of independence expected in their reading and the lack of 'checking up' meant that many students felt that they did less reading in the first year than they did at school. 'I know that you do have reading lists but you don't go to them unless you have an essay to do. So I don't think I have done as much as at school. At university it is not amplified enough, people do not pay attention to the reading list' (second-year A&H).

In the questionnaire, students were asked about the nature of their academic reading. The majority of respondents (70%) read the essential and/or recommended books/articles on the reading list often or very often, but did not read additional books/articles for general understanding of the subject regularly. When it came to reading additional books/articles on the booklist for specific purposes (e.g. assessment) 72% did read them often or very often. The majority of students (57%) never or sometimes read materials not on the reading list (including online) recommended by friends, but 59% read materials they found themselves often or very often. These results do suggest that students tend to focus their reading on what they perceive they have to read or around assessments, rather than for general reading.

When asked about their feelings and behaviours regarding reading for their course, the majority of students were sometimes (51%) or never (8%) excited about the ideas they were reading. However, the majority felt satisfaction after reading something (69% often/very often) but were not particularly motivated to read more (53% never/sometimes, 47% often/very often). A large majority of students had difficulty in understanding the language used in the texts they read sometimes or often (80%) and sometimes or often did not understand the ideas they were reading (83%) and the majority of students were overwhelmed by the amount of reading expected of them (42% sometimes, 40% often/very often). Students were ambivalent about their reading. The majority, said that, 'at least sometimes', they had difficulties with their reading, the language and the ideas and felt overwhelmed by the amount of reading given to them.

In a free question, students were asked how they overcame any hurdles they had with their reading. The most commonly occurring response (122 mentions) was to ask for help, the first people to ask were friends and family and then lecturers. Other methods to improve understanding of their reading were to look for additional information to clarify their reading (93 mentions). The additional reading could be print materials found in the reference section of the book, but most commonly students wanted to find something that would be easier to read and searched the Internet, the most popular sites being Google, YouTube and Wikipedia. When searching for definitions of words or phrases, students also commonly used electronic resources (64 mentions); namely Google, dictionaries and the thesaurus. Many students persevered with their reading and re-read (63 mentions), often after taking a break (53 mentions). Other common tactics for understanding their reading were making notes (12 mentions) and breaking the reading down into smaller chunks or reading summaries (8 mentions). Very few students 'gave up' (7 mentions) but many students persisted with their reading, often using phrases such as 'suffer through it' or 'grit my teeth and do it' (22 mentions).

2.6.2. *Writing*

With the exception of those A&D students who attended an Arts Foundation course, many students felt that the amount of writing they were expected to do at university was lower than pre-university. They did find the writing difficult, however, and particularly the demand to 'find their voice':

> I don't find the actual pace or the amount of writing and assignments I have to hand in is as intense as it was at college, but the quality of writing — trying to learn to write in an academic way ... we knew that we needed to be more concise — we would have less words to get all our information in, but it is changing the tone of your voice, from your voice to what is acceptable in an essay, that is what I find really difficult and that is not what I was expecting so much. (first-year A&H)

One part of this 'academic way' is referencing and the possibility of plagiarism. 'You never had to do that at sixth form, you literally wrote "by so and so" and you did not have to do anything else' (second-year A&H) and all students struggled with the concepts of 'citing' and 'bibliographies'. In addition, students, very early on, recognised disciplinary differences when reading and found this difficult when it came to their writing:

> [You] take information from many sources; different terminology, different ways of people writing about it. So to put it all together in one coherent piece of writing is difficult. (first-year A&D)
> Referencing is completely different for English and History — I did not understand how it worked. ... Before I came to university, I never had to do the whole referencing thing, and that was a big shock. (first-year A&H)

Other students were not prepared for the different kinds of writing they were expected to do, much of it very different from what they had previously experienced, '[I had] no experience of the different kinds of writing required ... so it took me a while to grasp what they wanted me to do' (first-year A&D). This is particularly true of international students. MA students in A&D, from India, found that the ways of studying in the United Kingdom were very different '[there is] not much focus on academic writing at home — over here the emphasis is on referencing. This is the first time I will be doing a literature review; I have never done that before' (MA student A&D). They found particular difficulty with paraphrasing and summarising and were concerned about plagiarism and experienced 'confusion over quotations and when I could give my own opinions and how to blend everything' (MA student A&D).

Although they were working with greater 'depth' from level 2, overall, students found the subsequent years easier than the first, particularly in terms of the writing '... I don't know if it is because I have stepped up a notch, but I don't feel there has been that step up, or it has not been as difficult anyway' (second-year A&D). By the end of their degree they found that writing had enabled them to 'find their voice'. 'The more I wrote, the more I found my voice. Learning the language of the subject/discipline' (final-year A&D).

> I think my writing is more informed. In the first year I had not picked up anything about somebody being critical. The extra reading, you are in the mode of reading widely around the subject, just generally in the habit of being aware of the debates going on. [My writing is] more sophisticated. In the first year I had no experience and in the final year it is second nature. You know your primary sources, but I have a confidence with extra reading and my voice. (final-year A&H)

In the questionnaire, students were asked to reflect on the last piece of writing they undertook on a scale of 1 (strongly disagree) to 6 (strongly agree). These reflections give some insight into the process of writing at university. When writing, the students felt that they read a lot of materials (68%) and made a lot of notes (68%), and a large minority found difficulties in starting the writing (46%) but did not leave it to the last minute (49%). Seventy-eight per cent referenced all the information that they used from other sources, but did not use work they had read without understanding it because it sounded good (65%). Regarding help and advice from the tutors, a large minority (32%) said that they were not told how to structure the work or advised what should go into the work (31%), with 35% being given advice on structuring and 43% on content. However, students did discuss the structure with other students (41%) and also what should go into the work (47%). When it came to working with other students, the majority (64%) did not; they also did not get other students to read their work before handing it in (73%) or members of their family (65%).

2.7. Academics' Experiences of Student Literacies

Staff frequently expressed disappointment with student literacies, both their reading and writing.

> First years do not like to read and find it a chore, they have to be coerced or it has to be demonstrated that the reading is specifically required for their assessment. Third years are expected to read around the subject, but they generally look at the core text and on the internet rather than using good academic sources.

> Generally I find that having accumulated more knowledge and with a fixation of their final degree mark, [final year] students engage with more reading but this tends to be very limited and restricted to what the need to read; or they perceive they need to read. Broadly speaking, students don't read enough regardless of year or the reading material. If students are prepared to read in the first year they are much better in the third year but for some [reading] is a novelty and they don't [do it].

There was criticism of student writing, with many tutors believing that the first years were not well prepared for writing at university:

> First year students, in my view, don't understand how important writing is as the vehicle for their knowledge; they don't understand the difference between different genres of writing (i.e. academic versus journalistic); they often have no experience of academic conventions (ie evidence all statements); no knowledge of their discipline's practice. The 'hidden curriculum' is not on their radar. Third years should have grasped all of this.

But many tutors were critical of student writing at all levels, their abilities and their attitudes, indicating a lack of 'commitment to academic conventions such as referencing, writing in an academic style etc'., an inability to construct sentences and arguments and to use feedback to improve their writing.

> For the most part students don't write very well or often enough. Writing is treated as a chore and is engaged with in a utilitarian fashion (they only do it when they have to and when a mark is attached to the work). The standard of English and grammar is poor.

2.8. Support for Writing

2.8.1. *Student Perspectives*

In the schools of A&D and A&H, writing support is provided centrally by a specialist who works closely with the programmes of study. This support is individual and group-based offered within and without the courses and open to all students. In the focus groups, students were asked about support for writing, the support they currently received from the university and other sources and also what they felt would be useful to improve their writing.

Students reported that they were given guidance on their assessments in course documentation, but often did not find this useful, as they did not understand what it meant or what the lecturer was looking for 'I use that and hope for the best I guess' (first-year A&D). What they found most useful was direct engagement with staff, including the feedback that they received on their work. Regarding feedback, all students felt that there should be more feedback, and some reported that they only received a mark and no comments on their work. When comments were made on the work itself, students often found them confusing. They did not always understand obscure comments or annotations, such as the bald statement 'grammar?', the use of question marks or the practice of circling words.

> I read everything, not just the comments but what has been circled, question marks etc. and sometimes I don't understand why they are there, what I have done wrong. (second-year A&H)
>
> One of the comments I get is 'you need to write in a scholarly way' but what is a scholarly way? I don't understand it — what they want I am not capable of giving. (first-year A&H)

One student had to write a document response and gave a particular example of unhelpful feedback, '[the tutor wrote] 'this is not a document response, but an essay', but what is a document response? We did not get it defined in seminars or lectures' (second-year A&H).

Some students were given the opportunity to discuss the feedback in one-to-one tutorials, which they found very helpful '[you can] speak to your tutor directly and get out of that session exactly what you needed to get' (first-year A&D), but the majority did not have this timetabled opportunity, or received formative feedback on their work instead. They wanted to have more timetabled opportunities to discuss the feedback they received or tutorials to explain assessment/writing requirements; 'then you know you are on the right track, as you could end up doing all this work and at the end have done it completely wrong' (first-year A&D). Many students did not feel comfortable asking their tutors for help, they did not want to show their weakness 'it would take me a long time to get the courage to go, it is a pride thing really' (second-year A&H) and so sought help from other sources. The most common were peers within the programme of study, where they checked requirements and/or read each other's work and had a discussion about it. Other sources of informal support for writing included family, friends and students who were at a higher level. Many students found family support limited due to the lack of disciplinary knowledge of their chosen reader, but useful when asked to explain what the work meant and also for proofreading.

When asked about assessment and feedback in the questionnaire, 57% of students said that they received written feedback on their last piece of marked work on a feedback form, 30% received comments written on the work itself and 22% did not receive any written feedback. When they did receive written feedback, 91% said they read the feedback finding it useful for understanding where they could improve their work (58%) and would use it to inform future assignments (62%). However, when it came to discussing the feedback with their tutor, the majority of students did not do this (76%).

When thinking about support for writing, many students would like to see compulsory essay writing in the course 'to really apply it to what you are doing on your specific course, the specific essay etc. It gives you ideas on how to develop your points' (first-year A&H), with worked examples. This should be in a seminar or tutorial setting rather than the lecture as the lectures should be subject based:

> ... it frustrates me in subject lectures when they are doing something other than the subject. I feel that the lecture time is valuable and so prefer to be doing something on the subject as we do not have a lot of contact with the lecturer. (second-year A&H)

All students felt that academic support was useful for those who need to go, particularly drop-in sessions, where they could talk about their work with someone who is separate from their programme of study with another perspective.

In the questionnaire, students were asked to indicate whether they used various sources of support for their reading and writing. The most popular source of support were online or printed materials with 68% of students accessing online materials from various sources often or very often, and 61% accessing university support materials either online or printed. Specialist support such as dyslexia support and support for international students can only be accessed by the students for which it is targeted; 88%

and 92% respectively of students never accessed this support. There is a university-wide peer mentoring scheme available to students, and some students can access peer mentoring in their school or academic support, but a large majority of students never accessed these services (83%, 92% and 82% respectively). Regarding support from tutors, the majority of students (74%) sometimes or often used feedback for support, whereas 10% never did. Twenty-three per cent of students never actively sought out their tutor and asked for help, 44% sometimes did and 33% did often or very often. Students often asked others for help, with 75% asking their peers sometimes or often (14% never) and 61% asking their friends and family (33% never).

When asked an open question about what support would be most useful for reading and writing, the most common suggestion was subject tutor help which was mentioned 101 times, with more feedback being mentioned 33 times and more detailed requirements mentioned 31 times and giving examples 4 times. Peer help was mentioned 20 times and help from friends and family 14 times. Students often indicated where they wanted help including referencing, grammar, structure, presentation, and felt that in addition to tutor help there should be more help at university level with workshops (21 mentions) maybe mandatory at the beginning of the course and academic support (8 mentions) being the most common. Students also wanted more materials, ranging from books in the library to specific materials, but they also wanted more online materials and help (22 mentions). When asked about how they would prefer their support, 52% said that they would like it face-to-face, with 19% preferring online support and 29% showing no preference.

2.8.2. *Academic Perspectives*

Academics were asked a series of questions about the support they provide for students. From the answers given, it appears that tutors often gave guidance to the whole cohort that was specifically targeted at the assignment, such as sample answers or a discussion of the work required for different grades. Fewer tutors give formal lectures on aspects of writing (editing, referencing, structure), with 36% never giving them. Sometimes previous students were invited in to discuss assignments with current students. Regarding individual help, tutors referred students to online materials for help with their writing, but the majority did not offer drop-in sessions, mark draft submissions or comment on work if asked to, and peer review of work was not standard practice. When marking work, 41% of respondents said that they edited the work.

Some tutors provided writing exercises in scheduled teaching slots using various methods such as those shown in Table 2.3.

Table 2.3: Writing exercises used by tutors.

Peer review in sessions	Brainstorming	A short synopsis or summary
Mind-mapping	Outlines or plans for assessments	Bullet points and seminar presentations
Practice essays	Online discussions	Online assessments
Blogs	Group writing	Poster presentation
Summary of discussions	Pre-set work and sharing in seminars	Rewriting paragraphs in different tenses
Reflection	Group essay plans	Free writing
'Fill in the missing word' exercises	Writing across the curriculum activities	Analysis of reading and presentation
Editing exercises		

Some tutors offer formative feedback on student work, which includes group feedback sessions, peer review either by using blogs or in tutorials, commenting on essay plans and individual comments on work. One tutor offered formative feedback sessions but commented that few students turn up.

2.9. Academics' Perspectives on the Barriers to Student Reading and Writing

The majority of respondents recognised that students had many hurdles with reading and writing at university which they had to overcome. There was a criticism of reading in terms of there being a 'deficit' of some kind in the student; mainly the lack of concentration, 'reading in depth and with care', lack of ability to read critically, lack of cognitive ability and lack of vocabulary and poor literacy skills. This was attributed to a general lack of reading and 'spoonfeeding' at school with an over-reliance on Internet sources, such as Wikipedia and distractions both virtual and 'real'. There was a consensus that there was no preparation at school for the type of reading required at university. In addition, there was a recognition that the texts that students were expected to read at university were often inaccessible and with 'unfamiliar words and discipline-specific terminology'.

> They are used at A-level to reading from one or two key textbooks and find the expectation at university to read more widely confusing and difficult.

Again, as with reading, there was a consensus that students had a deficit of the skills required for writing at university and a poor grasp of the conventions of written English. This included grammar, sentence structure, punctuation, paragraphs, a tendency to write how they speak, not being able to reflect on or critically review their own work, lack of coherent argument or structure and a limited vocabulary. This lack of skills was attributed to their previous educational experiences, particularly the perceived lack of teaching literacy at school.

In addition to poor literacy skills, there was a feeling that their previous educational experiences had encouraged them to search for a 'right answer' rather than engage in debates.

> Following A-level they are fixed on "what do I have to write" rather than how best to write and convey their ideas and understanding. The modular approach to A-levels leads them to expect a constant reshaping and handing back process.

> The use of sources causes the main problem; how to cite them and incorporate the work of others into essays. Also, the degree of analysis required rather than descriptive prose. Finally, the appropriate academic, dialectical tone is something that some of them struggle with, sometimes opting for an inappropriately opinionated approach.

There was also a recognition of the students' frequent 'fear of not getting it right' and a 'lack of confidence in finding their own academic voice', and an appreciation of the difficulties that students experience with writing requirements at university, with a lack of explicit expectations and 'detailed criteria' being of no help:

> They don't know what we expect; because we don't tell them or we all have different expectations. We don't do enough writing with students or analysis of texts within their disciplines so they don't realise how important it is.

Academics frequently stated that the lack of writing ability caused them extra work 'I often spend twice as long marking assignments because I am correcting all their writing' and also expressed a disappointment with the current educational system:

> ... every hurdle we put in students' way increases the barriers to reading and writing and generates anxiety ... There are more and more expectations of the tutor about reading drafts,

---

and this has been fostered in schools. This is likely to add to our burdens, and lecturers will probably respond by using other forms of assessment which neglect the development of critical writing skills.

Students come to university these days hampered by a lack of earlier training in the importance of accurate reading and accurate writing — thus it is not entirely their fault that they have initial problems. A more significant issue is the resistance of so many to accepting the importance of conveying their meaning in essays in accurate prose. If they have now become somewhat obsessed with plagiarism as a concept, it has not translated into a desire to write well on their account, sadly.

... you can lead a student to books but you can't make them think. They are the products of a school system that has robbed them of initiative and an internet culture that works against depth and seriousness. We work with the flow by offering them workshops, endless sessions on how to write and research etc. instead of challenging them. Maybe the horse has bolted, however. Sad days.

Students are increasingly lecturer-dependent. We find ourselves entering a double-bind: in attempting to help them more (providing scanned materials for them to read online etc.), we run the risk of de-skilling them; of undermining the need for them to develop intellectual independence, a spirit of enquiry, the experience of undertaking risk. (I don't have an answer to this)

2.10. Discussion

To succeed at university, students must demonstrate their learning and thinking through academic writing and this requires an understanding of and expertise in various genres and writing conventions. For the majority, of students, though, this, represents an abrupt change from the limited and directed reading and supported writing practices pre-higher education to, largely, independent reading and writing in higher education, where they are expected to read widely, synthesise that reading into their writing to structure coherent arguments and reference appropriately with little or no guidance.

Students do understand that reading and writing will be different at university, but are unclear about those differences. They expect reading to be 'harder', independently sourcing a greater quantity of texts and to read them in 'more depth' and writing would be 'completely different' in that it should replicate the styles of writing found in their readings, with a wider vocabulary and be more 'elaborate', 'sounding academic'. These findings are congruent with findings about expectations of university generally, with students being 'vague about what university learning and teaching involved' (Hardy, Hand, & Bryson, 2008, p. 86). It was not clear where the limited and vague expectations of reading and writing at university came from, but it is possible that they are based on 'stereotypical conjecture rather than anything firmer' (*ibid.*, p. 86); possible sources of these expectations could be teachers, friends and family. Indeed, some students in our sample indicated that they felt their pre-university experiences had prepared them well for university; that it would be a continuation of what they did at school and so felt confident in their abilities, and, as we have said, this confidence prior to their arrival at university has been reported elsewhere (Cook & Leckey, 1999; Lowe & Cook, 2003; Smith, 2005). However, the majority of students did not feel prepared for reading and/or writing at university and were anxious about it, feeling intimidated.

On the other hand, the academics in our sample were very explicit in their expectations of first-year students' reading and writing. They expected reading to be focused and narrow, but for students to engage with good quality textbooks and to read with understanding. They expected the first piece of writing to be well structured to lead to a coherent argument, and to be referenced appropriately, following the conventions of their discipline. There was recognition that first-year students were not prepared for this, but academics still expressed disappointment with student reading and writing, feeling that first-year students found it both a chore and had to be coerced to do it. They felt that the students did not have the ability to undertake the reading required at university with a lack of concentration, ability to read critically, cognitive ability, vocabulary and literacy skills generally. Much of this was attributed to their pre-university experiences (which they described as one of spoonfeeding), a general lack of reading, an over-reliance on Internet sources and distractions (virtual and real). They felt that students did not understand how important writing is 'as the vehicle for their knowledge' and were critical of student writing at all levels, their abilities (particularly the standard of English and grammar and lack of vocabulary), attitudes and commitment to academic conventions. Academics were disparaging of pre-university education (particularly A levels), in that it did not prepare students for the independence required at university or levels of literacy required, but fostered in students a state of dependency.

This lack of preparation for students entering higher education is recognised across the sector; the Flying Start Project produced a draft scoping paper in April 2009 *Recommendations for Changes to UK Education Policy to Help Students Make More Successful Transitions to Academic Writing in Higher Education* to address this issue. They presented 'ten recommendations for the development of UK post-16 education policy ... intended to promote smoother student transitions to academic writing in Higher Education'. These included recommendations on A level teaching and assessment, alternatives to A level in FE teaching and assessment, preparation for academic writing in HE and staff training and development (see Appendix 2.A for full policy recommendations). While these developments should be lauded for those students entering higher education, it must be recognised that not all students who stay on at school do go onto higher education. In the academic year 2009/2010, 84% of 16-year olds were in full-time education (43% at school and 41% in further education) and 70% of 17-year olds were in full-time education (32% at school, 38% in further education) (Department for Education, 2011); however, the number of 18-year olds in higher education was 22.5% and 19-year olds was 11.1% (Department for Business Innovation and Skills, 2011). With the recent changes in the fee structure for higher education, there is some uncertainty about the number of A level students who will be attending university. A recent poll in the *Guardian* showed, for example, that '... 47% plan to go straight to work while 12% still uncertain about university education' (Insley, 2011). Therefore, only a minority of students who stay on in full-time education will go onto university, and with the increase in the school leaving age, this is set to decrease, so if the calls for changes to pre-university education to include preparation for higher education are adhered to, school students may be alienated from their studies, as they do not intend to go onto higher education, or alternatively, may not be offered a place in an increasingly competitive environment. Although higher education establishments could and do offer schools some assistance to those students who intend to go to university, such as 'taster sessions', or preparatory sessions within schools, we argue that the responsibility for transition lies with higher education itself. This could be some form of preparatory course during extended induction periods, set firmly within the disciplines that they will be studying. The situating of these preparatory programmes is important bearing in mind the multitude of different genres of writing students is required to undertake at university, which vary quite considerably in the conventions expected and the style of writing: academic, journalistic, reflective, summary, critique, argument, literary and business. However, these induction periods should not be restricted to first year, as students struggle with writing transitions at all levels of their studies.

Preparation for reading and writing at university is imperative, as the described lack of it left the students in our sample struggling with reading and writing, and for some this caused anxiety and stress, which could lead to students avoiding modules and jobs that require writing or impact negatively on their learning (Clarke, n.d.). A particular difficulty was in 'independent learning' and the requirement to move from guided to self-directed study, which for many was problematic (Cook & Leckey, 1999). This manifest itself in the amount of reading they felt they had to undertake from the reading lists given and the lack of guidance on the purpose of the reading; they therefore felt that the reading was 'pointless' as they were not sure what they were going to do with the reading and there was no 'checking up' by tutors. Many students could not keep up with the reading and so only read for relevance, mainly assessments or seminars and, due to this, many felt that they were doing less reading than pre-university. This reading for relevance continued throughout their time at university, with very few students reading around the subject. All students struggled with writing at the beginning of their time at university; it was not the quantity (the majority of students did less writing at university than pre-university), but learning to write in an 'academic way', particularly referencing and finding an 'academic voice' that caused the difficulties. Very early on, they recognised disciplinary differences from their reading and from their tutor guidance/feedback and found this a particularly difficult arena for them when constructing their own writing and following the relevant conventions.

Academics felt that they gave guidance to students on their written work, but there was recognition that expectations are not sufficient. Many students did not find course documentation useful; they did not understand what it meant or what the lecturer was looking for. The majority of staff gave guidance on assignments, structure and requirements to the whole cohort, and students found this useful. Some tutors integrate writing support, including exercises, into scheduled teaching slots, but only a few gave formal lectures on aspects of writing. The majority of tutors do not offer one-to-one support or other forms of help with student writing, and when offering drop-in sessions, were disappointed at the lack of take up of the support provided. Students, when needing help with their reading and writing tend to approach their peers or friends and family, not feeling comfortable approaching their tutors as they did not want to show their weaknesses. This lack of trust between student and tutor is something that has been reported elsewhere; Hardy and Bryson (2010) in their study concluded that 'Relationships with peers became increasingly important, particularly for clarification of what was required of them or for academic support, contacting academic staff would be a last resort and then it would probably be by email'.

Many students reported that reading did not 'excite' them. Some did report that they felt 'satisfaction' following their reading, but were not motivated to read more. If they did experience difficulties in understanding their reading, then, in addition to seeking help, they would look for additional information, most commonly something that would be easier on the Internet; the most popular sites being Google, YouTube and Wikipedia. Over half of students received written tutor feedback on their writing and found it useful for improving their work, but a large minority did not receive any written feedback. Some students commented that the feedback they received was obscure and confusing, with comments such as 'grammar', 'you need to write in a scholarly way', question marks and the circling of words not being explained. Some students were given the opportunity to discuss the feedback in one-to-one tutorials, which they found useful, but the majority had no such opportunity.

Students themselves had clear ideas about the type of support they needed and they included the following:

- Compulsory sessions in their programme of study, in a seminar or tutorial setting but not a lecture, as those were for the delivery of content
- Tutor feedback on their work
- More detail about tutor requirements for a piece of work
- University workshops
- Drop-in sessions with someone separate from their programme of study
- Online or printed support materials

2.11. Conclusion

The struggles that many of the students in our research described regarding their academic literacies, often cause anxiety and distress, and this affects their learning and their overall experience of university. Academics are critical of the students' ability to read and particularly write in the genres and conventions expected of them, but do recognise that there is a lack of preparation for writing, both pre-university and at university, and that any guidance given to the students is limited. It is imperative for the student to succeed at university and develop their full potential, for them to be fully conversant of the requirements for each piece of their writing. There are some overarching principles that the students need to deploy, but in addition there are specific requirements within the disciplines and the tutors, which are often in conflict with the overarching principles (e.g. those concerning specific referencing requirements or the ways in which the writing is to be structured) and these need to be made explicit for the student. The responsibility for teaching academic writing within the university lies with all involved: the academy and senior management, the department, individual academics and designate support staff. The university should make provision for providing support centrally focusing on transitions to university, 'independent learning' and specialised academic writing support for those who require it; the departments should work with support staff and/or offer specific disciplinary support; and individual lecturers should make explicit their expectations and requirements through briefings, transparent feedback to individual students and a greater discussions with their students that fosters 'trust' relationships around writing. Academic literacies should be top of the academy's agenda for learning and teaching as it is too important an issue in terms of engaging students to be left to chance.

References

Adams, J. (2008). *How do students learn to write in UK higher education and how does this influence my practice as a professional teacher of academic writing?* Retrieved from http://www.actionresearch.net/writings/tuesdayma/jaULLfinal0508.pdf

Ahmad, R., & McMahon, K. (2006). The benefits of good writing: Or why does it matter that students write well. In S. Davies, D. Swinburne & G. Williams (Eds.), *Writing matters. The royal literary fund report on student writing in higher education* (pp. 1–6). London: The Royal Literary Fund.

Bartholomae, D. (1985). Inventing the university. In M. Rose (Ed.), *When a writer can't write: Studies in writer's block and other composing-process problems (perspectives in writing research)* (pp. 34–65). New York, NY: Guilford Publications.

Baxter Magolda, M. B. (2010). The interweaving of epistemological, intrapersonal, and interpersonal development in the evolution of self-authorship. In M. B. Baxter Magolda, E. G. Creamer, & P. S. Meszaros (Eds.), *Development and assessment of self-authorship: Exploring the concept across cultures* (pp. 25–43). Sterling, VA: Stylus Publishing.

Cabral, A. P., & Tavares, J. (2002, September 11–14). Reading and writing skills in higher education: Lecturer's opinions and perceptions. *European conference on educational research*, University of Lisbon, Portugal.

Clarke, D. C. (n.d.). *Explorations into writing anxiety: Helping students overcome their fears and focus on learning.* Retrieved from http://zircon.mcli.dist.maricopa.edu/mlx/warehouse/01401-01500/01411/clark_rpt.pdf

Coffey, M., Merryweather, D., Itua, I., & Foxcroft, A. (2010). *Context specific writing solutions, participatively designed for first year undergraduates.* Flying Start End of Project Report (online). Liverpool Hope University. Retrieved from http://www.hope.ac.uk/collaborativeprojects/flyingstart/component/joomdoc/doc_details/29-context-specific-writing-solutions

Cook, A., & Leckey, J. (1999). Do expectations meet reality? A survey of changes in first-year student opinion. *Journal of Further and Higher Education, 23*(2), 157–171.

Davies, S., Swinburne, D., & Williams, G. (Eds.). (2006). *Writing matters. The royal literary fund report on student writing in higher education* (pp. 27–34). London: The Royal Literary Fund.

Flying Start. (2009). *Recommendations for changes to UK education policy to help students make more successful transitions to academic writing in higher education.* Retrieved from http://www.hope.ac.uk/collaborativeprojects/flyingstart/the-strands/the-policy-strand

Francis, H., & Hallam, S. (2000). Genre effects on higher education students' text reading for understanding. *Higher Education, 39*, 279–296.

Frean, A., Yobbo, Y., & Duncan, I. (2007). A-level students unable to write essays [online]. *The Times*, August 15. Retrieved from Lexisnexis.com. Accessed on 28 November 2011.

Ganobcsik-Williams, L. (2004). *A report on the teaching of academic writing in UK higher education.* The Royal Literary Fund. Retrieved from http://www.rlf.org.uk/fellowshipscheme/documents/TeachingWritingUKHE.pdf. Accessed on 23 January 2012.

Great Britain. Department for Business Innovation & Skills. (2011). *Participation rates in higher education: Academic years 2006/2007–2009/2010 (Provisional).* London: Department for Business Innovation & Skills. Retrieved from http://www.bis.gov.uk/assets/biscore/statistics/docs/p/participation_rates_in_he_2009-10.pdf. Accessed on 12 January 2011.

Great Britain. Department for Education. (2011). *Education and training statistics for the United Kingdom 2011.* London: Department for Education. Retrieved from http://www.education.gov.uk/rsgateway/DB/VOL/v001045/index.shtml. Accessed on 12 January 2011.

Haggis, T. (2006). Pedagogies for diversity: Retaining critical challenge amidst fears of 'dumbing down'. *Studies in Higher Education, 31*(5), 521–535.

Hardy, C., & Bryson, C. (2010, December 14–16). The social life of students: Support mechanisms at university. In *Society for research into higher education annual research conference 2010: 'Where is the wisdom we have lost in knowledge?'* Exploring Meaning, Identities and Transformation in Higher Education, Wales.

Hardy, C., Hand, L., & Bryson, C. (2008, May 7–9). I'm going to work really hard: Expectations and reality checks. In *Third annual European first year experience conference.* University of Wolverhampton, Wolverhampton.

Hounsell, D. (1997). Contrasting conceptions of essay-writing. In F. Marton, D. Hounsell & N. J. Entwistle (Eds.), *The experience of learning* (2nd ed., pp. 106–125). Edinburgh, UK: Scottish Academic Press. Retrieved from http://www.docs.hss.ed.ac.uk/iad/Learning_teaching/Academic_teaching/Resources/Experience_of_learning/EoLChapter7.pdf. Accessed on 23 January 2012.

Husain, S., & Waterfield, R. (2006). The first year of higher education. In S. Davies, D. Swinburne & G. Williams (Eds.), *Writing matters. The royal literary fund report on student writing in higher education* (pp. 27–34). London: The Royal Literary Fund.

Insley, J. (2011, May 3). Half of A-level students shun university: Poll of 16–18-year-olds shows that 47% plan to go straight to work while 12% still uncertain about university education. *The Guardian*. Retrieved from http://www.guardian.co.uk/money/2011/may/03/a-level-students-shun-university

Kember, D. (2001). Beliefs about knowledge and the process of teaching and learning as a factor in adjusting to study in higher education. *Studies in Higher Education, 26*(2), 205–221.

Lea, M. R. (2004). Academic literacies: A pedagogy for course design. *Studies in Higher Education, 29*(6), 739–756.

Lea, M. R., & Street, B. V. (1998). Student writing in higher education: An academic literacies approach. *Studies in Higher Education, 23*(2), 157–172.

Lillis, T. (1997). New voices in academia? The regulative nature of academic writing conventions. *Language and Education, 11*(3), 182–199.

Lillis, T. (1999). Whose "Common Sense"? Essayist literacy and the institutional practice of mystery. In C. Jones, J. Turner & B. Street (Eds.), *Students writing in the university: Cultural and epistemological issues* (pp. 127–147). Amsterdam: John Benjamins.

Lillis, T., & Turner, J. (2001). Student writing in higher education: Contemporary confusion, traditional concerns. *Teaching in Higher Education, 6*(1), 57–68.

Lowe, H., & Cook, A. (2003). Mind the gap: Are students prepared for higher education? *Journal of Further and Higher Education, 27*(1), 53–76.

McMahon, K. (2004). *What's going on with student writing: A study commissioned by the royal literary fund*. London: The Royal Literary Fund.

Murray, N., & Kirton, B. (2006). An analysis of the current situation. In S. Davies, D. Swinburne & G. Williams (Eds.), *Writing matters. The royal literary fund report on student writing in higher education* (pp. 7–14). London: The Royal Literary Fund.

Read, B., Francis, B., & Robson, J. (2001). 'Playing Safe': Undergraduate essay writing and the presentation of the student 'voice'. *British Journal of Sociology of Education, 22*(3), 387–399.

Smith, K. (2005). School to university: An investigation into the experience of first-year students of English at British universities. *Arts and Humanities in Higher Education, 3*(1), 92–93.

Vardi, I. (2000, July 5–7). What lecturers' want: An investigation of lecturers' expectations in first year essay writing tasks [online]. *The fourth Pacific Rim — First year in higher education conference: Creating futures for a new millennium*. Queensland University of Technology, Brisbane. Retrieved from http://www.fyhe.com.au/past_papers/abstracts/VardiAbstract.htm. Accessed on 25 November 2011.

Winch, C., & Wells, P. (1995). The quality of student writing in higher education: A cause for concern? *British Journal of Educational Studies, 43*(1), 73–87.

2. A. Appendix

Flying Start: Potential Policy Recommendations for Development by the Policy Group
These are the areas identified by Flying Start where we believe there is the potential for changes in educational policy to impact on student transitions into academic writing in HE. We welcome feedback on any aspects of the scoping paper, but these are the key areas we ask respondents to focus on when providing feedback.

A Level Teaching and Assessment

1. Incorporate analysis, evaluation and critical thinking more systematically in the assessment criteria for written A level work.
2. Link the synoptic paper and the extended project qualification more explicitly to preparation for post-A level work.
3. Include more items of extended written composition in sections of A level assessment other than the synoptic paper.
4. Review A level assessment in light of increasing uptake of alternative programmes, including the International Baccalaureate (IB).
5. Incorporate in A level curricula those aspects of non-A level qualifications that prepare students better for HE.

Alternatives to A Level in FE Teaching and Assessment

6. Make non-A level qualifications more widely available to cater for the widening range of students and learning approaches.
7. Commission research on the likely impact of increased use of the IB and other qualifications providing access to HE.

Preparation for Academic Writing in HE

8. Provide and ensure the delivery of preparatory courses on academic writing for those FE students who are most likely to benefit and are expecting to progress to HE, having entered the UCAS system.

Staff Training and Development

9. Provide protected time for HE lecturers, A level and other FE tutors to liaise and collaborate with HE staff to share and develop good practice.
10. Provide training for HE staff in students' pre-HE experiences of writing for assessment in the wider context of epistemological and disciplinary requirements.

Chapter 3

Writing in the Disciplines

Hilary Nesi

3.1. Introduction

One of the central tenets of genre studies is that the writer's choice of text structure, grammar and lexis is governed by his or her own role and purpose, and the context and audience for which the text is produced. This means that writing tutors should always customise their advice according to the situation of the individual writer, bearing in mind that even slight changes in writing purpose and context will affect the way in which a socially successful text unfolds. While it is true that student writers are developing as individuals, and need to learn to produce prose that "'has a voice" or "sounds like a person'" (Elbow, 2007, p. 7), students also need to learn to write like members of their own discipline, reflecting the particular values and conventions of their discourse community. Writing tutors who are familiar with the various genres associated with a given discipline, and with the values and conventions these genres reflect, can help to empower their students so that they do not simply follow a prescribed format, but employ it as an effective and efficient means of communicating with their readers.

Gaining familiarity with the conventions of disciplinary writing is not always easy, however. Student assignments belong to the category of 'occluded' genres (Swales, 1996), in that they are generally only available to their own authors, and to a few designated readers. Many students never see a proficient example of the genres they attempt to produce, and many writing tutors feel forced to rely for genre information on inauthentic

Writing in the Disciplines: Building Supportive Cultures for Student Writing
in UK Higher Education
ISBN: 978-1-78052-546-4

textbook models, enhanced by memories of their own student writing experiences relating to a different place, time and discipline. The British Academic Written English (BAWE) corpus[1] was created to help address this problem, containing just under 3,000 proficient university assignments, fairly evenly distributed across four levels of study and more than 20 major disciplines. The BAWE texts have been grouped according to disciplinary domain and assigned to 'genre families' according to their form and educational purpose, and this enables us to compare and contrast them, identifying not only disciplinary differences but also common generic features which can be introduced and practised in the discipline-specific or multi-disciplinary writing class.

This chapter aims to describe the BAWE corpus holdings, discuss some findings that are relevant to writing tutors and demonstrate how tutors can benefit from corpus access in various ways.

3.2.   The BAWE Corpus and Its Context

A corpus is commonly regarded as a collection of texts in electronic form, selected to represent a language or language variety in order to provide data for linguistic research. Corpora help language specialists identify genre-specific and discipline-specific linguistic features, and can therefore be very useful for tutors who seek to build a supportive environment for academic writing.

The corpora most commonly referred to in academic writing programmes are collections of articles from academic journals and science magazines. In *English for Specific Purposes* (ESP), there has been a long tradition of research article analysis, dating from Swales' initial research into the structure of article introductions (1981), and based on the assumption that international student writers need to write in the research article style. Moreover journal articles have the added advantage of being readily accessible in electronic format and quite easily convertible into subject-specific corpora, albeit without the copyright permission necessary to preserve them for future use. Thus, in Tim Johns 'kibbitzer' series, dating

---

1. The British Academic Written English (BAWE) corpus was developed as part of the project 'An investigation of genres of assessed writing in British Higher Education', funded by the Economic and Social Research Council (project number RES-000-23-0800) from 2004 to 2007, under the directorship of Hilary Nesi and Sheena Gardner (formerly of the Centre for English Language Teacher Education, University of Warwick), Paul Thompson (formerly of the Department of Applied Linguistics, University of Reading) and Paul Wickens (Westminster Institute of Education, Oxford Brookes).

from the 1990s, home-made collections of articles from the *New Scientist* and *Nature* were commonly used as an impromptu source of linguistic evidence to resolve students' writing queries (see http://lexically.net/ TimJohns and Johns, 1991a, 1991b), and in Lee and Swales' (2006) study of a writing class for students of pharmacology, biomedical statistics and educational technology the students themselves were able to compile and analyse collections of research articles to make up for the lack of relevant discipline-specific information in academic writing textbooks.

Corpora of journal articles are clearly very useful resources for doctoral students who are aiming to continue their careers in academia, and for scholars around the world who are increasingly required to publish their research in the medium of English. However, most of the writing produced by university students differs in important ways from published article writing. Even at postgraduate level, very little of the students' written output presents the findings from their own original research, and whereas academic experts argue for the centrality of their topic and the importance of their contribution to the field, there is rarely any need for students to follow suit. As Lee and Swales (2006, p. 68) point out, student texts generally have a different purpose and a different readership in mind, and 'writers who are new to the field can hardly be expected to make confident claims, expertly survey the literature, draw strong conclusions etc. in the same way as an established writer can'.

Collecting large amounts of student writing from a range of disciplines is a more laborious process than downloading articles from an online source. The BAWE corpus project drew on over 1,000 volunteer student contributors over a three-year period in order to gather enough examples of proficient coursework to represent all four levels of British university coursework in a range of disciplines. Student writing can be collected more easily if it is gathered automatically, for example, via online submission procedures, but, apart from issues relating to intellectual property rights, there is a danger that essential contextual information will be lost if coursework is collected in this way. The BAWE corpus files are annotated with contributor details (age, gender, first language and length of UK schooling) as well as information about the module and department for which the coursework was produced. This was obtained from the contributors when they gave written permission for their work to be included (see Alsop & Nesi, 2009), and has proved useful when exploring small subsections of the corpus in greater depth. Dissertations and theses were not collected for the BAWE corpus, because these are often already in the public domain and are therefore not fully 'occluded'. However, there is scope to compare the BAWE texts with the writing of both expert research article authors and research students, because alongside numerous collections of research articles compiled by individual researchers, several small collections of dissertations and theses have been created in recent years, for example, by Thompson (2000) and Charles (2003, 2007).

The contents of the BAWE corpus are outlined in Table 3.1. Holdings are grouped into four disciplinary domains: Arts and Humanities, Life Sciences, Social Sciences and Physical Sciences. The levels in this table refer to the first, second and final year of undergraduate study (Levels 1–3), and taught masters programmes (Level 4). Some pieces of assessed work contain multiple texts, a portfolio of lab reports for example, so the corpus actually contains 2,897 texts, somewhat more than the number of assignments.

The texts in the BAWE corpus (excluding front and back matter, formulae, tables, footnotes, references, appendices etc.) increase steadily in length from level to level. The average length of a text is 1,788 words at Level 1, 2,324 words at Level 2, 2,637 words at Level 3 and 2,903 words at Level 4.

Table 3.1: Overview of assignments in the BAWE corpus.

	Level 1	Level 2	Level 3	Level 4	Total
Arts and Humanities (AH) Archaeology; Classics; Comparative American Studies; English; History; Linguistics/ English Language Studies; Philosophy; others	239	228	160	78	705
Life Sciences (LS) Agriculture; Biological Science; Food Science; Health; Medicine; Psychology	180	193	113	197	683
Physical Sciences (PS) Architecture; Chemistry; Computer Science; Cybernetics/ Electronic Engineering; Engineering; Mathematics; Meteorology; Physics; Planning	181	149	156	110	596
Social Sciences (SS) Anthropology; Business; Economics; Hospitality, Leisure and Tourism; Management; Law; Politics; Publishing; Sociology	207	197	166	207	777
Total number of assignments	807	767	595	592	2761

Table 3.2 shows the frequency of some interactive features across the corpus, generated by the text analysis tool *LIWC* (Pennebaker, Chung, Ireland, Gonzales, & Booth, 2007). The use of personal pronouns is higher in all the domains than in Pennebaker et al.'s sample of articles from the journal *Science* (0.8%), but much lower than in their sample of novels (10.3%) and in their transcriptions of talk 'in real world unstructured settings' (13.6%). The students use question marks with roughly the same frequency as in the *Science* articles (0.05%), but much less than in the novel sample (3.39%). Perhaps unsurprisingly, writers in the Arts and Humanities are slightly more likely to use personal pronouns and the first person singular pronoun 'I'.

References to the reader ('you') are uniformly low in frequency, but it is worth noting that the form *i* (usually the first person singular pronoun, but also a Roman numeral in numbered lists) occurs more than 10 times more frequently in the BAWE corpus than in the British National Corpus. Although not every instance is pronominal, its extreme frequency does seem to contradict the advice given by some tutors that the first person pronoun is to be avoided in academic writing, at any cost.

Table 3.3, reproduced from Nesi and Gardner (2012), shows scores at each level of study across the five dimensions first described by Biber (1988). Biber developed these dimensions with reference to various types of text, including conversation, broadcasts, fiction and published academic research,[2] but not university student writing. Further details of the linguistic features associated with each dimension, and their factor loadings, are provided in Biber, Conrad, Reppen, Byrd, and Helt (2002). Dimension 1, which contrasts verbal 'involved' and nominal 'informational' styles, is characterised by contractions, present tense verbs, first and second person pronouns and 'private' verbs such as *believe*, *think* and *know*. The scores for conversation are usually high on this dimension, while the scores for published research are usually low. Dimension 2, which measures narrative features such as third person pronouns, past tense verbs, perfect aspect verbs and 'public' verbs such as *say* and *tell*, produces positive scores for fiction and negative scores for published research. Dimension 3 contrasts 'elaborated' and situation-dependent styles. Published research is usually elaborated because it is explicit about context, using relative clause constructions, nominalisations and adverbials to facilitate interpretation of the text independently of a specific place and time. Conversations and broadcasts do not need to do this, of course, so these kinds of texts usually have negative scores on Dimension 3. Dimension 4 measures persuasive

---

2. Taken from the Lancaster-Oslo/Bergen (LOB) corpus.

Table 3.2: Means for selected interactive features (means are expressed as a percentage of total word use in the disciplinary domain).

	Personal pronouns	First person singular pronoun	First person plural pronoun	Second person pronoun	Question marks
Arts and Humanities	3.0 (s.d.1.9)	0.4 (s.d.0.6)	0.4 (s.d.0.7)	0.1 (s.d.0.2)	0.08 (s.d.0.1)
Life Sciences	1.6 (s.d.1.7)	0.2 (s.d.0.8)	0.2 (s.d.0.6)	0.1 (s.d.0.3)	0.05 (s.d.0.1)
Physical Sciences	1.2 (s.d.1.4)	0.3 (s.d.0.7)	0.4 (s.d.0.7)	0.1 (s.d.0.2)	0.05 (s.d.0.1)
Social Sciences	1.7 (s.d.1.4)	0.2 (s.d.0.8)	0.2 (s.d.0.4)	0.0 (s.d.0.2)	0.07 (s.d.0.1)

Table 3.3: Dimension scores by level in the BAWE corpus.

Level	1. Involved	2. Narrative	3. Elaborated	4. Persuasive	5. Abstract and impersonal
1	− 12.7	− 2.7	5.1	− 1.4	5.9
2	− 13.9	− 2.8	5.6	− 1.4	6.2
3	− 14.7	− 3.0	5.7	− 1.5	6.4
4	− 17.2	− 3.2	6.3	− 2.0	5.5

features typical of argumentative texts such as editorials, including verbs such as *agree*, *ask*, *insist* and *recommend*, conditional subordination, and modals expressing prediction, necessity and possibility. Finally, Dimension 5 measures features that are typical of written as opposed to spoken texts, such as passive constructions, conjuncts such as *thus* and *however*, and adverbial and postnominal clauses. Published research will usually have a high score on this dimension.

Table 3.3 reveals that assignments in the BAWE corpus become more informational and elaborated, and less narrative and persuasive, as students progress through their course of study. The table shows consistent change at each level on every dimension except Dimension 5, where masters students (Level 4) appear to write in a less abstract and impersonal style than undergraduates. This could be because the distribution of assignment genres changes somewhat at postgraduate level, with an increase in the number of assignments preparing students for professional practice.

These findings suggest that the proficient university assignments in the BAWE corpus are highly informational, elaborated and abstract, with relatively few narrative or persuasive features. It seems sensible to assume, however, that most students who attend academic writing skills courses will be most familiar with informal, interactive, implicit language features, in other words those that occur most commonly in conversation and fiction. Learning the techniques of academic writing means learning to craft text which is less reliant on the reader's understanding of the context in which it was produced, and more impersonal and densely informative.

3.3. Genre Families in the BAWE Corpus

Each assignment in the BAWE corpus is considered to represent one of the many student writing genres, distinguishable linguistically and structurally. These genres have been grouped into 13 'genre families', and these in turn have been grouped into five broad categories which aim to encapsulate the fundamental purposes of student writing. These are as follows:

1. Demonstrating knowledge and understanding (Explanations and Exercises)
2. Developing powers of informed and independent reasoning (Critiques and Essays)
3. Developing research skills (Research Reports, Literature Surveys and Methodology Recounts)
4. Preparing for professional practice (Problem Questions, Proposals, Design Specifications and Case Studies)
5. Writing for oneself and others (Narrative Recounts and Empathy Writing).

The purposes and characteristics of the 13 genre families are discussed in detail in Nesi and Gardner (2012). Table 3.4 indicates their distribution, frequency and range across the 24 departments represented by at least 50 assignments in the BAWE corpus.

The corpus contains examples of all the genre families in all the domains except Arts and Humanities, where there are no Case Studies or Problem Questions. Table 3.5 compares the spread of assignments in the corpus across four disciplines, one from each domain. Quantities are expressed in percentages, as different numbers of texts were collected in each discipline.

All students have to write essays, but all departments use a range of other genres too, particularly in the Physical Sciences, where students tend to write less than in other domains, but in a greater variety of different styles. Also a greater diversity of genres is required at each successive level of academic study. In the Arts and Humanities, for example, 91% of Level 1 texts are Essays, but at Level 4 this decreases to 61%. In the Life Sciences 25% of texts at Level 1 are Explanations, but at Level 4 this decreases to 9%. Almost half the Level 1 and 2 texts in the Physical Sciences are Methodology Recounts, but at Levels 3 and 4 the proportions change, with greater use of other genres such as Design Specifications, Research Reports and Empathy Writing.

Each different genre of assignment has a different social purpose, and this difference affects the way the text is constructed, and the language used. Gardner and Holmes (2009), for example, discuss the effect of genre on the use of section headings, in response to the question 'Can I use headings in my essay?'. They found that in some genre families the use of section headings is more or less compulsory, while for others the use of headings is optional, or dependent on the practice for different genres within the same broad family. Table 3.6 shows the percentage of assignments with section headings in each of the genre families. It indicates relatively little use of

Table 3.4: Genres and genre families in the BAWE corpus.

Genre family	Frequency	Range	Examples of genres
Essay	1225	24	challenge; commentary; consequential; discussion; exposition; factorial
Methodology Recount	347	15	data analysis report; experimental report; field report; forensic report; lab report; materials selection report
Critique	319	24	academic paper review; interpretation of results; legislation evaluation; policy evaluation; programme evaluation; project evaluation; review of a book/film/play/website
Explanation	198	15	legislation overview; instrument description; methodology explanation; site/environment report; species/breed description; account of a natural phenomenon
Case Study	194	12	business start-up; company report; organisation analysis; patient report
Exercise	114	15	calculations; data analysis; calculations + short answers; short answers; statistics exercise
Design Specification	92	7	building design; game design; product design; website design
Proposal	76	15	book proposal; building proposal; business plan; catering plan; marketing plan; policy proposal; research proposal
Narrative Recount	72	14	accident report; account of literature or website search; biography; creative writing: short story; plot synopsis; reflective recount
Research Report	61	17	research article; research project; topic-based dissertation
Problem Question	40	7	law problem question; logistics simulation; business scenario
Literature Survey	35	11	annotated bibliography; anthology; literature review; review article
Empathy Writing	32	11	expert advice to industry; expert advice to lay person; information leaflet; job application; letter; newspaper article

Table 3.5: Genre families in four disciplines.

Genre family	English	Business	Biological sciences	Engineering
Case Study		21.2		13.9
Critique	0.9	19.9	11.8	13.0
Design Specification		1.4		11.8
Empathy Writing	4.7			0.4
Essay	84.0	33.6	6.5	6.7
Exercise	6.6	8.2	4.1	4.2
Explanation		3.4	37.3	6.7
Literature Survey	4.7		1.8	0.4
Methodology Recount		1.4	34.3	34.9
Narrative Recount	3.8	2.7	1.2	5.0
Problem Question		6.2		2.5
Proposal	0.9	1.4	1.8	4.2
Research Report		0.7	4.7	1.7

Table 3.6: Assignments using section headings.

Genre family	% with headings	Genre family	% with headings
Essay	31	Problem Question	78
Narrative Recount	42	Exercise	79
Empathy Writing	49	Proposal	87
Critique	59	Methodology Recount	88
Explanation	63	Case Study	91
Literature Survey	71	Design Specification	95
		Research Report	98

headings within Essays, but more or less obligatory use in Research Reports, Design Specifications and Case Studies.

Gardner and Holmes (2009) also found that in all the disciplinary domains except Physical Sciences the use of section headings increased with each level of study. This was particularly the case in the Arts and Humanities, where only 6% of Level 1 students used section headings, rising to over 70% at Level 4. This may be because upper-level students produce longer assignments, in a greater variety of genres, but it also suggests that upper-level students are more aware of the conventions of published academic writing, where section headings are the norm. Moreover, students with more experience of writing genres which require subheadings tend to transfer the subheading habit to other genres they produce. In the Arts and Humanities, for example, 82% of texts are Essays, and of these only 14% have headings. Students in the Physical Sciences produce Research Reports and Methodology Recounts which are conventionally divided along the lines of the IMRD structure (Introduction, Method, Results and Discussion). Only 11% of Physical Science assignments are Essays, and 58% of these have headings.

The assignment genre also affects students' choice of source material, and the way that this material is referenced. In some genres, writers are expected to reproduce received knowledge, whereas in others the focus is on the validity of source claims, or the analysis of authentic data. Bizup (2008) proposes a categorisation system which construes sources in terms of the functional roles they play. According to this system, 'Background' sources are materials used for general information or for factual evidence, 'Exhibit' sources are materials the writer analyses or interprets, 'Argument' sources are sources which present claims for the writer to discuss and 'Method' sources are sources which provide the theories or methodologies which the writer follows. The same source may be categorised in different ways, depending on how it is used by the writer.

In the BAWE corpus, Explanations are most likely to rely on received knowledge, and therefore to draw on sources such as textbooks and reference material which play a Background role. Narrative Recounts, which often contain personal reflection, are more likely to draw on sources which describe Methods of study, teamwork or professional practice. Critiques and Essays refer to primary data from Exhibit sources and critical claims from Argument sources. Problem Questions, Proposals, Design Specifications and Case Studies are all problem-solving genres, and are likely to identify problems manifested in primary Exhibit sources, and explain approaches to these problems in terms of Method sources.

The type of the source the student uses has implications for the choice of referencing procedure. Naming the author of the source and attributing to him or her a stance in relation to the information reported (as in, e.g., 'Nesi (2010) argues ... '; 'Hardy and Clughen (2011) claim ... ') is a method particularly suited to the Argument source type, as it characterises the source author as an independent and original thinker whose opinion can be accepted or challenged by the student writer. Placing within parentheses the author's name and the date of publication reduces the focus on the author, and referencing numerically rather than by name removes attention from the source author entirely; these alternative approaches may be more appropriate when the assignment draws on Background, Methods or Exhibit sources. The authors of sources used for background information are neutral figures, and their names and opinions are not particularly relevant to the student's aim to present uncontroversial, universally received knowledge. Similarly the author is often of little relevance in sources describing standard scientific procedures, although methods in the Social Sciences can be closely associated with individual scholars, and may be discussed in the manner of Argument sources. Exhibit sources are sometimes difficult to accommodate to any of the conventional referencing systems. Primary non-academic texts such as company reports, software code, speech transcripts and advertisements often lack essential information about authorship and the place and date of publication; and so the best approach for ease of retrieval by the reader may be simply to label the source text and append it to the assignment.

3.4. Differences Across the Disciplines

The division of the BAWE corpus into disciplinary domains is intended to assist the identification of broad differences in register across the disciplines. Table 3.7, reproduced from Nesi and Gardner (2012), shows scores for each of the disciplinary domains across the five dimensions described by Biber (1988).

The scores align quite closely with Biber's 1988 findings for published academic journals, books and reports.[3] Biber's sample scored − 15 on Dimension 1, between − 2 and − 3 on Dimension 2, between 4 and 5 on Dimension 3 and between 5 and 6 on Dimension 5. The score for Biber's sample on Dimension 4 was unmarked (zero), however, whereas the scores in the BAWE corpus are all negative, indicating that student writing has considerably fewer overtly persuasive features, particularly in the Arts and Humanities. Table 3.7 indicates that assignments in the Life Sciences have the heaviest informational weighting, and those in the Arts and Humanities are most like narratives. Assignments in the Physical Sciences are the most abstract and persuasive, while those in the Social Sciences are the most explicit.

These considerations could help writing tutors to create more appropriate writing tasks for their students. Argumentative essay topics such as 'Money is the root of all evil' and 'Crime does not pay' (both titles of essays in LOCNESS, the *Louvain Corpus of Native English Essays*) or 'It is important for college students to have a part time job' and 'Smoking should be completely banned at all the restaurants in the country' (from CEEAUS, the *Corpus of English Essays Written by Asian University Students*) seem to invite the use of involved and persuasive features, and possibly also the use of narrative, because the focus is on the writer's own personal experiences

---

3. Taken from the Lancaster-Oslo/Bergen (LOB) corpus.

Table 3.7: Dimension scores by disciplinary domain.

	1. Involved	2. Narrative	3. Elaborated	4. Persuasive	5. Abstract and impersonal
Arts and Humanities	− 13.4	− 2.1	5.7	− 2.3	5.5
Life Sciences	− 15.6	− 3.0	5.7	− 1.5	5.7
Physical Sciences	− 13.4	− 3.7	4.4	− 1.2	6.5
Social Sciences	− 15.3	− 3.0	6.5	− 1.3	6.2

Table 3.8: The 20 most frequent lexical words in each of the disciplinary domains.

Arts and Humanities	Life Sciences	Physical Sciences	Social Sciences
Make	Result	Value	Law
Language	Show	System	State
New	Cell	Figure	New
See	High	Time	Social
Man	Time	Show	International
Woman	Study	Result	Make
Time	Food	Data	Market
Example	Patient	Make	Woman
World	Health	Model	Country
State	Cause	Design	World
People	Need	High	See
London	Make	Give	Economic
Show	Research	Take	Case
Form	Increase	Number	Policy
First	Find	Process	Time
Social	Different	Find	Political
Society	Protein	Order	Group
Take	System	See	Need
Word	Group	Increase	Work
Life	Due	Method	High

and opinions. The titles of all 2761 BAWE assignments can be viewed in the 'Contents' section of the BAWE website at http://www.coventry.ac.uk/bawe. None of them suggest this type of response; instead most writing tasks seem to encourage an objective and distanced perspective on the topic.

Table 3.8 presents the most frequent words across the four disciplinary domains, illustrating differences in the topics students write about. In broad terms, the lists suggest that Arts and Humanities students write about language and the individual in society; Life Science students write about variation and change in living things; Physical Science students write about systems and numerical data; and Social Science students write about law, the market and social and economic policies.

Table 3.9 presents a keyword list of the statistically most significant words in each of the disciplinary domains. These are largely technical terms and proper names. Literary figures are key in the Arts and Humanities, diseases and organisms in the Life Sciences, companies and equipment parts in the Physical Sciences and nations and subject experts in the Social Sciences.

Table 3.9: Top 20 key words in each of the disciplinary domains, in comparison with the corpus as a whole.

Arts and Humanities	Life Sciences	Physical Sciences	Social Sciences
Poem	ATP[a]	Renold	Tourism
Ranke	Elegans	Kidde	Hospitality
Narrator	Asthma	Pixel	Denning
Pronoun	Pie-1	Bohr	Hofstede
Plutarch	Chloroplast	Amplitude	Nepal
Verb	Skn-1	Hexagon	Arendt
Aeneas	Blastomere	Microneedle	Expatriate
Sublime	Weed	Detector	Hotels
Athenian	UHT[b]	Led	NPV[c]
Athens	Pneumophila	Algebra	Ikea
Eliot	Mitochondria	Turbine	Shostak
Poet	Protein	Modulus	Simmel
Lenin	Abdominal	Cantilever	Hotel
Poetry	Cytochrome	Piston	Chancery
Gothic	Antioxidant	Beam	Kenya
Utterance	SHH[d]	Radstone	Lashley
Wordsworth	Bowel	Birthweight	Korea
Brecht	Medication	Microcontroller	Nisa
Archaeologist	Ewe	Stylus	Buttle
Bolsheviks	Aquaponic	Gearbox	TNCS[e]

[a]ATP = Adenosine triphosphate.
[b]UHT = Ultra-high temperature/Ultra-heat treatment.
[c]NPV = Net present value.
[d]SHH = Sonic hedgehog homolog.
[e]TNCS = Transnational corporations.

Word lists such as these can be generated online for each discipline represented in the BAWE corpus, using the corpus query tool *Sketch Engine*. Writing tutors work in different ways, according to context and their students' needs, and some may not consider the lexis of the discipline a major area of concern. Certainly writing tutors cannot be expected to advise on technical terminology in every field. The lists may be useful for those creating teaching materials, however, perhaps as a starting point for exploration of the use of the keywords in context.

3.5. Epistemological Differences

Alongside the division into the four domains (Arts and Humanities, Life Sciences, Physical Sciences, Social Sciences) an alternative categorisation system groups disciplines in terms of whether they are 'hard' or 'soft', 'pure' or 'applied' (Becher, 1989; Becher & Trowler, 2001). The soft and pure distinction is a matter of epistemology. In the soft–pure qualitative disciplines such as Classics, English and History new knowledge is developed through interaction between disciplinary experts, and there are many different approaches to the same field. The hard–pure quantitative disciplines such as Biological Science, Chemistry, Mathematics and Physics, on the other hand, follow a single paradigm; knowledge tends to develop steadily and cumulatively, so that new knowledge builds on old knowledge. Applied disciplines, whether they are hard or soft, involve a qualitative element because they are concerned with the application of theory in the real world rather than under controlled experimental conditions. Hard-applied disciplines solve problems and create processes and products; soft-applied disciplines are traditionally concerned with professional practice. In the BAWE corpus, disciplines such as Agriculture, Business, Medicine and Engineering are largely applied rather than pure, but the hard/soft, pure/applied categorisation does not work perfectly because applied disciplines offer theoretical modules on their degree programmes, and pure disciplines offer modules of a more practical nature. Moreover, although reflection is typically associated with soft-applied studies, most departments require students to produce some reflective writing as part of their degree programmes, regardless of whether they represent hard or soft, pure or applied disciplines. Some disciplines such as Linguistics, Archaeology and Philosophy contain both soft and hard elements, and the departments that teach these disciplines can be located within Arts, Science or Social Science faculties, depending on the organisational structure of the university.

Holmes and Nesi (2009) compared words expressing reaction and reflection in two 'pure' subsets of the BAWE corpus: History, a soft discipline, and Physics, a hard discipline. For this study, the 'saying' and 'internal cognition' words listed in WordNet (Fellbaum, 1998) were identified in the keyword lists for the two disciplines. These had been created using WordSmith Tools Version 4.0 (Scott, 2004), and contained all the words that occurred significantly more or less frequently in these disciplines when compared with the BAWE corpus as a whole. Strikingly, a great many of the keywords which occurred unusually frequently in History were unusually rare in Physics, and *vice versa*. For example, *argue*, *belief*, *support* and *claim* were positively key in History but negatively key in Physics, and *determine*, *know*, *calculate*, *find* and *show* were positively key in Physics, but negatively key in History.

The History students typically turned to the opinions of individuals to support their arguments, as can be seen from the following examples containing the keyword *argue*:

- Gareth Steedman Jones provides the seminal work. He *argued* that social movements, such as Chartism, could be constituted on ideological and political platforms ...
- In this sense, it can be *argued* that for Marx and Engels, a primitive idea of democratic, or majority, rights served to justify a complex social theory of inevitable revolutionary struggle.
- I would *argue* that the 1917 revolution would not have occurred without it.

Most of the positive keywords in Physics, on the other hand, referred to the establishment of facts through data analysis, as in the following examples for *determine*, *calculate* and *show*:

- Gamma ray photons are uncharged and create no ionisation or excitation of any material they pass through and hence the methods of *determining* their energies are somewhat limited.
- ... and this data was used to *calculate* a value for Planck's constant.
- Table 3.1 *shows* that as the intensity was decreased, the stopping voltage measured increased.

Holmes and Nesi (2009, p. 67) conclude that:

> In physics the identities of agents are commonly suppressed, to emphasise the fact that knowledge is derived from replicable laboratory activities, observations and measurements rather than from interpretation or discussion. On the other hand the KWs [key words] in history were more likely to have explicit agents; the identities of the authorities and sources referred to were important in establishing their validity and relevance.

In Holmes and Nesi's study, 'saying' and 'internal cognition' keywords were further compared across pure disciplines (History and Physics) and applied disciplines (Engineering, Medicine, and Hospitality, Leisure and Tourism Management). Applied approaches to knowledge are 'functional' and 'pragmatic' (Becher & Trowler, 2001, p. 36), because practitioners have to make decisions based on only partial and imperfect evidence. This is demonstrated in Holmes and Nesi's study by the fact that the positive keywords in the applied disciplines expressed greater uncertainty than those in the pure disciplines. For example, the following contexts for the keywords *indicate*, *unlikely* and *uncertain* all come from applied disciplines:

> There were no abnormalities in other systems, which **indicate** that this diagnosis is less likely. (Medicine)

> Although the shaft and thrust bearings are being designed to take 50% body weight, it is **unlikely** that this will be thrust onto the drill in its lifetime. (Engineering)

> Comprising mainly small businesses that rely on fluctuating demand, profitability is **uncertain** and production, wages and skills are low. (Hospitality, Leisure and Tourism Management)

Hard–soft and pure-applied distinctions are never rigid. Disciplines have fuzzy boundaries, and university departments often wish to broaden their students' experiences and skills by introducing approaches from a different disciplinary type (preparation for the world of work in the pure disciplines, for example, or reflection in the hard disciples). Nevertheless an understanding of hard, soft, pure and applied approaches can help writing tutors to appreciate departmental expectations. For example, there is probably more need to teach methods of 'hedging' assertions to students of applied disciplines, and it is probably not a good idea to insist that students from every discipline use the same referencing system, because whereas the identity of the source author is important information in the soft disciplines as a means of establishing the student writer's stance, in the hard disciplines theories or procedures often conform to recognised standards and do not need to be associated with a particular individual, at least in the body of the text.

3.6. Conclusion

This chapter has shown some ways in which academic corpora can be used to inform the design of academic writing syllabuses and the teaching and learning of academic writing skills. By drawing attention to differences in writing practice across the genres and the disciplines, it discourages a 'one size fits all' approach to academic writing support. Clearly, strategies that will gain a student high marks in one context can be irrelevant or even undesirable in another. Students need to develop the ability to write differently to meet different expectations, especially as these expectations grow more diverse at higher levels of study, and beyond the university into the world of work.

The BAWE corpus is freely accessible, and writing tutors, materials writers and course designers can explore it in more detail, with more specific questions in mind. It is possible to download the corpus from the Oxford Text Archive for use with concordancing programmes such as *Wordsmith Tools* (Scott, 2004); it is listed in the Archive as resource number 2539. Alternatively the corpus can be searched online using the open access version of *Sketch Engine* (http://ca.sketchengine.co.uk/open/) or the subscription version which provides the facility to create new subcorpora, and to compare BAWE with other subscription-only corpora such as the BNC. The manual *Using Sketch Engine with BAWE* (Nesi & Thompson, 2011) is written especially for novice users, and demonstrates all the major query types.

The chapter might also inspire readers to create their own corpora, perhaps in collaboration with their own students, to reflect more exactly a specific writing context. Whether they opt for the strong version of data-driven learning, or simply mine the corpus holdings for examples of appropriate usage, corpus evidence is a powerful means of dispelling false beliefs about academic writing conventions, and shedding light on disciplinary practice.

References

Alsop, S., & Nesi, H. (2009). Issues in the development of the British Academic Written English (BAWE) corpus. *Corpora, 4*(1), 71–83.
Becher, T. (1989). *Academic tribes and territories: Intellectual enquiry and the culture of disciplines*. Buckingham, UK: The Society for Research into Higher Education and Open University Press.
Becher, T., & Trowler, P. (2001). *Academic tribes and territories: Intellectual enquiry and the culture of disciplines*. Buckingham, UK: The Society for Research into Higher Education and Open University Press.
Biber, D. (1988). *Variation across speech and writing*. Cambridge: Cambridge University Press.
Biber, D., Conrad, S., Reppen, R., Byrd, P., & Helt, M. (2002). Speaking and writing in the university: A multidimensional analysis. *TESOL Quarterly, 36*(1), 9–49.
Bizup, J. (2008). BEAM: A rhetorical vocabulary for teaching research-based writing. *Rhetoric Review, 27*(1), 72–86.

Charles, M. (2003). 'This mystery': A corpus-based study of the use of nouns to construct stance in theses from two contrasting disciplines. *Journal of English for Academic Purposes*, *2*, 313–326.

Charles, M. (2007). Argument or evidence? Disciplinary variation in the use of the noun *that* pattern in stance construction. *English for Specific Purposes*, *26*, 203–218.

Elbow, P. (2007). Voice in writing again: Embracing contraries. *College English*, *70*(2), 168–188.

Fellbaum, C. (1998). *WordNet: An electronic lexical database*. Cambridge, MA: MIT.

Gardner, S., & Holmes, J. (2009). Can I use headings in my essay? Section headings, macrostructures and genre families in the BAWE corpus of student writing. In M. Charles, S. Hunston & D. Pecorari (Eds.), *Academic writing: At the interface of corpus and discourse* (pp. 251–271). London: Continuum.

Holmes, J., & Nesi, H. (2009). Verbal and mental processes in academic disciplines. In M. Charles, S. Hunston & D. Pecorari (Eds.), *Academic writing: At the interface of corpus and discourse* (pp. 58–72). London: Continuum.

Johns, T. (1991a). From printout to handout: Grammar and vocabulary teaching in the context of data-driven learning. In T. Johns & P. King (Eds.), *Classrooom concordancing* (pp. 27–37). Birmingham: ELR University of Birmingham.

Johns, T. (1991b). Should you be persuaded: Two samples of data-driven learning materials. In T. Johns & P. King (Eds.), *Classrooom concordancing* (pp. 1–16). Birmingham: ELR University of Birmingham.

Lee, D. Y. W., & Swales, J. (2006). A corpus-based EAP course for NNS doctoral students: Moving from available specialised corpora to self-compiled corpora. *English for Specific Purposes*, *25*, 56–75.

Nesi, H., & Gardner, S. (2012). *Genres across the disciplines: Student writing in higher education*. Cambridge: Cambridge University Press.

Nesi, H., & Thompson, P. (2011). *Using sketch engine with BAWE*. Retrieved from http://trac.sketchengine.co.uk/wiki/SharedResources

Pennebaker, J. W., Chung, C. K., Ireland, M., Gonzales, A., & Booth, R. (2007). *The development and psychometric properties of LIWC2007*. Retrieved from http://www.liwc.net/LIWC2007LanguageManual.pdf

Scott, M. (2004). *WordSmith tools*. Oxford: Oxford University Press.

Swales, J. (1981). *Aspects of article introductions*. Aston ESP Research Reports no 1. Language Studies Unit, The University of Aston at Birmingham. Republished by University of Michigan Press in 2011.

Swales, J. (1996). Occluded genres in the academy: The case of the submission letter. In E. Ventola & A. Mauranen (Eds.), *Academic writing: Intercultural and textual issues* (pp. 45–58). Amsterdam: John Benjamins.

Thompson, P. (2000). Citation practices in PhD theses. In L. Burnard & T. McEnery (Eds.), *Rethinking language pedagogy from a corpus perspective* (pp. 91–102). Frankfurt: Peter Lang.

Chapter 4

The Embodied Writer: Merleau-Ponty, Writing Groups and the Possibilities of Space

Patrick O'Connor and Melanie Petch

> Communities of practice do not reduce knowledge to an object. They make it an integral part of their activities and interactions, and they serve as a living repository for that knowledge.
>
> (Wenger, McDermott, & Snyder, 2002, p. 9)

As we sit and write, innumerable things are occurring to our body, our physicality. As we sit and type, there are numerous events both political and social outside our door, as much as there are baroque channels of nerves, blood and tissues and so forth which constitute our embodied being. It strikes us as odd that, given these dramatic regions, the image that most springs to mind when we think of the writer is that of the figure hunched over the desk with pen in hand.[1] This restricts our understanding of writing in a very profound way. The key traditional understanding of the writer is one that is essentially passive. The writer is isolated and removed from the social and political sphere as much as from everyday life. Furthermore, there is a certain monastic perversity at work here; the writer in this image is alone, accessing in an abstract way the entire region of time and space. Such a notion of writing presupposes that the writer is wholly autonomous in

---

1. The most cursory image search for 'writing' on any reliable Internet search engine will confirm this.

Writing in the Disciplines: Building Supportive Cultures for Student Writing in UK Higher Education
Copyright © 2012 by Emerald Group Publishing Limited
All rights of reproduction in any form reserved
ISBN: 978-1-78052-546-4

imagination. Here, writing becomes individualised rather than thought of as embedded within a social context. Writing, thought of in this way, is not socially situated in the practical tasks of everyday life but utterly disembodied. Writing is simply cognitive, devoid of an appreciation of its situation, its social atmosphere, as much as its relationality to the world of others and things. Why writing is thought of in this way is something that we are going to explore in this chapter. It is our contention, along with Merleau-Ponty, that the idea of the autonomous writer is part of the legacy of Cartesian subjectivism.

From the perspective of the higher education (HE) teacher, the simple truth is that we have a tendency to forget about the embodied writer when we teach. When we have our attention fixed on a number of student faces when lecturing, we do not tend to take account of what is fully involved in the process of writing itself. Writing is always something done in another place; it is merely an adjunct to the learning process. It is subordinate to the ends and means of educational outcomes. Writing happens in some shadowy circuit between the impartation of knowledge and the return of that knowledge in the presentation of student assessments. There are two things that we can say here. Firstly, university teachers and even students themselves do not on the whole reflect on the very process which takes up a relatively large portion of their time at university. Secondly, writing is thought of as one of the activities in which university students engage in their home lives. These two points illustrate something very banal but hugely significant. In the time span of a student's university career, the activity that is most entangled with a student's experience of both the university and extra-mural environment is the writing process itself. Whether students are scrawling some notes on a bumpy bus ride, doing group work in class, in their flats searching Wikipedia, cutting and pasting bibliographies from the Internet, note-taking at lectures, or drumming out essays on their laptops in their rooms, the most significant common denominator is the writing process itself. That the writing process is thought of as secondary, as something that can be left to the individual, is something which we would like to challenge in this essay. We will argue that a much more nuanced appreciation of academic writing can be gained by thinking of writing as socially generated, contextual and embodied within particular practices.

The most basic recommendation of this chapter is that the Cartesian mind-set should be changed. Writing should be considered as fundamental within the domain of HE. There are a number of ways of achieving the primacy of writing, but in this chapter we will concentrate on one aspect and that is the idea of the embodied writer. It is our contention that concentrating on the physical and embodied nature of writing is something that allows teachers to create flourishing educational environments.

We shall draw on the theoretical work of French phenomenologist Maurice Merleau-Ponty which we argue is useful to demonstrate how an understanding of embodiment is essential for conceptualising academic writing, and furthermore it will allow us to recommend practices for ways in which the embodied writer may learn and develop in HE. The chapter will be laid out as follows: firstly, we will present a brief summary of the Merleau-Ponty's phenomenology. Secondly, we will look at how the body can be thought of as a site of possibility, as this will allow us to conceptualise the idea of the embodied writer. Finally, the theoretical work will allow us to recommend practices for creating supportive learning environments for embodied writers. Here we will look at the numerous different practical applications which might cultivate the notion of the embodied writer. To this end, we will look at writing in relation to doctoral writing groups.

4.1. Maurice Merleau-Ponty's Phenomenology

If we are to look at the philosophy of Merleau-Ponty we see at once the most banal but striking insight: the body is forgotten individually, socially and historically. This is because of what Merleau-Ponty calls 'intellectualism' (rationalism) and empiricism which have become the dominant paradigms of intellectual life in the twentieth century (Merleau-Ponty, 1962, pp. 26–28, henceforth, *PP*). Both for Merleau-Ponty are intellectual dead ends. Rationalism with its focus on cognitive conscious structures and empiricism with its emphasis on incoming sense data are both hewn from a common deadly error: they separate consciousness from the world. Meaningful knowledge is, therefore, split into a subject–object distinction. We are forced into the false alternative of thinking that the only options for understanding the human is either as an isolated ego or as a passive subject receiving experiences from the external world. The idea that there is a subject in my head and a world out there and that never the twain shall meet is a divorce that is too costly for Merleau-Ponty. Such a world view is deeply entrenched, however. For instance, if we look at the case of writing in HE, we can think of student writers as simply thinkers who observe the world from inside the windows of their own eyes, experiences upon which they report their findings at a later date.

Merleau-Ponty's phenomenology, then, and specifically for our purposes his notion of the body, tries to mediate between subjectivity and objectivity, our minds and world. Merleau-Ponty's phenomenology is characterised by being anti-mechanistic and anti-reductive in nature. His phenomenology remains profoundly reticent about disinterested knowledge. In essence, disinterested knowledge is in some way a form of dead knowledge — it is inert and without vitality. Objective knowledge is by definition aspecific. It is not dependent upon perception or apprehension, but holds for everyone because it is non-particular (Merleau-Ponty, *PP*, p. 61). Such disinterestedness is a form of abstraction and entails a huge cognitive dissonance within the human being as it promotes the idea that the human being is separate from the world. This dissonance is essentially the legacy of Descartes' splitting of the human being into two irreconcilable substances: mind and body. If we pursue this logic to its end, it means that our essential understanding of the world is one of two wholly alien and irreconcilable worlds. This means that the human being, and indeed the thinking human being, is always essentially estranged from the world. That such a division is entrenched has more macabre consequences, as it presupposes a separation that cannot be healed.[2] The most perverse consequence of Cartesian dualism is the implantation of a torrid separation between mind and world. Merleau-Ponty speaks of this in quite violent terms: 'Our science and our philosophy are two faithful and unfaithful offshoots of Cartesianism, two monsters born of its dismemberment' (Merleau-Ponty, *PP*, 1993, p. 138).

Merleau-Ponty looks at the rich world of perceptual experience in order to overcome what he perceives as the inadequacy of empiricism and rationalism. Both approaches are in effect two sides of the same coin, implicated in objectifying human experience. For Merleau-Ponty, scientific knowledge makes of consciousness nothing more than an object amongst others in nature. Consciousness is here only accountable in terms of mechanistic processes and causal descriptions (Merleau-Ponty, *PP*, pp. 73–90). Rationalism and empiricism therefore contribute to a desiccation of experience by objectifying it, making of the body a mere thing amongst other things.

Alternatively, Merleau-Ponty wants to propose a dynamic account of human experience, one where the body has a central function. Consciousness, before it is anything, is embodied for Merleau-Ponty. It is inherently

---

2. Here Merleau-Ponty is following a very basic Husserlian point. For Husserl, all consciousness is intentional. This means that all consciousness is consciousness of something. Consciousness is always directed towards something; it is immediately enmeshed in the world. The basic point is that we are unable to understand our conscious apprehension of an object in the world as a cognitive event occurring in my mind separate from some kind of physical reality in the world. It is absurd for Husserl to argue that an external object which the subject perceives is something that gets added to consciousness; consciousness is not intentional by having something from the external world placed inside of it. Husserl's point is that consciousness and what it is conscious of are given together. Put basically, when we experience a cup we do not experience this or that representation of the cup but we experience *that* cup. Thus, consciousness is not separated from the world but utterly at one with it. When I am conscious of an object I perceive the thing itself, not my own perception of the object. See Husserl (1983).

relational and operates on a contextual basis. For Merleau-Ponty, this is because one of the most primordial experiences is that we take up space and depth. If this is the case, it entails that we are embodied beings. His claim is that modern science and Cartesian philosophy divest humans of the lived experience of their body. Our body necessarily takes up space and depth and is therefore the origin of any understanding we can have of perception. We cannot think without thinking 'body' first and foremost. Here we must understand that the human body is not a passive empirical body, calmly sorting impressions that come from the outside world. The body for Merleau-Ponty is active. It reaches out to the world of experience, habituating itself to the organisation of the spaces in which it is embedded. Put in the most basic terms, the body ties the human being to place. The fact that I cannot but take up space reveals that the body has a 'thereness.' The fact that the subject takes up space and depth means that it cannot be an abstract entity with free reign over the entire domain of time and space. It is embedded in the here and now the very fact that we have a body reveals our embodied being-in-the-world. The body is therefore of the utmost importance for Merleau-Ponty. Consciousness cannot be revealed in any meaningful way without a true understanding of how the body operates. It is because I have a body that the 'I' is always located in a specific context or situation. Having a body means that I am tied to a historical time and place, to events and situations, to a perspective that is open to manifold arrangements of the world. In other words, prior to anything else, the human being is an embodied being.

4.2. The Body and Possibility

While the human being is first and foremost an embodied being, it is of the utmost importance that we remain vigilant against considering this embodiment in passive terms. It might remain somewhat counter-intuitive to think of the body as merely something with which we are encumbered: the body, as Merleau-Ponty points out, is a nest of activity in its own right. The body is constantly remoulding and adapting itself to the world in which it is enmeshed. The body operates within the constraints of habituation and sedimented experiences but also remains open to emerging spaces and environments. As we will later see, as teachers when we think of the student writer, we must take this active and dynamic sense of the body into account when constructing embodied writing environments. We must realise that the body in itself has its own traditions and history in as much as it is open to new possibilities. The body that writes is situated at the intersection of both practice and possibility.

As embodied beings, our relation to the world is always one of activity; the body in its most visceral, existential nature is one of natural possibility and motility (movement) as much as it is of habitual disposition. A simple example will demonstrate this. When we are taught to drive it is in a specific space and time, say, two years' ago in Nottingham. The skills and capacities which we acquire in attuning our bodies to how the car works are essentially transferable. When we drive anywhere, we do not need the skills we have built up in Nottingham. When we drive years later after our initial lessons, we do not need to drive in the same way in the same place. Our bodies are regulated to driving, but they are also adaptable to new contexts. In essence, this means that the body is actively relational. It exists in relation to movement. What we must understand is that the body is essentially not static, our embodied being is constantly grasping out to things in the world. One of Merleau-Ponty's examples will show what is at stake here:

> The bench, scissors, pieces of leather offer themselves to the subject as poles of action; through their combined values they delimit a certain situation, an open situation moreover, which calls for a certain mode of resolution, a certain kind of work. The body is no more than an element in the system of the subject and his world, and the task to be performed elicits the necessary movements from him by a sort of remote attraction. (Merleau-Ponty, *PP*, p. 106)

For Merleau-Ponty, the body is always active and attempting to cope with the arrangement of its context of involvement. This would even be the case when the body is still. When we are still, the body has a sense of the distance between me and the desk or chair within the room in which I am sitting. The body is the origin of all understanding since it is always attuning itself to the context in which it is involved in. The body is the main mode in which we get a sense of what is possible within a context. For example, when we sleep, our body is habituated to the dimensions of our bed. If we are habituated to sleeping in a double bed, our body adapts to the length, breadth and dimensions of the bed. It is quite possible to imagine that, if we stay in a friend's house in a single bed, we could roll out, since the body has not acquired a sufficient degree of habituation to the new bed's dimensions. The most elementary point here is that embodied beings are constantly regulating themselves self in relation to sets of possible tasks. Habit becomes important because it orients the body to a world in both general and particular ways (Merleau-Ponty, *PP*, p. 84). The spaces and environments which we inhabit are not abstract and disinterested spaces but wholly vibrant lived spaces. The very rooms in which we are enmeshed are not neutral and detached but operate by confining us to certain spaces while opening us to others. It is this dynamic which we should attempt to harness. Again, as we will see, Merleau-Ponty's account of embodiment will allow us to consider much more engaging and significant ways of organising writing spaces.

That the body encounters the world in terms of possibilities entails that its most fundamental aspect is one of action. As embodied humans, we encounter the world as the intersection between received practices and a virtual space of possible movements. The body always remains sensitive to its specific history of networks and practices, as well as adapting to new situations. Prior to conscious control, our bodies are always adapting. Merleau-Ponty's famous example of the phantom limb demonstrates this. If one who has an arm amputated walks towards a doorknob, the absent arm reaches to open the doorknob (Merleau-Ponty, *PP*, pp. 73–90). This shows that the body is constantly reaching out to the world, and more significantly it demonstrates that humans as embodied beings are recalcitrant to mechanistic reduction. The body is always in some way in excess of the pure mechanistic features of the body. The point is not that I have an arm which is a means to open a door, what is important is its most primordial being resists mechanistic reduction. The body considered in its optimum capacity is the body engaging in transformative possibilities; the body is always the body emergent. We are thus never absolutely free, but free in so far as our body is the site from which we can liberate ourselves in relation to our historical context. The human being is free, but free in so far as our bodies are the most crucial sites from which we can liberate ourselves from the past in relation to that very past.

4.3. Writing the Possible

In terms of literacy cultures and spaces of writing, what can we draw from Merleau-Ponty? As stated at the outset, what Merleau-Ponty's phenomenology combats is the notion of the abstract and disengaged writer. To think of the embodied writer is to think of a writer as both a site of constraint and possibility. When one writes, irrespective of the context, one is writing with a series of practices and habits. The point is that these habits and practices are open to transformation and possibility. To think of the writer in an abstract, reductive or predetermined way is precisely to take away the very possibility of writing, since the writer is utterly decontextualised, whereas, as Merleau-Ponty argues, the body is always there, contextualised in the world. This is especially the case in an educational context where possibility is the oxygen upon which teachers and students thrive. Essentially, to disengage the writer is to disembody the writer, it is to make the writer immune from transformation and activity, thereby ensuring that the writer cannot liberate their prose from the tyranny of the abstract and predetermined. The idea then of the disinterested writer and reflective writer presupposes a sense of disinterest and disavowal. A writer and specifically a student writer cannot get a sense of how they are engaged in the world without coming to understand their writing as both practice and possibility. This means that writing is always embedded and habituated to diverse practices, but it is this very diversity which opens new possibilities and horizons for the student to engage with. Indeed, an abstract and scientific model of the writer is thoroughly limited in this respect since the body is removed from the very site in which possibility is at stake.

In the context of HE, the scientific model of a disinterested writer has a wholly pernicious effect on how we can understand student writing environments. Students are beings who are in the process of self-development. Put in Merleau-Pontyian terms, they are at the intersection of habitual dispositions and practices while sensitive to their developing needs. To recycle the image of the cold, abstract and neutral writer is to conceive of the student writer as a writer who has immediate access to a wealth of knowledge without the disciplinary practices to make that knowledge tangible. Such an understanding assumes that the student writer is the finished product, rather than thinking of the writer in a state of development. In short, the notion of the abstract thinker disengages from a comprehension of an actual human being developing. If we do not think of students as embodied writers, then we cannot think of their writing environments as having any transformational capacity.

The model of deterministic knowledge which Merleau-Ponty bears suspicion towards, as seen in the case of writing in HE, requires thinking of student writers as a means to an end. In short, you have a pen or laptop which will produce an essay. Within the discourse of HE in the United Kingdom, the discourse of learning outcomes very much complements this model. The most pervasive model in HE at the moment is that of learning outcomes and acquired skills. In essence, the student writer will achieve a particular end for every input. The HE sector as a whole has willingly attempted to develop this mode of thinking. At base, this involves the adaptation of industrial and mechanistic models to nominally improve the educational process by optimising its efficiency. If the methods used successfully in business and industrial sciences become applied to education, then surely universities will enhance their performance in a similar way. Certainly, it should be noted that there is an element of self-legitimisation at work here. In an unstable economic climate university management teams will be disposed to adopting this model, since it enables management to create regimes of success in order to make apparent their courses general economic utility.[3] This elicits the wholesale adoption of pseudo-scientific language in an effort to legitimise the educational experience. Unfortunately, this opposes the qualitative idea of the embodied writer. In terms of students writing, it is our claim that the mechanistic model diminishes the experience of writing and environments in which we write, and also the quality and enjoyment of the courses students take.

Writing we hold, following Merleau-Ponty's analysis, is a qualitative disposition. This means that writing environments should aim to produce practices and techniques which can produce a range of effects in students. Hence, different writing practices should be implanted within different curricula. The task for the best HE teacher is to foster writing environments that remain sensitive to the developing nature of students, as they move from sedimented bodily habits to newer forms of intellectual development. This claim may seem counter-intuitive since if one takes writing to be bodily, it therefore must also be mindless and unreflective. In our view, this misses the point of the writing experience, since the idea that the student is embodied also entails that the student is actively situated in diverse situations and contexts. In terms of Merleau-Ponty that we have bodies entails that we are exposed to numerous transformative situations. It is the very plurality of these situations which illuminates in a beneficial way the student writing process. If we adopt the idea that writing is empty and simply a means to an end, there will be a concomitant diminishment of the intellectual experience, since by definition writing becomes disembodied and does not adapt to numerous different contexts and situations. That embodiment is significant for writing is demonstrated in the most elementary way. If students are writing, they are temporal or transitive beings who begin within a situation and move into a different one. This is not to say that students are merely protean, but that writing begins embodied within a specific history and develops into a new context within a specific time and place. Whether what is written is a quickly jotted note or a more careful exegesis is tied to a past, a very visceral present and an open future. When students write they are engaged in procedural knowing rather than mindless rote repetition (Bains, 2004). The very embodiment of the student and their developing habituations is precisely that which mitigates mindless repetition. Writing must thus be thought of as a form of truth as emerging self-development rather than as a repetitive carrying out of predetermined ends or objectives. It is thus beneficial to consider writing

---

3. This point is owed to Elliot Eisner (1969) who examines the shifts brought about in education in the post-Taylor model of American schools. See http://eric.ed.gov/ERICDocs/data/ ericdocs2sql/content_storage_01/0000019b/80/37/e2/25.pdf, p. 4

as an embodied activity, since a procedural or emergent understanding of writing entails the distinct understanding that the writing process is exposure to a lively range of ideas and thoughts as opposed to a simple set of learning objectives which are mindlessly repeated.

Support can be drawn for this embodied notion of writing in Elliot Eisner's (1969) essay 'Instructional and Expressive Educational Objectives: Their Formulation and Use in Curriculum.' Eisner distinguishes between 'instructional objectives' and 'expressive objectives' (pp. 16–21). Instructional objectives are those where the educator is dedicated to implementing the means to achieve a certain set of behaviours. What characterises this method is a means-end or learning outcomes model. The teacher here generates behaviour according to pre-established objectives. For Eisner, the consequence of this is the homogeneity of delivery. It would entail that learning outcomes become aspecific and decontextualised. Insofar as outcomes are created they will be generic and thus disembodied. They will be known in advance; there will be a repetition of behaviour across students; and thus in some way the educational experience is not embodied as situational or as an encounter. In contrast, Eisner speaks about what he calls expressive objectives those which do not specify the outcomes of the teaching process. Eisner prefers to think of the expressive objective as an encounter, one which does not specify the behaviour the student is expected to acquire. Expressive objectives provide teacher and student with an 'invitation to explore' (Eisner, 1969, p. 18) In essence, Eisner is advocating the embedding of the contingency of knowledge and understanding. The more situational and contextual the teaching environment is the more evocative rather than prescriptive becomes the teaching and learning experience.

For our purposes, Eisner's analysis corresponds to our understanding of the embodied writer. The writer is a transitive being moving from one writing environment to another. As with expressive objectives, what is demanded for creating a flourishing writing environment for students is a resistance to the homogeneity of student experience. While instructional objectives fall back into the reflective subject–object dichotomy, expressive objectives operate within a context of an embodied writer. Thinking of the writer as expressive allows us to generate events and encounters in which students develop meanings which become personalised and questioned. Writing should thus be considered as an emergent discipline, where one actively reflects on one's written artefact in an effort to reveal its meaning and significance. By thinking of the writer as an embodied writer, one is made aware most significantly of the student's situational involvement. Student writers are at the intersection of their habitual dispositions and tendencies, but the task of the teacher is to embed a diversity of phenomena within writing seminars, which will allow an unfurling of their existing knowledge in relation to new possibilities. Central to this notion is that the written text is not just a text that operates in linear fashion. The task of the teacher is to embed the invention of new intellectual tools in order to create the context in which imaginative variation and creative contributions can flourish. The embodied writer can thus become the writer who is devoted to interpretation, appraisal and situational and spatial adaptability. In this instance, writing becomes alive rather than moribund. In order to create an environment in which student writing flourishes, it is therefore incumbent on HE teachers to generate situations in which writing may be encountered in this way.

We should attempt to avoid as much as possible the romantic idea of the sole writer. Writing is not something students just do themselves. This would be the view that Merleau-Ponty might rail against, the view that writing is not social, not expressive and not something students have a very material stake in when coming to understand a diversity of approaches. Lectures, seminars, and indeed lecturers, should be more attuned to the possibilities of thinking about notions of embodied writing. Rather than thinking of writing as something that students are sent away to do, we think it would be more productive to think of writing, and indeed writing environments which lecturers and students utilise, as dynamic and vibrant spaces in order to foster the nuance, appreciation and deliberative capacities that can be earned from embodied and transformational contexts.[4] If we consider writing as embodied, and as part of a developing second nature, then writing can be thought of as a capacity. Put in this way, writing can be thought of as an enabling discipline. Like the car driver who learns in Nottingham, the habit of learning embeds the possibility of transformational and procedural knowing within newer contexts. Writing is a very visceral and embodied experience that is continually fresh and new. It is thus apt to develop more HE environments and spaces which allow writing to flourish as 'expressive objectives' instilled in students through practice and exemplification.

In phenomenological terms, writing is therefore a form of *praxis* rather than *theoria*. Here writing becomes a *practical art*.[5] When students write, we must understand the process as temporal and procedural. This means that teacher and student writer may become sensitive and responsive beings. As Eisner demonstrated, teachers will have a more fruitful educational experience if they focus on the qualitative rather than generic outcomes and goals. Fostering supportive writing environments requires the teacher to

---

4. Patrick O'Connor has developed this notion in terms of autonomous learning in another context (see Crome, Farrar, & O'Connor, 2009).
5. This point is owed to a conversation with Keith Crome.

respond to the specificity of contextual educational encounters, rather than in terms of predetermined objectives. This is not to say that general rules and behavioural outcomes do not have their utility, only that they are valuable insofar as they are subservient to supporting expressive outcomes. Indeed this entails that predetermined instructional objectives are useful insofar as they render their instrumentality unapparent.

4.4.   Writing Groups as Spaces of Possibility

Cultivating vibrant learning spaces in the HE environment where both the writer and writing can flourish takes mindful consideration. While productive writing spaces may, in some cases, happen upon the writer by chance — more often than not, they are consciously established with a community of writers' needs in mind. Such communities must propagate shared values, experiences or processes if they are to resonate with their intended participants. Etienne Wenger et al. (2002, p. 5) notably calls these spaces 'communities of practice' and perceives them as sites of shared experience that reinforce the idea that an individual is truly understood. Likewise, for learners in HE, environment and climate is deeply important to the learning process and can impact heavily upon the students' motivation to participate and to envisage themselves as learners within this environment (Biggs & Tang, 2007, pp. 37–38). Earlier we identified that Merleau-Ponty perceives how the embodied writer will reach out and actively participate in the world of experience. For Merleau-Ponty all knowledge accrual is in some sense second nature. Prior to reflection, there is a tacit accrual of knowledge that takes place in learning environments always informing the sense in which the writer may learn. We must thus surely also expect the world of experience to hold up a reflection of tacit understanding and the shared values that appeal to the writer. Learning environments, then, have enormous potential as both the writer and the writing community can potentially coexist together and act as a 'living repository' for the creation of knowledge. Indeed, for Merleau-Ponty communication and social interaction is never only an interior monologue. Speech is as much a form of bodily expression within different media such as language, art, painting, film and poetry.

Writing groups, in this light, can thus offer a way of foregrounding the social aspects of writing. As we have already witnessed, Merleau-Ponty is profoundly aware that writing is often seen as a separate entity to disinterested and neutral knowledge production. As we know, he contests the idea that writers are disembodied and isolated from the world and rather sees them as fully responsive beings reaching out to a world that extends beyond the confines of their writing desk. Echoing Merleau-Pontyian views and the need for reaching out, writing groups explicitly address the questions of knowledge, textual practice and identity in the context of peer relations (Aitchison & Lee, 2006, p. 266). What is more, within this peer-assisted environment, writing and knowledge creation can be seen as something that is socially generated and even co-produced. Writing groups, therefore, can offer a plethora of expressive spaces, forms of action where group participants can perform and test out their knowledge within the parameters of a like-minded community.

4.5. Writing Groups and the Doctoral Student Experience

In order to assess such a type of community, we will now reflect on a recent Postgraduate Researcher Symposium (hosted by the UK Council for Graduate Education at the British Library, November 2011); the most recurring message of the event was the call from doctoral students to have more opportunities to join communities of practice with other students who share the same experience. Given the nature of the doctoral writing process, this response is hardly surprising. The intensified nature of thesis writing involves the production of some 80,000 words of scholarly work, which is often done in isolation, and most usually, over a sustained period of time. It is no wonder then that for many doctoral students, writing is seen as something that upsets the balance of the natural flow of 'punctual and effective completion of the doctorate' (Aitchison & Lee, 2006, p. 265). Often writing is seen as something that needs to be endured in an attempt to *verify* the thinking process and not something that *develops* the thinking self. Furthermore, without some form of formal or informal support network, the doctoral student is a prime candidate for slipping into the role of the disembodied writer. Without the regularity of seminars, lectures, tutorials and opportunities for informal discussions — a feature of the undergraduate learning experience — doctoral students have little opportunity (other than supervision meetings) to speak out their thoughts *on* and approaches *to* their research. Even then, many supervisory discussions are governed by content and subject matter rather than the mechanics and processes of writing.

It is clear that once postgraduates do 'start to share information, skills and tactics for research and writing, there is a dynamic increase in productivity, and even in enjoyment' (Murray, 2002, p. 147). With this in mind, might writing groups open up the possibility that writing is in itself a form of knowledge production? Might they also offer outlets for socialising the process of writing and even evoke the pleasure and productivity that Murray refers to? In this section of our chapter, we aim to consider how the participants of one particular writing group developed collaborative approaches to knowledge-building and in doing so displayed characteristics of Merleau-Ponty's embodiment of writing.

4.6.   The Writing Group for Research Students (WGRS) at De Montfort University (DMU)

4.6.1.   Background

The Writing Group for Research Students (WGRS) was established in November 2009 and is convened by Melanie Petch, Senior Lecturer in Writing Development, in the Directorate of Library and Learning Services at De Montfort University (DMU). The group was initiated in response to the increasing number of doctoral students who were attending academic writing workshops aimed primarily at undergraduates; in some cases, as many as 25% of attendees were doctoral students. Feedback from this particular body of students indicated that their very specific writing needs were not being met in the workshops and they needed more opportunities to interact with other students undergoing the same experience. This feedback also challenged our own misguided assumptions that PhD students 'just know how to write' (Caffarella & Barnett, 2000, p. 39). To identify how some of these needs might be conceptualised, an evaluation was initially carried out to gauge doctoral students' levels of confidence in terms of their writing. The responses showed that 96% of research students identified with one or more 'writing anxieties' which included topics such as 'critical analysis', 'structuring a thesis/chapter' or 'writing in an academic style'. While these topics do not differ greatly from undergraduate concerns, what we began to realise was that postgraduate research students needed these concepts framed within the context of doctoral writing. As a result, this offered us a clear rationale for writing development provision that was steered towards the specialised writing concerns experienced by research students. We were also mindful that doctoral students welcomed opportunities to meet other students in less formal outlets. In response to these concerns, the WGRS was established later that year.

4.6.2.   Aims of the Group

From the outset, the WGRS had as its focus on the need for cultivating an environment where doctoral students could normalise the practice of doctoral writing by interacting and sharing their experiences with other group participants. Although not initially intentional, each of the aims below has an embodied writing, or in other words, socialising, experience at its core:

- *To foster a community approach to writing at research level*
- *To increase the output and quality of research students' writing through objective setting, discussion, practice-based activities and peer reviewing*
- *To provide a forum for information exchange*
- *To create an environment where students can assimilate and practise the academic language and culture of their disciplines*

4.6.3. Group Identity

The WGRS is now an established component of the research provision that Library and Learning Services offer to doctoral students. The group meets for two hours on a monthly basis in a central library location. It is multi-disciplinary in nature with participants spanning all four faculties as well as two institutes.

The WGRS attracts doctoral students at all stages in their research, with a particular interest from those in their first year of study and also those at the writing-up stage. The benefit of bringing together more experienced students with those who are less experienced is documented by Maher et al. (2008, pp. 265–266). They suggest that the more experienced doctoral students bring 'more experience and knowledge ... and general know-how', whereas new students 'bring enthusiasm and new ways of doing'. From our experience, this blend of experience and enthusiasm has been largely positive, with salient questions from newer members giving those with more experience the opportunity to make sense of their own approaches to writing and then to pass on their knowledge. The reciprocal nature of this transaction is beneficial to both parties, and the talking out is reminiscent of truth emerging collectively rather than governed by one single voice of authority.

4.6.4. Pedagogic Principles of the WGRS

- *Setting writing objectives*: At the beginning of each meeting, participants share their monthly writing output. In doing so, they discuss some of the barriers to their writing over the past month and also share what has gone well. They then set clear, realistic objectives for the following month which are recorded on paper so they can be revisited at the next meeting. This open and public commitment to writing seems to be a key motivator in terms of increasing the writing output of the group.

- *Discussion*: The focus of each meeting is based on discussion topics that group participants have identified as being particularly relevant. All the topics are student initiated and discussions are student led, creating opportunities for group members to 'learn and share the management' of a particular task at hand (Aitchison & Lee, 2006, p. 272).
- *Peer-reviewed activity*: Group participants are invited to share their work-in-progress with the rest of the group. This provides an opportunity for them to gain confidence in practising the language of their disciplines via a more informal channel. It also enables them to receive feedback from their peers on the mechanics and process of writing.

4.7. WGRS Participants as Embodied Writers: Emergent Themes

By utilising the pedagogic principles above, some interesting themes have emerged from the WGRS which chime with Merleau-Ponty's characteristics of the embodied writer.

4.7.1. The Habitual Nature of Writing

What we found was that the act of setting writing objectives and evaluating them at the next meeting enabled students to make a public commitment to the rest of the group. Making a promise to others to write can have a significant impact on how regularly writing occurs. Indeed, Lee and Boud (2003, p. 195) stress the necessity of making writing seem like 'normal business.' The response from one of the group participants shown below shows that writing now forms part of their daily routine or daily habit:

> The group has highlighted the importance of writing con-tinuously as I go along, and there were occasions when an upcoming meeting of the writing group was my motivation for writing that week.

There is a sense that the transformative space of the writing group can encourage writing as an emerging habit, even if it is not yet second nature. However, speaking out writing objectives in a public arena is not always a driver to increased motivation. One participant noted that while setting writing objectives did allow him/her 'to focus more' on writing as a process, in terms of the 'actual product' he/she still found this 'difficult'. What is clear is that for some group participants, despite talking out their intentions, those painful, isolating spells of putting words on the page to shape a 'product' are not always harmonised by the commitments made to writing in front of the group. For others, writing does not become habitual without the drive of the community's 'knowingness' of their intentions.

4.7.2. The Body

The public act of speaking out one's intentions is not only an incitement to habitual ways of writing but also intrinsically connected to the concept of imprinting one's own intentions on the outside world. In a Merleau-Pontyian sense, the writer is willingly reaching out to the world by sharing their rudimentary writing processes with others outside their physical self. In the WGRS, through peer review, open discussions and setting writing objectives, there is always a sense that the body is not immune from the transformative capacity of the community but is actively feeding into it and finding nourishment as a reward for its investment. Group participants often use others' inputs to enrich their own work. One member recorded that one of the benefits of peer review had been that

It is helping as I have used others idea in [my] writing.

In fact, one of the most prominent themes to have emerged from writing group activities reflects the most primitive human impulse to give and to share and, in return, to receive. All these transactions are of course heavily loaded with emotion and anxiety seeing as writing carries so much of the internalised self. Murray (2002, p. 149) also recognises how painful it is to release one's work out into a community. It was an intention of the WGRS that our writing community would be a safe environment where embodied writing practices could develop freely. Mindful of the need to establish trust, the group collectively drafted set of peer-reviewed guidelines to support participants who gave feedback to others and received feedback on their own work in return.

Interestingly, through peer review, the socialisation of writing also becomes an iterative process as knowledge that is imparted by the writer is then critiqued and returned by other participants and then finely tuned and batted out once again in the presentation of writing. As such, participants are developing a shared vernacular to talk about the process of writing (Maher et al., 2008, p. 269). This process is not without its complexities; of course, there are disagreements over the implication of wording a question a certain way in a participant's work, for example, but the process of justifying why one perspective might be more valid than another reinforces the collaborative nature of peer review. What is clear is that in most cases the body displays an openness to interact with the manifold arrangements of the world even if they are unfamiliar.t

4.7.3. *Knowledge as Truth Emerging*

Placing knowledge outside the body with the aim of reformulating and refining it also gives way to the idea of truth emerging rather than it being a static, unchangeable concept. Peer review in the WGRS, for example, focuses on participants' writing-in-progress rather than a polished piece of finished work. This opens up the idea that participants' writing is an ongoing dialogue that might go back and forth and also converge with, and diverge from, other voices. Aitichison and Lee (2006, p. 272) define the peer-learning approach as a 'horizontalising' process. This is in contrast to the 'vertical' view that perceives the student in a subordinate position to the expert. The notion of both 'being and becoming' (Aitchison & Lee, 2006, p. 272; Maher et al., 2008, p. 263) is also reflected in peer review, with participants sharing the act of 'becoming' doctoral researchers while also witnessing moments when members, interchangeably, assume the temporary role of 'expert'. Drawing upon Eisner's perspectives mentioned earlier, what this collaborative knowledge-building process does is to reinforce the qualitative learning experiences rather than the generic outcomes and goals.

This need for democratic learning feeds into the idea of facilitation. The WGRS, as mentioned earlier, is convened and facilitated by the Lecturer in Writing Development at DMU. A facilitator might help chivvy the group along when activities need to progress and also help participants to feel 'supported' (Maher et al., 2008, p. 265), but this role perhaps plays out more effectively when it is taken on by someone who understands the specific needs of this particular group (Murray, 2002, p. 147). The facilitator of the WGRS has been through the doctoral experience, but is sensitive not to impose her own experience on the group and hold it up as the only doctoral experience to be had. Rather, as Wenger et al. (2002, pp. 13–14) stresses, the role of the community, and indeed the facilitator, is to nurture and elicit participation rather than manage or control it. In the WGRS, if one member is consistently looked to for a definitive answer to a query, it is the role of the facilitator to open the question out to the rest of the group to fully ensure that truth is free to emerge rather than to be 'unlocked' from a perceived voice of authority.

4.7.4. *Performance*

Through the socialising activities of peer review and setting writing objectives, the performative aspects of these activities can have a positive impact on motivation. The public commitment participants make to writing are particularly important for one member who points out that

> Setting monthly writing objectives [is] very helpful because I announce them in front of everyone.

It is the very act of speaking out one's commitment to writing that gives it a sense of permanence that would be easy to ignore if it were to remain internalised. Performance, therefore, reinforces the writer's embodied connection with the world, giving them a sense of a writing identity. 'I have performed the act of a writer, therefore this makes me one' is the implicit message here.

Performing and speaking out is also important in the forming of other identities that constitute the doctoral student experience. Lee and Boud (2003, p. 188) speak of how 'academic identities, including identities as researchers, are forged, rehearsed and remade in local sites of practice'. Furthermore, they note the importance of contextualising practices for these formations to have true resonance. Contextualising practice has been one of the biggest challenges for the WGRS which operates as a multi-disciplinary group. This is reflected in the participants' comments below:

> The only disappointment for me in attending the group, is the lack of Humanities students to discuss writing with.
> It would be better to find those working with similar philosophical approaches and proposed methodologies. Little benefit of discussing quantitative research with someone in engineering, but that's because I'm a qualitative researcher in social science.

Performances then seem more valuable if the performee feels that he or she is truly understood. Cleary, there is a need for disciplinary writing communities that might complement the practices of the WGRS. However, the multi-disciplinary backdrop of the WGRS does aim to cultivate a safe space outside the participants' discipline for them to rehearse their disciplinary narratives. The participants' 'pure' disciplinary environment could be viewed as more censored and competitive perhaps in the light of competition for funding, and for continuing personal development and teaching opportunities. In other words, performances a doctoral student might make in front of experts in their own field will need to be polished and intellectually rigorous, whereas the WGRS offers a rehearsal space for trial and error in front of a receptive yet sensitive audience.

4.7.5.   Space and Movement

The performative activities of the WGRS very much inform the arrangement of the room and the way the movement of the body manifests within this space. Assembling the room has become very much an opening activity of the group. The group often begins with the arrangement of chairs and/or tables in a circular or rectangular style. The key idea here is that no particular seat is located outside the formation of the rest of the group. This is to ensure that the group includes all members into its core and also to ensure that potential power relationships between 'expert' and 'student' do not seep into the group dynamics.

At the peer-reviewed stage, the group splinters into several smaller reading groups to allow time for all participants who are sharing work to receive detailed feedback from their peers. In this phase, it has been interesting to note how the group personalises the space in the room. There is an almost implicit desire for groups to head for a handful of comfortable chairs at the far end of the room. There are not enough comfortable chairs for all the groups, so the remaining ones focus on 'building' their own spaces with the remaining furniture in the room. The initial circular set-up is always abandoned. This need for 'home-building' is expressed by Gaston Bachelard (1994, p. 91) in *The Poetics of Space* when he writes that a 'human being likes to withdraw into his corner ... and it gives him physical pleasure to do so.' Indeed, this nesting behaviour seems to reflect the intimacy of exchanging knowledge but also demonstrates the respect individuals feel for the work of others. Voices lower, bodies move closer together and non-verbal body language becomes more intimate and more intense. Eye contact is strong; head nodding is more frequent, and pensive characteristics such as chin stroking and the expressions of agreement are common. At this stage, coffee and tea cups are always refilled and cakes are revisited once more. In terms of Merleau-Ponty's embodiment of writing, the WGRS displays a visceral and dynamic representation of this. The exchange of knowledge is wholly humanised and writing is seen through the organic process of speaking out and listening reflectively with others.

4.7.6.   Sharing Food

Taking this humanising element further, food is a symbolic feature of the WGRS. At each group meeting, members are invited to volunteer for baking duties. Often, although not exclusively, we find that those bringing along their work for peer review will also bake or bring food for the group. This might seem like a trivial act, but through this act of feeding and nurturing others, the embodiment of writing might be realised most profoundly. Food becomes a Eucharistic gesture where participants give thanks for the feedback they have received on their work. The exchange of food seems to replicate the exchange of knowledge. The implicit message here is that: 'In return for your consideration of my work, I will feed and nourish you'. Echoing themes mentioned earlier giving and receiving is a basic human impulse. This is seen most readily in the intimate act of baking for the group and eating the food together. The cultural diversity within the group also makes the baking of food an opportunity to share a little of one's own culture. From a traditional German cake to an Arabic dessert, food has become a signature theme for the WGRS.

4.8. Conclusion

What the phenomenology of Merleau-Ponty brings to our understanding of the learning environment is the raw and immediate permeation of body and intelligence. The sphere of body and reflection is mutually dependent spheres and cannot be separated from each other. The body, and its tangible relation to its environment, is one of emerging possibility. As we mentioned at the beginning, writing is as much about thinking of the body within an environment as it is of thinking of the body as a fleshy mess of sinew and nerves. Merleau-Ponty's phenomenology allows an understanding of embodied writing as something that may be cultivated in expressive environments. In the *Phenomenology of Perception*, Merleau-Ponty gives the example of a blind person's use of a cane. For Merleau-Ponty, he says that the 'the acquisition of a habit is [...] the grasping of a significance'.[6] The blind person's cane is something that becomes an extension of the body; it imbues objects and things in the world with a degree of possibility. If we substitute the writing pen or the laptop for the cane, we have an apt metaphor for the student as an embodied writer. The mere object or instrument can be a thing pregnant with possibility once appropriate and vibrant writing environments are cultivated. That with which we write is part of a vital and creative instrument opening ourselves to different contexts, ideas and possibilities. There is of course no separation between body and world for Merleau-Ponty. There is no longer a separation between the mind of the student and the object that is a pen; there is instead the idea

---

6. 'The blind man's stick has ceased to be an object for him, and is no longer perceived for itself; its point has become an area of sensitivity, extending the scope and active radius of touch, and providing a parallel to sight. In the exploration of things, the length of the stick does not enter expressly as a middle term: the blind man is rather aware of it through the position of objects than of the position of objects through it' (Merleau-Ponty, *PP*, p. 143).

that the pen is part of a lived space. The pen or keyboard or palm-pilot is now permeated with the possibilities and inventions which the body is open to. The writer here is no longer the isolated individual but wholly entwined with a vibrant space of possibility.

On practical terms, in this chapter we have given consideration to the ways of constructing expressive and social spaces where writing can be conceptualised as a fully-embodied act. The theories of both Merleau-Ponty and Eisner have informed our discussion on how we might best cultivate learning environments that enrich and deepen our students' writing experiences. Our concern has predominately rested with the doctoral student and the need to open up more opportunities for this particular group with very distinct writing needs, so that they may experience fully the benefits of embodied writing. Writing groups were identified as one way of cultivating a sense of community and identification with others who share the often painful and isolating process of writing a thesis.

As we have seen, the approach used by WGRS at DMU illustrates how the embodiment of writing is actualised most significantly in the group's desire to give and to receive. This takes the form of talking out and sharing experiences, work-in-progress and even food. Knowledge-building is seen as a humanising behaviour that has evolved organically and creatively within the writing group environment. Peer-reviewed activities in particular demonstrate how both space and movement reflect the intimate exchange of knowledge and how it is possible to imprint it on the world of experience.

While the embodied writer can be seen to value this environment, and in particular, feel motivated to write while there, we can also see that there are limitations to this particular approach. We have identified the need for contextualising spaces that also enable students to rehearse their narratives to an audience that understands the deeper philosophical approaches and methods that underpin their subject matter. These contextualised communities would, we recognise, complement the features of identity formation and sense of shared experience that are already practised and valued in the WGRS. An embodied writing environment therefore can empower and increase productivity in doctoral students, but more importantly it can go some way to extending learning beyond the writing desk. Above all, it encourages a vibrant and meaningful two-way interaction between writer and the environment he or she inhabits.

References

Aitchison, C., & Lee, A. (2006). Research writing: Problems and pedagogies. *Teaching in Higher Education, 11*(3), 265–278.

Bachelard, G. (1994). *The poetics of space.* Boston, MA: Beacon Press.

Bains, K. (2004). *What the best college teachers do*. Harvard: Harvard University Press.

Biggs, J., & Tang, C. (2007). *Teaching for quality learning at university*. Maidenhead, UK: Oxford University Press.

Caffarella, R. S., & Barnett, B. G. (2000). Teaching doctoral students to become scholarly writers: The importance of giving and receiving critiques. *Studies in Higher Education, 25*(1), 39–52.

Crome, K., Farrar, R., & O'Connor, P. (2009). What is autonomous learning? *Discourse: Learning and Teaching in Philosophical and Religious Studies, 9*(1), 111–126. Retrieved from http://prs.heacademy.ac.uk/view.html/PrsDiscourse Articles/113

Eisner, E. (1969). *Instructional and expressive educational objectives: Their formulation and use in curriculum*. Retrieved from http://www.eric.ed.gov/ERICWebPortal/search/detailmini.jsp?_nfpb−true&_&ERICExtSearch_SearchValue_0=ED 028838&ERICExtSearch_SearchType_0=no&accno=ED028838. Accessed on 14 November 2011.

Husserl, E. (1983). In F. Kersten (Trans.), *Ideas pertaining to a pure phenomenology and to a phenomenological philosophy* (pp. A.87–90, 93–95). Hague: Springer.

Lee, A., & Boud, D. (2003). Writing groups, change and academic identity: Research development as local practice. *Studies in Higher Education, 28*(2), 187–200.

Maher, D., Seaton, L., McMullen, C., Fitzgerald, T., Otsuji, E., & Lee, A. (2008). 'Becoming and being writers': The experiences of doctoral students in writing groups. *Studies in Continuing Education, 30*(3), 263–265.

Merleau-Ponty, M. (1962). *The phenomenology of perception* (C. Smith, Trans.), London: Routledge.

Merleau-Ponty, M. (1993). Eye and mind. In G. Johnson & M. B. Smith (Eds.), M. B. Smith & C. Dallery (Trans.), *The Merleau-Ponty aesthetics reader: Philosophy and painting*. Evanston, IL: Northwestern University Press.

Murray, R. (2002). *How to write a thesis* (2nd ed.). Maidenhead, UK: Open University Press.

Wenger, E., McDermott, R., & Snyder, W. M. (2002). *Cultivating communities of practice: A guide to managing knowledge*. Boston, MA: Harvard Business School Press.

Chapter 5

Writing in the Virtual Environment

Helen Boulton and Alison Hramiak

5.1. Introduction

At the heart of this chapter, as with the rest of the book, is the student. We will explore how students utilise technology for writing in an academic world, and how that usage might change (or not) when the student transfers it to and from their personal world. The advent of technology and its increasing use by so many people in an academic context has meant that literacy practices which are viewed in a socio-cultural context must also include that of the digital world, where many students spend a proportion of their time. If we view language as a resource to make meaning depending on the context in which we use it, then this must also apply to digital literacy which arises from the use of language in the virtual world.

Learning to write virtually requires new literacy skills for new audiences, an ability to read critically and synthesise research, an ability to navigate the web and an ability to understand how to use multimedia in our learning, teaching and assessment, which are supported within virtual spaces. These new skills are increasingly being referred to as network literacy, digital literacy and information literacy, which are defined in the next section.

Students born after 1990 are viewed by some as the 'Net generation' (Tapscott, 1998) 'Millenials' (Howe & Strauss, 2000) or 'Digital Natives' (Prensky, 2001) and seen as immersed in a culture which is rich in technology. More recently there has been recognition that this immersion in technology is related mainly to the use of communication technologies rather than a high level of technology that may be viewed as academically related

Writing in the Disciplines: Building Supportive Cultures for Student Writing in UK Higher Education

(Bennett, Maton, & Kervin, 2008), hence the need to consider carefully any technical skills that may be required by tutors and/or students prior to using some of the technologies referred to in this chapter (Sharma, 2010).

The purpose of this chapter is to provide the reader with a grounded understanding of how students construct communications using technologies, and how they build relationships, connecting to each other virtually, and continue with their studies online, in a virtual environment. It examines the way attitudes may or may not change, and with them, the physical practice of writing in a virtual environment when students move between the two worlds of academia and personal. It also considers the consequences for both students and tutors as we move into a progressively virtual world where students are increasing using multi-modal text. In the face of the growth in Web 2.0 technologies and mobile technology and the increasing use of 'text' language, we consider the impact these are having on student writing styles and discuss both what might be considered acceptable in higher education (HE) and how tutors might encourage learners to develop appropriate writing skills for their audience.

Students using virtual technology for communications might alter their language which may or may not affect the language they use for their academic work. Within this chapter, we include a comparison of social writing with standard academic writing in HE by examining language and literacy as it changes when we write in virtual spaces, moving on to the types of virtual spaces that students might use, what they are and how are they are defined as such. From here we discuss the mobile types of virtual spaces, the ones that allow you to take and use them anywhere, and how this affects the way they are used, and why. We will then consider the use of web logs, particularly with a view to developing reflective writing skills, and how learners are using wikis for collaborative, social learning and considers the language they need to develop for this activity. We then move on to examine ePortfolios which are still relatively new in HE and consider how ePortfolios help students to develop their writing and individual identity which they can then choose to share with the external world.

5.2. Languages of Technology

Today's students can be thought of as being 'transliterate', that is, they can communicate and learn across the boundaries of multi-modal technologies (McDougall & Potamitis, 2010). Tutors who are unable to keep up with this pace of technology often find themselves unable to relate to, and engage, such students. Even when teachers receive training in curricular uses of technology, they do not necessarily receive training about new mind-sets, identities and practices that come with new technologies and forms of communication (Lewis, 2007). This matters most when their teaching relationship breaks down as a result of their inability to communicate on the same level in the virtual environment as their students.

It is agreed by some that information and communications technology (ICT) is insulated from all else, and that the same applies to literacy and that in sending a message from a mobile device, we are concerned only with pushing buttons, not how the technology actually works (McDougall & Potamitis, 2010). Should we therefore apply this to how we view technology in teaching and learning? Should we view ICT as a range of easy to use tools perhaps, and not be concerned about how it affects the actual teaching and learning, rather bringing technology to the classroom in the form of mobile devices, instead of booking physical information technology (IT) rooms? This chapter focuses on the social constructivist aspects of using ICT in teaching and learning, rather than the more insulative aspects. Should we, as some think, view IT as media things, not as technologies, but as ways of representing the world, and communicating within it, rather than primarily as technical? (Buckingham, 2007). In doing so, we might be allowing ourselves to relate more to our students and thus enable the teaching learning relationship with our students to keep up with the speed of change.

In the previous section, the terms 'network literacy', 'digital literacy' and 'information literacy' were introduced. If we are to define a specific set of capabilities as a 'literacy' we are claiming that they are needed for other capabilities, are critical in life, essential to making and sharing culturally significant meanings and consequently, at some level, there should be a society-wide entitlement to these capabilities. When we think about literacy, we generally tend to think in a traditionalist way, with 'being literate' being defined as being able to read and write. When we think of literacy in terms of ICT, however, this can take many forms and there is a whole range of adjectives that can be applied, such as ICT literacy, using or programming computers, digital literacy, using digital information, multimedia literacy, moving between text, graphics and sound, and network literacy, accessing and creating and interpreting web-based documents, to name a few (Weigerif & Dawes, 2004). As argued by Buckingham (2008) a much broader reconceptualisation of what we mean by literacy in a world that is increasingly dominated by electronic media is needed (Buckingham, 2008).

Digital literacy can also be thought to define those capabilities which fit an individual for living, learning and working in a digital society. There are various definitions of digital literacy, such as that provided by JISC which states that 'digital literacy defines those capabilities which fit an individual for living, learning and working in a digital society' (Beetham, 2010). The now widespread use of Web 2.0 technologies and accompanying social practices have shifted the focus somewhat of what we might mean by digital literacy, such that any current definition should now include participation in social networks as a pivotal part of knowledge acquisition and transfer (Beetham, 2010). Eisenberg (2008, p. 39) defines information literacy as 'a set of skills and knowledge that allows us to find, evaluate, and use the information we need, as well as to filter out the information we don't need' (Eisenberg, 2008). This definition by Eisenberg links closely to that of Beetham above, who makes the transition of these skills to digital media.

For each of the literacies described above, however, a basic level of classic literary competence is required, the language for which is developed through listening and speaking. Taking this further, one might argue that the capacity for developing this literacy in this way is arguably being detrimentally affected by the use of the virtual world. If students prefer to communicate online through text, which in itself is frequently not written in a grammatically correct way, rather than through speaking and listening, then they are unlikely to further develop their literacy skills beyond that of the primary classroom.

The Internet allows users to create text that is accessible by millions (if not billions), and it has the potential to influence them all, with a capacity for a sort of power (Weigerif & Dawes, 2004). For example, think about how students look to see how many 'friends' they have on Facebook©, or how many followers they have for their latest tweet or blog entry. The capacity for 'power', conceivably, is that which facilitates online popularity through the means of having followers in their virtual spaces. To acquire this type of agency in the virtual world, stems, arguably, from a meta-awareness of how your domain works and how you might work it (Lewis, 2007).

This type of sharing enabled by ICT is a crucial aspect of ICT literacy and is almost entirely dependent on a students' ability or capacity to collaborate with others through this medium (Weigerif & Dawes, 2004). The more you can share with others through a variety of media, applications, sites and so on, the more others can share with you, and, arguably, the capacity for this sort of power increases. There are three aspects that computers offer learners that can arguably be said to be the key to literacy online:

1. The opportunities to create and modify text easily — unlike pen and paper, digital text can be written and changed repeatedly with ease.
2. The opportunities to engage in dialogue (learning or social) with others — text is used across many different types of media from many different types of devices enabling communication to be far easier than it used to be.
3. The opportunities to read and write with a high level of support from software — spell and grammar checks, specialist software packages that type while you speak and so on, offer tremendous support for digital text.

Captured text, be it shared on a blog, wiki, discussion forum (see later in this chapter for explanations of these terms) and so on, is then available for discussion, reflection and evaluation, which could lead to the thought processes often associated with higher order thinking such as synthesis and evaluation (Weigerif & Dawes, 2004). Thus, an increase in ICT literacy, while it has its negative connotations, also has its positives for students, as long as tutors engage with it in teaching, learning and assessment.

In terms of language, students do write differently depending on the type of virtual space they are using. Student blogs, texts, messages on MSN© or Facebook© do not (rarely) contain the same level or type of language that is handed in with their assignments (Irwin & Boulton, 2010). Virtual space is generally viewed as informal space, and as such the language used is adapted to this. As we hear and use words creatively in new combinations to express ideas and thoughts our vocabulary shifts, adapting itself along the way. One aspect of becoming literate is our contribution to this change, and the increased use of ICT has created its own language with new words and words with extended meanings being produced (Weigerif & Dawes, 2004), for example, login and download are new words, while buttons and surfing have taken on new meanings. In addition to this, hybrid forms of words have also been developed, as these are easier and quicker to use when writing informally through the medium of text, instant messaging, or Twitter© for example, 2nite (tonight) and lol (laugh out loud) and ur (your).

Such exchanges of language are characterised by a lack of conventional grammar and spelling, and by a mutual understanding of other conventions; developed to increase the rate of interaction so that it almost matches the speed of talk (Weigerif & Dawes, 2004). This mutual understanding does not always cross generations, or even the roles in teaching and learning, and it might be that parents are unable to read (and write) text messages that can be understood by their children. It might also be the case that academic tutors are unable to do the same if students are themselves unable to differentiate between academic and informal social practices when it comes to reading and writing. This shift in registers, between academic and personal writing, as suggested by some writers, often parallels the way in which students change the way they shift their speech between talking to tutors and talking to peers (Crystal, 2001).

Exchanges between students on phones, MSN© and so on contain erratic instances of grammar, punctuation and spelling, and do not always take sequential turns; they do, however, have their own rationale of syntax and grammar. As such, these exchanges, so common amongst students, have created their own online language and dialogue, and as with all languages, the best way to learn them is to immerse oneself in them, by being involved in its community of use. This is in no way to suggest that all tutors should suddenly get on Facebook©, text or tweet during lectures and so on; however, it might be useful if they could learn some of the key phrases, and words, if only to correct them in academic assignments. If we understand more about our students, we can help them differentiate if they are having problems doing so in the virtual spaces they inhabit.

Participants in such exchanges, for example, between students on Facebook© organising a social gathering of some kind, draw on their understanding of their own culture, on the cultural models of their peers (and possibly the celebrities of the day) and also draw on their developing classic and ICT literacy to generate this exchange (Weigerif & Dawes, 2004). Having done this and made the transition to 'text speak' students may require academic writing support to help them to revert to a 'proper form' of writing for academic purposes such as essay writing. There may therefore be a need for higher education institutions (HEIs) to assist learners to bridge the gap between their informal practices with ICT (and the accompanying informal knowledge practices that run in parallel with these), and the demands of academic study that incorporate ICT. However, some learners may actively choose not to engage totally with technology for either social or academic practices, for whatever reason, they may prefer face-to-face learning and socialising. Learners also expect to use technology for academic purposes in very different ways from that in which they use it for other (social) settings, preferring to keep the two separate, and are very dependent on their experience of the use in academic settings — led by tutors, course structures and quality assurance requirements, to determine their expectations. This preference may be due to students being aware of the different contexts in which communication happens, adjusting their patterns of communication in line with this awareness. That would be consistent with a socio-cultural approach to writing.

In adapting their classic literacy for electronic media, we are expecting students to put literacy to use for its own purposes, and the form that this takes depends on the medium in which it was created and the context of the communication and community in which it was written. It may be that as this adaptation by students develops, the problem may become one of meeting students half way rather than trying to push them back towards an ideal academic literacy which may be less used than the language of text in their everyday lives. Work by JISC on student expectations found that prospective students were not certain about what role ICT would play in their academic work (Beetham, 2010). The general picture, however, seems to be one of rising expectations that technology will be used appropriately and well. This includes their expectations of their tutors' capabilities and skills with technology which are expected, by students, to be high.

As a society, we are knowledge and discourse based, with people increasingly so, in their expectations about how people should lead their private lives and conduct their personal relationships (Simpson & Mayr, 2010). Indeed, one might argue that privacy itself has become a rarity rather than the norm because of the ease with which (and the inclination with which) personal information can be and is shared through online media. Students, like the rest of the population, have an expectation to live and lead much of their lives online (often during lectures!). The knowledge(s) and discourses which have the capacity to shape people's lives are disseminated through texts of various sorts and transmitted through the media and modern ICTs (Simpson & Mayr, 2010). Applying this to students, we might be unable to deny that some adaptation is also required on our part, as academic tutors, if we are to maintain good working relationships with our students. It might not, given the speed of change and the increasing usage of online media for text (for reading and writing maybe not so much in classic literacy terms, but an ICT based one that reaches them in their everyday lives) be acceptable for us to demand correct English grammar and spelling for all pieces of work. We may, one day (if we do not do so already), have to meet our students part or half way on some assessments if we are to continue to interact with them in a mutually beneficial way.

Having covered aspects of the language used in virtual spaces, we now move on to look at the types of spaces in which this language is used and changes.

5.3. Types of Virtual Spaces

What is a virtual space? Defined by some as 'cyberspace', virtual space is space that does not physically exist, rather, it exists in the 'ether', as part of a virtual world; a connection of wires and cables, or via other means such as Wi-Fi that enables us to have a presence online. Virtual space is that which we use when we go online, when we use the Internet to connect to others from within our and their virtual worlds. As such, currently, virtual space, as with real space, is infinite, and, because of this, its possibilities are also arguably seen as endless by users of this type of world. Students are no exception to this, and with open arms, have embraced the technology that allows them such freedom.

Virtual space is not easy to define, and not easy to look up in order to find a definitive definition — many exist, but none seem to focus in on the space aspect of this term. More so, definitions focus on virtual worlds and what we can do in these. The purpose of this chapter, however, is to give the reader an overview of the types of virtual spaces that exist, as they apply to students.

The kinds of virtual spaces that students use include Facebook©, MSN© instant messaging, YouTube©, MySpace© and Twitter© (the list is not exhaustive). These are generally deemed to be 'social spaces' for students, not necessarily to be confused with the type of spaces that they might use for academic purposes. That is, spaces where students can meet and communicate in the virtual world to talk about the personal rather than the academic parts of their lives. The types of virtual spaces that students associate with academic work and life would be those such as virtual learning environments (VLEs) used by universities to communicate with students, common ones are those such as Moodle[©] and BlackBoard[©].

Some research has shown that students do not like to necessarily mix academic and social spaces (Crook & Cluley, 2009), despite a current trend within some HEIs to reach out to students, before and after they begin their studies, using social networking sites such as Facebook[©]. For most students, their social networking sites are purely for the purpose of connecting to others and having conversations via the web, rather than for academic work. Often on courses, students will contribute to a VLE, via discussion boards, blogs and wikis, but would rarely use this to arrange their social life or give much away about themselves on such sites to their peers. They prefer, instead, to create a separate world for this in what are 'traditionally' seen as spaces for social networking as listed above. The consequences of this might be that for some courses, the balance between contributing online to social and academic leans more to one side than the other and students might prefer to use their time to socialise virtually rather than contribute to a VLE. Given that students only have so much time to spend online, tutors who run interactive VLE sites might discover that online contributions and interactions for academic work suffer when this balance moves to social sites — possibly more so as students become more familiar and friendly with one another as a course progresses. In such cases, academics may need to resort to a more mandatory aspect for contributions online and associate them with assessments and other features of the course in order to engage the students in using the VLE as they would like.

From here we move on to look mobile virtual spaces, the type of virtual space that is accessible wherever you might be via mobile technologies.

5.4. Mobile Virtual Spaces

The virtual spaces represented above might arguably be considered less mobile than others. Adding to the university VLE, for example, whether it be for a blog or a discussion forum, might be something done at home or in a library (learning resource centre) rather than on the move. However, as mobile technology develops universities are investing in applications ('Apps') to enable learners to access these on the move. What we aim to do in this section is to look at smaller technological devices that can be used to access virtual spaces, including the ones described above, from wherever you are.

Technology is getting smaller, devices such as iPods©, iPads©, mobile phones, Notebooks© and iPhones©, mean that accessing web sites for social networking and communications is getting easier. There is now, as they say, 'an app for everything' and as such access is no longer a barrier. The rise of 'Twitter©' and the decrease in the costs of using phones for texting means that students can embrace this technology without fear of cost or inconvenience. If, for example, you stood at the rear of a lecture room or classroom, and observed students, how many, do you think, would you see using a small mobile device, and not necessarily for taking notes?

This in itself can cause problems for academic staff as students feel they can skip listening to the lecture, get onto Facebook© or MSN© and still catch up on the content as the notes will be on the VLE for them to cut and paste and use at leisure. In doing so, however, a step in thought processing is missed, and arguably some understanding is lost. When taking notes and then writing them up, we force ourselves to reread, reword and understand content in order to make sense of it for future reference. When that step is lost because we cut and paste, then print or save, with no real reading because we don't need to reword, vital understanding is lost along the way. While mobile devices and the applications they contain are not totally to blame, they could be argued to be part of the problem rather than part of the solution.

What might also conceivably be viewed as part of the problem and not the solution — in terms of the totality of the technology available through which to deliver the written word — is the lack of boundaries. The choice available could be viewed as a double-edged sword, in that boundaries tend to disappear with virtual text. The use of hyperlinks, cutting and pasting between applications, different mobile spaces and the sections within them makes it difficult to differentiate where text came from and who wrote it in the first place. The same text, for example, can look different depending on which application you view it from — compare, for example, how text looks on various Twitter© feeds. Add to this the transient, almost 'half-life' quality of the texts, which disappear, for example, to the bottom of a long list of entries in a blog or email, and suddenly a different approach might be needed for academics and students alike.

The issues, described above, can cause problems to academic tutors and may lead to what is termed 'slippery' text — text which mutates and evolves across different media (Mackey, 2007) being handed in as part of assignment work. Literacies are changing, and the ever-changing combination of literate capacities exhibited by contemporary media users is not the same as, and not as simple as a collection of personalised skills (Mackey, 2007, p. 319). It may be that academic tutors will have to learn a new vocabulary for these combined skills and attitudes, before our students leave us behind. New developments in this area are looking at ways in which such 'patchwork' texts (also referred to as intertextuality) might be assessed (Wolverhampton, 2011), thus moving with the times rather than against the tide.

In the early parts of this chapter, we made reference to a range of learning and teaching technologies. These are explained more fully in the following sections of this chapter which focuses on blogs, wikis and ePortfolios. These three aspects have been chosen as the focus for this chapter following discussions with academic colleagues from five universities as the technologies they would most like to know more about with a view to using in their teaching.

5.5.   Using Blogs for Reflective Writing

Web logs (blogs) are defined as allowing 'individuals to chronologically record their writing and reflections' using online digital media (Sharma, 2010). Each entry into a blog is stored in chronological order, hence the likeness to a journal; originally the term 'log' was taken from a ship's log with daily entries made and recorded in chronological order. Blogs look quite different from a web page and may be 'owned' by an individual or a community. One definition describes blogs as 'an easily created, easily updatable Web site that allows an author (or authors) to publish instantly to the internet from any Internet connection' (Richardson, 2010).

The benefit of a blog over the more traditional written journal is the way it can be accessed and shared with others, that is, it can remain private to the owner/creator of the blog, opened to a closed community such as a tutor group or opened to the world accessible via the web. In terms of learning and developing academic writing skills, this can make a blog a powerful tool for students who can access each other's blogs and share thoughts, resources, ideas and so on. Another benefit particularly in terms of learning, teaching and assessment in HE is that students or tutors can use a variety of multi-modal formats such as text, voice, image and video. Increasingly in practice, such as in teacher training and medical education, but the tool can equally be used to create communities of learning through sharing reflections. By using blogs tutors are often able to capitalise on students' desire to be online while developing their style of writing and the depth of their reflections: 'people like contributing and sharing ... ideas' (Rettberg, 2008).

Tutors are also joining the worldwide bloggers. Indeed, increasingly tutors in HE are embracing blogs to share their thoughts and opinions with their students, often beyond their immediate student group(s) to engage in discussions on specific discipline areas enabling wider discussions, across geographical and cultural boundaries, and introducing their students to new ideas, thus optimising the power of this tool.

Reflection, based on Schon's theories, has long formed part of assessment in HE courses, particularly those associated with professional training and development such as teacher training and training for the health professions (Schon, 1983). Traditionally, journals were kept by students but as Web 2.0 technologies have emerged these are providing alternatives to reflective journals (Bain, Mills, Ballantyne, & Packer, 2002) and are proving to engage some students more than the traditional methods of keeping reflective journals (Hramiak, Boulton, & Irwin, 2009). The increasing use of blogs for reflection and wider sharing of reflections enables a greater sharing of experiences and perspectives through the virtual and online nature of the blogs: 'When we write and reflect with others we can gain multiple perspectives' (Alterio, 2004). The process of opening blogs to others links to research by Rocco who found that 'Making reflection public seems to have had a positive impact on the quality and style of reflection and interactions' (Rocco, 2010).

There are many blogging providers who host blog spaces, which are generally free, such as www.journallive.co.uk, www.edublogger.org, www.blogger.com, www.wordpress.org, and www.edmodo.com. Some university VLEs may also have a blog tool, although if used for reflections, it is good practice to find out who has access to the blogs, which may often have private content. The types of blogs that can be used for reflection fall mainly into two categories: private blogs owned by individual students and community blogs. Generally, students will set up their own private blog but may need technical support with this (Sharma, 2010). The student then 'owns' their space and can give access to those they choose to give access to. A community blog, used in academic contexts, would usually be set up by the tutor, or administrator, to provide access to one blog shared by many which allows individual blog writing or the development of shared ideas within one blog area (Boulton & Hramiak, 2012).

Students will often have experienced blogs prior to university, but this may be limited to finding blogs as part of their personal research or through their online social communities. While there are some pioneering teachers in secondary education and further education who do draw on blog technology within the classroom, they are still in limited numbers. Introducing blogs as part of a learning experience to students may therefore require some technical support and an understanding of how the blog will help to engage them in their learning and writing.

As with all Web 2.0 technologies there is emerging research into how blogs are used in academic settings producing mixed experiences and findings. For example Martindale and Wiley used blogs as non-private spaces with their students and had some success, reporting that students' writing became more thoughtful and longer as the course progressed (2005). However, some research on supporting teacher education learning in the field using blogs reports limited use of blogs by students, and even more limited use of the blog as a reflective diary (Divintini, Haugalokken, & Morken, 2005). Other investigations explored the use of blogs as public reflective journals, which resulted in concerns from students around privacy and confidentiality, and that online reflective journals can be more time consuming for some students (Oti & Clarke, 2007). One study reports that blogs allow a broad spectrum of non-technical users to publish easily to a wide audience, giving examples of educational uses that include communication from the classroom/school to parents and the community, students practicing writing online and students communicating with students in different cultures (Catalano, 2005).

More recently, Kerawalla, Minocha, Kirkup, and Conole (2008) identified six factors that influenced blogging, in terms of the way students approached using the blog and their learning experience. These were perceptions of, and the need for community, perceptions of and the need for audience, the utility of, and need for comments, presentational style of the blog content, overarching factors related to the technological context and the pedagogical context of the course. The researchers also found that the blogging behaviours of their students were varied and depended on the way in which they addressed the factors identified, for example, some students chose not to blog at all, preferring to communicate with others via other means, while others used their blog simply because it was a convenient tool for making notes and so on, while others found the blogs increased their awareness of the technology and enabled them to devise strategies for using blogs in their own teaching (Kerawalla et al., 2008). Similar research by Churchill (2009) indicates that one of the main aspects of blogging that contributed most to students' learning was that of accessing and reading the blogs of others (Churchill, 2009). Sharma (2010) reported that her participants valued blogs finding that it helped them to think more deeply as well as articulate their ideas.

In terms of developing literacy within blogs, blogs will reveal the process of students' development and provide a virtual space where learning can be simply organised, can be easily shared and is searchable. As stated above, blogs generally comprise personal reflections and/or conversations that are regularly updated. These may be experiences of work-based learning, or reflections related to topics addressed in lectures, seminars, workshops and can also include summaries of reading. Students will therefore need support to develop skills in reflecting critically in developing skills that enable them to write with clarity and coherence. Students also need to be aware of how wide an audience their blogs can reach if they choose to make them public; this can be an empowering experience for students and enable them to reach out to new audiences and develop a wider community of practice than may have been possible through other forms of writing. Thus, blogs can be viewed as a form of connective writing. As students seek out and read the blogs of other bloggers, they will need to develop their reading skills and learn to be critical of what they are reading, thus again developing their literacy skills.

Students who are reluctant contributors in class may be much more willing to join discussions via blogs where they can compose and reflect on their contribution before uploading and sharing with others. Students therefore need to be very aware of the purpose of their writing and of the audience for their blogs. Hence, the role of the tutor may change to ensure equality of contribution more than may happen in class. Tutors will need to support the development of literacy skills such as research, synthesising ideas, organising reflections and analysis, as well as encouraging the development of skills in reading. As the number of blogs increases across the world, students will need to develop a good level of searching, and learn to read quickly and critically, learning to discard things which are inappropriate to their learning. As students develop their own blogs, they will also need to develop good organisational skills so that they can continue to develop and manage their blogs to become databases of learning with links outwards to other useful virtual resources. This genre of literacy will continue to develop as students receive responses to their blogs and may want to go back and review what they have written in the light of comments, developing knowledge and a deeper understanding.

Earlier in this chapter, we referred to the increasing use of blog writing by tutors. Some tutors regularly blog; for example, one tutor at Nottingham Trent University who teaches politics writes a minimum of 500 words each day reflecting on the day's political developments. The tutor encourages his students to follow and contribute to the blogs and also engages comment from beyond the university thus enabling a wider discourse than would generally be experienced by his students. The blog can therefore take learning beyond the university walls and connect groups of students and tutors who can share learning and experiences such as experiments and field trips in disparate geographical areas, inviting the input of discipline experts to share their learning, resulting in a higher level of metacognitive analysis and reflection. Richardson (2010, p. 30) draws together the differences in the genre of blogging to that of more traditional academic writing:

'Writing stops; blogging continues.
Writing is inside; blogging is outside.
Writing is monologue; blogging is conversation.
Writing is thesis; blogging is synthesis'.

From blogs we now move on to wikis and how they are used in collaborative ways to encourage students to work together to develop their writing online.

5.6. Wikis for Collaborative Writing

Wikis date back to the mid-1990s when they were seen as 'an easy authoring tool that might spur people to publish' (Richardson, 2010, p. 55). The term 'wiki' is a shortened form of 'wiki-wiki', a Hawaiian word which means quick. Wikis are now freely available social networking tools which are increasingly being used in HE as online collaborative learning spaces. One of the most well-known wiki spaces, which tutors in HE often advise students not to quote from in assignments, is Wikipedia (www.wikipedia.org). While this particular wiki may not be close to the hearts of HE tutors, and is criticised in academic circles because anyone can edit the content, the notion of students collaboratively creating a course or module wiki containing explanations of key terms is often used, based on the principle that anyone who has access to the wiki can edit it.

There are many free wiki host sites such as www.pbwiki.com, www.wetpaint.com, www.wordpress.com, www.elgg.com, which also integrate with the Moodle VLE, www.sharepoint.com and Google's$^{©}$ wiki available at www.sites.google.com. An alternative to a wiki is Google Docs$^{©}$ which enables collaboration in document creating provides a history and simple publishing to the world, but is less versatile than a wiki. Many VLEs also have their own wiki tool such as Blackboard$^{©}$. As with blogs, wikis can be kept private to a group or community or made open to the world.

As we move more towards online collaboration and knowledge creation, a wiki is a tool that has great potential for powerful, collaborative learning in HE. Pausing to consider the term 'collaborative learning', Dillenbourg (1999, p. 4) makes the distinction between the pedagogical and psychological aspects; viewing the pedagogical as being 'prescriptive' in requiring learners to work together with the expectation that they will therefore 'learn efficiently'; and he views the psychological as being 'descriptive' in that it is the 'mechanism which caused learning' (Dillenbourg, 1999). Pedagogically the tutor needs to support students in developing collaborative writing skills which include negotiation, editing synthesis and relevance.

According to some researchers, wikis are one of the most increasingly used Web 2.0 technologies in HE, particularly within 'post-92 institutions (73%), but less so for Pre-92 (59%) and HE colleges (56%)' (Brown, Jenkins, & Walker, 2006). Available to students 24/7 enables students to plan their time more effectively and access their learning at a time to suit their, often pressured, lives without being bound by geographical distance or time.

Increasingly wikis are being used not only for collaborative learning and group work assessments but also for pre-course engagement activities. It is possible to use other free media within a wiki; for example, at Nottingham

Trent University Google Maps has been integrated into a wiki to create a flexible resource for modern foreign language students; students are collaboratively developing this virtual space to provide information on potential work experience placements abroad.

In HE, wikis are most frequently used as a collaborative tool which can easily be used to plan, create, edit, revise, synthesise, append, critically reflect on learning processes and create links to articles or other multimedia that already exist, thus providing a tool for distance learners but also to complement face-to-face learning and teaching. As opposed to blogs, where users mainly have a personal identity, wikis can encourage contributors to become anonymous.

Through a wiki students can contribute to building knowledge and co-construct learning towards specific learning outcomes. Considerations in writing style, etiquette and group responsibility are often pre-requirements when introducing wikis for learning and teaching (Hemmi, Bayne, & Landt, 2009). As students create a wiki they become actively engaged through inter-action with content, and through interaction with tutors or other learners. A wiki can therefore also provide opportunity for peer review and peer feedback; for example, a student can write an assignment and ask others to comment on his writing style or other aspects; at Leicester University staff in the Law Faculty have been using wikis with first-year undergraduate law students encouraging them to work in groups, supported by a tutor, to develop a writing style appropriate to the law discipline's writing conventions. Another example of collaborative learning and co-construction of knowledge is at Nottingham Trent University where first-year undergraduates following a joint honours programme build a wiki comprising key terminology which they continue to build throughout their course, thus enabling a higher level of understanding of terminology as well as a quick reference. Some researchers report using wikis in Israel across three universities resulting in a wikitextbook with 564 sub-chapters, co-authored by undergraduate and graduate students in more than 20 classes offered by 7 academic departments over 2 years (Ravid, Kalman, & Rafaeli, 2008).

Peer assessment processes using a wiki can provide opportunity to foster metacognition and reflexivity (Kirschner, 2004), as well as how to be creative when working collaboratively as a community, and 'operate in a world where the creation of knowledge and information is more and more becoming a group effort' (Richardson, 2010, p. 69). These abilities are considered to be crucial for being successful in our modern knowledge and information society (Ebner, Kickmeier-Rust, & Holzinger, 2008). This type of learning experience can deepen levels of learners' engagement and collaborative writing within a digital learning environment. Hence, the utilisation of wikis provides opportunity for social constructivist learning as purported by Vygotsky (1978). Cole summarises the critical features of constructivist learning as follows:

1. All knowledge is constructed through a process of reflective abstraction.
2. Cognitive structures within the learner facilitate the process of learning.
3. The cognitive structures in individuals are in a process of constant development.
4. If the notion of constructivist learning is accepted, then the methods of learning and teaching must agree (Cole, 2009).

Vygotsky believed that individuals learn better if they do so with and through others such as their peers, or teachers (Tudge, 1990). In learning collaboratively through a wiki, learners are able to participate in such a style of learning through creating knowledge, reflecting and discussing with peers and thus mediating their own learning and progression as individuals. Vygotsky's ideas on the zone of proximal development (ZPD) also arguably align themselves with the idea of knowledge development through community (Vygotsky, 1978). The ZPD is defined as 'the distance between the actual developmental level as determined by independent problem solving and the level of potential development as determined through problem solving in collaboration with more capable peers' (Vygotsky, 1978). Thus, in relation to the use of a wiki in learning, teaching and assessment we would argue that by creating knowledge as part of a community, that is, with their peers, learners are capable of achieving more in terms of their development than if they had created knowledge working individually. Alongside, this is the development of their writing through feedback and working collaboratively.

A wiki would usually be set up by a tutor, administrator or member of a collaborative project team. Once a wiki has been created individual pages and layers can be created which can be hyperlinked to a 'home page'. Tutors without access to a VLE might adopt a wiki to share resources with their students. As with blogs, a range of media can be uploaded to a wiki such as text, voice, video and images. The use of images can provide a visually rich environment for students. One of the key features of a wiki when used collaboratively is that a page history can be viewed — this provides information on when changes were made, who made them and what was changed. While useful for tutors and collaborative groups to see who has edited content, this feature also provides support for tutors when assessing and needing to see what contributions individuals have made to group work projects. Most wikis will also have a 'discussion' area where group members working remotely can have a 'virtual conversation' relating to the project.

The main focus in writing using a wiki other than the collaborative aspect is that learners 'become publishers rather than merely consumers of information' (Cole, 2009, p. 141). A wiki not only enables learners to create, edit and reflect on materials either created by themselves or others, but this form of collaborative knowledge creation and sharing provides tutors with an opportunity to create tasks that can result in a higher level of social engagement than other, more traditional, forms of learning and teaching.

The following section examines how ePortfolios are providing a virtual space for students, which they own and control access to, to develop their own identity and writing which they can then choose to share with others.

5.7. ePortfolios

Paper-based portfolios have been part of HE for many years; used by students to provide evidence for assignments or in developing evidence for competency-based programmes such as teacher training, or in developing evidence for key professional skills. With the increase in the use of new technologies, ePortfolios are gradually replacing the traditional portfolio. This development is engaging students who prefer online multi-modal technology and are increasingly aware of the environment, the green agenda and sustainability issues. The ePortfolio provides an opportunity for students to have a virtual space that they 'own' where they can develop individual identity which they can then choose to share with the external world. Students are able to critically reflect on aspects such as professional development and formative feedback and evidence of individual development. Arguably, it may be that as the ePortfolio tool develops it will become a virtual space used by individuals to provide authentic multi-modal evidence of personal and professional development.

The term 'ePortfolio' has various definitions such as JISCs: 'An e-portfolio is the product, created by the learner, a collection of digital artefacts articulating experiences, achievements and learning' (JISC, 2008). Some research suggests that there are three different types of portfolio: an exemplary portfolio where students place their best pieces of work; a process portfolio which demonstrates the developmental process of the student's learning and a combined portfolio which contains examples of both exemplary work and developmental work (Falchikov, 2005). The authors' experience of using ePortfolios for a range of undergraduate and postgraduate courses in HE would suggest a fourth type that required for evidence in support of professional competencies such as those required by professional bodies. This fourth type would also reflect an ePortfolio for accreditation for prior learning where evidence is provided to support achievement of course learning outcomes, and that of students working towards national vocational qualifications who provide evidence of competencies. Others suggest different purposes of the ePortfolio, acknowledging the adaptation from the traditional 'portfolio' into the electronic domain, listing the different purposes such as 'developmental', 'presentation' and 'assessment' (Mason, Pegler, & Weller, 2004), while others identify a 'dossier portfolio', a 'training portfolio', a 'reflective portfolio' and a 'personal development portfolio' (Roberts, 2009).

In considering the introduction of an ePortfolio to any programme, the tutor team needs to carefully consider the purpose(s). Once the purpose has been agreed, a list of requirements can be drawn up so that a suitable ePortfolio tool can be identified. Many universities already have an ePortfolio tool within its VLE such as PepplePad$^©$ or Desire2Learn$^©$, but it may not necessarily suit the needs of the course. Tutors may need to trial the chosen tool and evaluate with students. It may be that course teams decide to turn to open-source, free software which is more suitable to the needs of their students such as ELGG$^©$ within Moodle$^©$ or Posterous$^©$. Involving students at an early stage in the introduction of an ePortfolio is therefore advantageous.

Ownership of the ePortfolio is an important aspect. With most systems the student is the 'owner' of this virtual space, although the tutor team will have input into the content of the ePortfolio. It will depend on the purpose(s) of the ePortfolio identified in the initial planning stages of using this tool as to whether the documents within this space are to be integrated into the course's assessment and feedback. Most ePortfolios will enable students to give access to the whole of their ePortfolio, or elements of their artefacts (an artefact is generally a document such as a video-clip, a text-based document and a sound file) to anyone whether inside or outside the university. Many students report that they give a wide range of people access to different elements such as potential employers, friends, relatives, peers and their tutors — as the 'owners' of the space this is their decision (Boulton, 2011).

Students will usually need support from tutors in how to set up and organise their ePortfolio. When the authors first started using ePortfolios with different groups of students, there was an assumption that as the ePortfolio would be owned and controlled by the students, they would want to organise it in their own way. This has not proved to be the case; the authors' experience is that students find it difficult to visualise how the ePortfolio might develop and therefore welcome support in the early stages of creating, structuring and organising their artefacts.

One of the main benefits of the ePortfolio is the range of multi-modal authentic artefacts that students can choose to put in their ePortfolios (Boulton, 2011). This multi-modal feature enables students to really think about how they want to present themselves and develop their identity through the ePortfolio. Most ePortfolios will provide an area where students can add commentary, often in the form of reflections, to link the different artefacts together. As they develop their ePortfolio, it starts to take on a web-based 'look' and tend to be navigated through different elements via hyperlinks.

Students may have used ePortfolios prior to starting in HE, but this will depend on their experience of ICT in their previous education institution. ePortfolios are not part of the secondary schools' National Curriculum, but some examination boards have built them into their assessment systems such as EdExcel who assess their Diploma in Digital Applications through an ePortfolio. However, as an ePortfolio tool is not viewed as a social networking tool wide experience of an ePortfolio by students prior to university is not common. Even on postgraduate courses it is common to find students have not used an ePortfolio tool and need an introduction to what it is, how to use it, organisation and how to draw documents together through reflective commentary.

As with wikis and blogs students are able to share artefacts and develop collaborative writing skills including negotiation, editing synthesis and relevance. Through sharing their work through their ePortfolio, they are able to receive peer and tutor feedback to develop their writing skills. The ePortfolio enables them to publish their work but only with those they give access to, rather than publishing to the world as with blogs and wikis. Skill in writing for different audiences, as discussed earlier in this chapter, is a further skill that can be developed and encouraged by tutors who may suggest specific persons such as employers to share their artefacts with for feedback and development purposes.

5.8. Conclusion

As HE moves towards a more student-centred learning environment, we are increasingly encouraging students to write using a range of virtual tools designed to encourage achievement of learning outcomes rather than content and increasingly considering different styles of learning (Kolb, 1984). The practice and use of Web 2.0 technologies such as those described in this chapter are very likely to have an impact on education in the future. Anderson (2007) predicts a number of ways in which this might happen. Firstly, there is the notion of the wisdom of crowds and the power of groups through the emergence of and increase in size of online social networking groups. These may come to threaten universities as traditional places for wisdom and knowledge creation — especially if it is perceived that you can so easily get this elsewhere. Secondly, there is the rise of user-generated content which increases the rise of the amateur, and a culture of do-it-yourself, and this in turn may also challenge the status of the academy as the elite source of knowledge (Anderson, 2007). The role of new technologies is providing new ways of learning and sharing (Johannesen & Habib, 2010). Encouragement of sharing virtual spaces to provide peer support to enhance student learning and gain multiple perspectives is also becoming more prevalent in HE (Alterio, 2004; Rocco, 2010). We should therefore identify where new tools will enhance the experience of students and engage them in collaborative co-construction of new knowledge through virtual spaces.

Literacy in the virtual world is increasing, and with it changes are coming that may or may not be welcomed by everyone, bringing with them, as they do, challenges to the old world order in education. It is up to those in HE to embrace these changes and in doing so rise to the challenges they bring. This will enable tutors to continue to support students in these new virtual ways of written communication and in doing so consistently keep learners at the heart of HE. In a world that is moving towards a model of collaborative learning and the social construction of knowledge, which is increasingly being reflected in HE as transition to roles of facilitator and co-constructors of knowledge with their students, the VLE is becoming increasingly powerful and is beginning to develop a new cultural literacy. Shared virtual spaces which provide opportunity for collaborative learning such as wikis, blogs and ePortfolios can also provide a far greater opportunity for students to really take ownership of their own learning in a way in which tutors are only just beginning to explore.

References

Alterio, M. (2004). Collaborative journaling as a professional development tool. *Journal of Further and Higher Education, 28*(3), 321–332.

Anderson, P. (2007). What is Web 2.0? Ideas, technologies and implications for education. *TechWatch Report.* Retrieved from http://www.jisc.ac.uk/publications/publications/twweb2.aspx.

Bain, J., Mills, C., Ballantyne, R., & Packer, J. (2002). Using journal writing to enhance student teachers' reflectivity during field experience placements. *Journal of Teachers and Teaching: Theory and Practice, 8*(2), 171–196.

Beetham, H. (2010, Sept.). *Review and scoping study for a cross-JISC learning and digital literacies programme.* Retrieved from http://www.jisc.ac.uk/media/documents/programmes/elearning/DigitalLiteraciesReview.pdf.

Bennett, S., Maton, K., & Kervin, L. (2008). The digital natives debate: A critical review of the evidence. *British Journal of Educational Technology, 39*(5), 775–786.

Boulton, H. (2011). The portability of ePortfolios in teacher education. Paper presented at the European Conference on Educational Research, Berlin.

Boulton, H., & Hramiak, A. (2012). E-flection: The development of reflective communities of learning for trainee teachers through the use of shared online web logs. *Journal of Reflective Practice.* Forthcoming.

Brown, T., Jenkins, M., & Walker, R. (2006). A longitudinal perspective regarding the use of VLEs by higher education institutions in the United Kingdom. *Interactive Learning Environments, 14*(2), 177–192.

Buckingham, D. (2007). *Beyond technology: Children's learning in the age of digital culture.* London: Polity Press.

Buckingham, D. (2008). Defining digital literacy: What do young people need to know about digital media? In C. Lankshear & M. Knobel (Eds.), *Digital literacies: Concepts, policies and practices.* New York, NY: Peter Lang.

Catalano, F. (2005). Why blog? *Time Higher Education Journal, 33*(5), 22–29.

Churchill, D. (2009). Educational applications of Web 2.0: Using blogs to support teaching and learning. *British Journal of Educational Technology, 40*(1), 179–183.

Cole, M. (2009). Using wiki technology to support student engagement: Lessons from the trenches. *Computers and Education, 52,* 141–146.

Crook, C., & Cluley, R. (2009). The teaching voice on the learning platform: Seeking classroom climates within a virtual learning environment. *Learning, Media and Technology, 34*(3), 199–213.

Crystal, D. (2001). *Language and the Internet.* Cambridge: Cambridge University Press.

Dillenbourg, P. (1999). Introduction: Collaborative learning cognitive and computational approaches. In P. Dillenbourg (Ed.), *Collaborative learning cognitive and computational approaches* (pp. 1–31). Oxford: Elsevier Science Ltd.

Divintini, M., Haugalokken, O., & Morken, E. (2005). Blog to support learning in the field: Lessons learned from a fiasco. Paper presented at the fifth IEEE international conference on advanced learning technologies (ICALT), Kaohsiung, Taiwan.

Ebner, M., Kickmeier-Rust, M., & Holzinger, A. (2008). Utilizing wiki-systems in higher education classes: A chance for universal access? *Universal Access in the Information Society, 7,* 199–207.

Eisenberg, M. B. (2008). Information literacy: Essential skills for the information age. *Journal of Library and Information Technology, 28*(2), 39–47.

Falchikov, N. (2005). *Improving assessment through student involvement: Practical solutions for aiding learning in higher and further education.* London: Routledge.

Hemmi, A., Bayne, S., & Landt, R. (2009). The appropriation and repurposing of social technologies in higher education. *Journal of Computer Assisted Learning, 25,* 19–30.

Howe, N., & Strauss, W. (2000). *Millennials rising: The next great generation.* New York, NY: Vintage.

Hramiak, A., Boulton, H., & Irwin, B. (2009). Trainee teachers' use of blogs as private reflections for professional development. *Learning, Media and Technology, 34*(3), 259–269.

Irwin, B., & Boulton, H. (2010). Analysing the development of professional identity in blogging discourse. Paper presented at the improving student learning: For the twenty-first century learner. *Proceedings of the 17th improving student learning symposium, Oxford.*

JISC. (2008). *Effective practice with ePortfolios*. Retrieved from jisc.ac.uk. Accessed on 12 December 2011.

Johannesen, M., & Habib, L. (2010). The role of professional identity in patterns of use of multiple-choice assessment tools. *Technology, Pedagogy and Education, 19*(1), 17.

Kerawalla, L., Minocha, S., Kirkup, G., & Conole, G. (2008). An empirically grounded framework to guide blogging in higher education. *Journal of Computer Assisted Learning, 25*(1), 31–42.

Kirschner, P. A. (2004). Design, development, and implementation of electronic learning environments for collaborative learning. *Educational Technical Research & Development, 52*(3), 39–46.

Kolb, D. (1984). *Experiential learning experience as the source of learning and development*. Englewood Cliff, NJ: Prentice Hall.

Lewis, C. (2007). New literacies. In M. Knobel & C. Lankshear (Eds.), *A new literacies sampler* (pp. 229–237). New York, NY: Peter Lang.

Mackey, M. (2007). Slippery texts and evolving literacies. *E-Learning, 4*(3), 319–328.

Martindale, T., & Wiley, D. (2005). Using weblogs in scholarship and teaching. *TechTrends, 49*(2), 7.

Mason, R., Pegler, C., & Weller, M. (2004). E-portfolios: An assessment tool for online courses. *British Journal of Educational Technology, 35*(6), 717–727.

McDougall, J., & Potamitis, N. (2010). *The media teacher's book* (2nd ed.). London: Hodder Education.

Oti, J., & Clarke, R. (2007). Dyslexia and online writing: Student teachers experiences of writing about themselves in a public forum. Paper presented at the British Educational Educational Research Association annual conference, University of London, London.

Prensky, M. (2001). Digital natives, digital immigrants. *On the Horizon, 9*(5), 1–6.

Ravid, G., Kalman, Y., & Rafaeli, S. (2008). Wikibooks in higher education: Empowerment through online distributed collaboration. *Computers in Human Behavior, 24*, 1913–1928.

Rettberg, J. W. (2008). *Blogging: Digital media and society series*. Cambridge: Polity Press.

Richardson, W. (2010). *Blogs, wikis, podcasts and other powerful tools for classrooms*. London: Sage.

Roberts, A. (2009). Encouraging reflective practice in periods of professional workplace experience: The development of a conceptual model. *Reflective Practice, 10*(5), 633–644.

Rocco, S. (2010). Making reflection public: Using interactive online discussion board to enhance student learning. *Reflective Practice, 11*(3), 307–317.

Schon, D. A. (1983). *The reflective practitioner: How professionals think in action*. London: Temple Smith.

Sharma, P. (2010). Enhancing student reflection using weblogs: Lessons learned from two implementation studies. *Reflective Practice, 11*(2), 127–141.

Simpson, P., & Mayr, A. (2010). *Language and power a resource book for students*. Oxford, UK: Routledge.

Tapscott, D. (1998). *Growing up digital: The rise of the net generation*. New York, NY: McGraw-Hill.

Tudge, J. (1990). Vygotsky, the zone of proximal development, and peer collaboration: Implications for classroom practice. In L. C. Moll (Ed.), *Vygotsky and educational instructional implications and applications of sociohistorical psychology* (pp. 155–172). Cambridge: Cambridge University Press.

Vygotsky, L. (1978). *Mind in society the development of higher psychological processes* (1st ed.). London: Harvard University Press.

Weigerif, R., & Dawes, L. (2004). *Thinking and learning with ICT raising achievement in primary classrooms*. London: Routledge.

Wolverhampton. (2011). *Digitally enhanced patchwork text assessment (DPTA)*. Retrieved from http://www.wlv.ac.uk/default.aspx?page = 24876. Accessed on 21 June 2011.

Chapter 6

Using Dialogic Lecture Analysis to Clarify Disciplinary Requirements for Writing

Lisa Clughen and Matt Connell

6.1. Introduction

> (...) in this place he did not know even how to reply to a
> simple question and gazed at the other clients as if it were their
> duty to help him, as if no one could expect him to answer
> should help not be forthcoming. (Kafka, 1999, p. 44)

Kafka's stark representation of the bewilderment that can issue from encounters with institutional structures and practices has a resonance for those trying to help students of Higher Education (HE) with their writing, for it also captures the way confusion breeds a need for help, especially when the questions being asked are by no means simple. Whilst students may see tutors as fonts of knowledge and sources of assistance, implicit in the Kafka quotation above is the suggestion that looking to one's peers is potentially supportive too. Of course in Kafka's dystopias, there is usually a failure of solidarity (the accused in *The Trial* do not help each other much), and in the academy too, students all too easily become competing supplicants rather than members of a community.

This chapter considers the confusions wrought by academic work and embraces the frequently advanced notion that social interaction is crucial for dealing with the opacities of academic writing (Bazerman, Elbow, Hillocks, & Blau, 2006; Sperling, 1996, p. 67). It draws from critical interest in dialogic forms of learning (Dysthe, 2007; Lillis, 2003), wherein knowledge, in this case knowledge about one's subject, about the specific expectations of the writing task and group knowledge about the different understandings and difficulties facing students as they write, is seen as 'emerging from interaction and the interpenetration of different voices' (Dysthe, 2007, p. 1). In the interests of building supportive communities for writing, it offers dialogic lecture analysis as a technique that aims, on the one hand, to promote a sense of solidarity and shared identity amongst students as, together, they face the challenges of academic writing and, on the other hand, to stimulate tutor–student dialogue that would open the ground for tutor understandings of student confusions around writing.

6.2. Clarifying Disciplinary Requirements for Writing

Trying to understand and forge a way through the workings of HE can seem a daunting task as students confront not a single Law, as Kafka's characters do, but a series of confusing cultures whose modus operandi might differ as frequently as they overlap (Ganobcsik-Williams, 2004) and with each one playing a somewhat different language game (Elton, 2010, p. 152–153; Haggis, 2006, p. 7; Read, Archer, & Leathwood, 2003, p. 271). Kafkaesque in their blind alleys, contradictory demands and threats (threats to identity, to self-esteem and to familiar ways of speaking and writing (Bowstead, 2009)), the many cultures that students negotiate in HE can generate endless confusion as they strive to meet university, faculty and subject requirements. Writing in the academy is, as many commentators have pointed out (see Chanock, 2001; Deane & O'Neill, 2011; Elton 2010, pp. 151–2; Haggis, 2006), a prime site for the materialisation of this confusion as student-writers strive to produce texts that conform to the rules of the correct language game. Writing, after all, is not a transparent process, an easy translation of one's thoughts onto the written page, but, as scholars from different disciplines and approaches to writing development argue, a craft that unfolds through time as writers grapple to discern and then situate themselves within the specific demands of the different writing cultures in which they are located (Bazerman et al., 2006). Such grappling may be particularly acute in disciplines where writing is the main output, such as in English literature, the specific context for this discussion, and which accordingly carries a heavy weight in terms of assessment (as opposed, perhaps, to writing in science or art and design subjects, where the weight may be more on what is written about than the writing itself).

Clarifying disciplinary requirements for writing is no easy task. Haggis, for example, suggests that such clarity might even elude academics: 'far from being self-evident, or something that academics can rightly expect students to be familiar with, such processes are partly hidden even from academics themselves' (2006, p. 9). Indeed, the complexities of identifying and then addressing the particular social and cultural inflections of writing seem unending. For one thing, writing, as Bazerman says (Bazerman et al., 2006), involves particular local decisions which generate specific disciplinary rules, and it is in this that the indeterminacies of writing and consequent confusion abound. Individual confusions cannot always be dealt with in general writing materials and generic skills sessions, especially for the many students taking multiple subjects: 'My English lecturers said they wanted my opinions in my essay, so I put them in more than I ever have before, and I got the worst mark I've ever got' (second-year English student); 'Can I include a quote from Peter Pan in my History essay?' (third-year history student); 'I'd like to begin my Linguistics essay with this anecdote from ethnography-is that ok?' (first-year Linguistics student). Facing what might feel like contradictory demands and wholly individual questions, some students may feel like they are going under, drowning like Kafka's characters, needing 'lifebuoys in a sea of confusion' (Kokkinn, 2001, p. 215).

Accordingly, a practically unanimous call, even from those who promote quite different approaches to writing development, is that disciplinary tutors and writing specialists need to make explicit the rules of the culture (Deane & O'Neill, 2011; Haggis, 2006, pp. 8–9; Levin, 2001), to make writing itself visible (Mitchell, 2010) and render 'tacit knowledge overt' (Elton, 2010, p. 152) with a view to transmitting it to students. This idea of socialising students into an academic culture has constituted a paradigmatic approach to writing development in UK HE (Lillis, 2006, p. 31). Whilst recognising that socialisation approaches can be problematic if they fail to address the dialogic nature of knowledge production, and also registering the sustained critique such approaches receive from UK scholars who work within an academic literacies perspective (Lea & Street, 1998; Lea & Stierer, 2000; Lillis, 2003, 2006), we nevertheless wish to reflect constructively on the merits of such an approach.

We will therefore offer a consideration of what is at stake in the notion of being socialised into — or, ideally, of choosing to join — a community of practice such as a writing culture. Seeking to work within socialisation paradigms of writing development, we argue that socialisation into a culture, despite the rhetorical violence inherent in the grammar 'I socialize you' (subject/verb/object), may not be as exclusive or injurious as critics of the socialisation paradigm might suppose. After all, it is through socialisation, through an understanding of disciplinary requirements that students can participate in a culture and begin to develop their voice enough to contribute to a culture and even to challenge it. Indeed, in terms of being socialised into the academy, one of the key notions into which students are to be socialised is that debate and critique, including debate and critique about disciplinary requirements, are vital for scholarly culture. Conventions have to be taught before they can be deconstructed. For example, one can be certain that the writer bell hooks knew how to capitalise before she decided not to.

6.3. On Joining a Writing Culture and 'Unconscious Competence'

> Helping students see themselves as members of the academic community may be the most important challenge faced in the university at large and in the writing classroom in particular. (Penrose, 2002, p. 443)

More than simple socialisation into a course, then, what we are aiming for is what Penrose points to above: a scenario in which students feel genuine members of the academic community. An important element of this is that they understand disciplinary requirements, but what does 'understanding disciplinary requirements' mean if it is to move beyond simple socialisation? We suggest that ultimately it means to belong to a community of practice to the point where its conventions become not only 'second nature' but are also open to critique, rather than those conventions being treated as an external force to which one must submit. Students can find themselves in an in-between position with regard to writing conventions — they are both part of a specific writing culture and are expected to write as such, but are often aliens to it too, like travellers in a new country. As Purcell-Gates notes:

> the concept of *foreigner*, or the *outsider*, captures in important ways the experience of many learners who have difficulty learning to read and write. Not only do they struggle to gain control over a strange code, but they also experience the world encoded by print as unfamiliar and unpredictable. (1997, p. 181)

Of course, in these days of increased 'internationalisation', many students are not merely metaphorical but literal outsiders struggling with a whole new culture, not just an academic corner of it.

If education is experienced as an alienating and external demand (Mann, 2001), then students may simply want to use words to pass, rather than desiring to really join in, to be the 'members of the academic community' of which Penrose speaks. Some students feel stuck, caught in a dialectical paradox like one of Kafka's logical twists, as though they cannot join without a password, but cannot get the password until they have fully joined, and remain outside. This is one theme of Kafka's rich parable 'Before the Law' (1992), which is also incorporated within *The Trial* (1999, pp. 120–121). In the parable, a man seeking entry through a door to the Law (often taken to be wisdom or enlightenment) is intimidated into waiting outside all his life by the stern demeanour of the doorkeeper. The man keeps trying to work out what is required of him, but receives no direct help from the doorkeeper and communication between the two becomes curiously out of joint. But the implication revealed as the man draws his final breaths is that, if he had only realised it, he was free to enter all along. Similarly, students may feel that intimidating tutors demand understanding as the price of entry to the culture of the academy, but conversely, like Kafka's doorkeeper, tutors may feel impatient that students do not realise that the door is open if only they would push on it.

In order to help stuck students to understand disciplinary requirements, tutors have to generate a movement by taking a step into the students' worlds (Haggis, 2006, p. 10). It is not enough to stay aloof like Kafka's doorkeeper. Here, as Laing (1967) pointed out in the field of psychotherapy, until we can enter 'their' worlds, 'they' can't enter 'ours'. As tutors of writing, we need to go to the students and try to explicate what our cultural worlds are, and to find ways of interacting with them that will allow them to speak of their worlds in their own terms *as well as* in ours. The best writing comes from the intersection between these worlds, as the conventions of a writing culture and the worlds outside it illuminate each other through a productive dialogue.

One factor of particular relevance to 'post-92' institutions in the UK is the question of who exactly our new students are, and from what cultural worlds they come. Some of them, perhaps from less traditional routes to entry, have not necessarily identified with academic culture, and in fact may have already marked themselves as outside of the culture despite their decision to attend university (Read et al., 2003). As such they may perhaps already be 'gameplayers' concerned with getting through a system perceived as alien, rather than being motivated by an intrinsic interest in a subject (Haggis, 2006, p. 6). The transformative moment with such students can be when they really do get interested. For this to happen, dialogue between their world and the culture of the academy is essential so that students can begin to internalise the culture, and then, crucially, make it their own and begin to intervene in it. In other words, it is not enough that students merely understand the culture of an academic discipline, as this still presupposes a 'them and us', with the student remaining outside the discipline as his/her own understandings and contributions are rendered stagnant. When they really enter the discipline, students become practitioners within it, and may then influence the community by being part of it and acting within it. Our main point here is that socialisation into a discipline *is* important, and that it need not be considered authoritarian if it is done with dialogues that lead to democratic citizenship.

Explaining the rationale behind cultural demands is essential if what we are proposing to be a democratic form of joining is to occur. Dealing with referencing is an interesting example in this regard. One of the more formal and burdensome of academic requirements, the demand to properly reference can easily feel like an estranging imposition that is only done to show you can play a certain language game, to impress, to avoid accusations of plagiarism: all are real enough concerns, and are not without merit. But the real story behind referencing is a much more interesting one — it is about open access to sources, about 'standing on the shoulders of giants in order to see further', about the possibility of checking context and accuracy, about entering a dialogue with not just an immediate author, but with the whole community of scholars, living and dead, with whom a written text is in conversation. Referencing is not about exclusion, but inclusion: it is about becoming a member of a communication community which has a certain way of pursuing the democratic notion of the 'unforced force of the better argument' (Habermas, 1998, as cited in Thomassen, 2010, p. 70). It is about 'understanding where we are coming from', which not coincidentally is a phrase also apposite for the project of understanding across cultures. The point is that students need to reference to be part of the academic community. At this historical juncture, no amount of debate will change this — they are not free to reject this cultural requirement. Impositional socialisation occurs, perhaps, when students are merely told to reference, or even how to reference. However, if the rationale for referencing is discussed with them, then they can hold informed opinions over referencing, its importance and its operations.

To help students understand academic culture, tutors have to find a way of understanding this culture more clearly themselves, and to try to see what it might mean through the eyes of a student. Tutors need to render what they take for granted explicit, and may learn something themselves when they do this. 'Walking in the shoes of the other' is a neat slogan, but a real challenge. It is difficult for academics to imagine themselves into a pre-academic space (Haggis, 2006, p. 9). Most have a certain cultural capital that well predates their academic careers — this is what got them where they are in the first place. Usually succeeding at scholarly tasks, they have generally found that their writing gains some degree of approval. 'Unconsciously competent' (Howell, 1982 as cited in Bhawuk, 1998, pp. 637–639) in their culture, they may take it for granted, having usually been willing participants in their own cultural socialisation. To support writing, however, staff have first to forget what they already know to imagine they are foreign to their own worlds and have to start anew within them. They have to alienate themselves from what they do, so they are outside looking in, deconstructing their own practices. Brecht's (see Willett, 1964) ideas about using dramatic form to generate an 'estrangement' or 'defamiliarisation' effect (*Verfremdungseffekt*) is the type of thing we have in mind. We suggest that a fairly simple method of dialogic lecture analysis can begin to facilitate such a process and that this can be especially productive within a writers' group or seminar situation.

6.4. Using Dialogic Lecture Analysis to Render Unconscious Competence Conscious and Help Students Understand Disciplinary Requirements

Building on the notion that Brecht's theory of dramaturgy might be of relevance here, we could say that the lecture is the stage of the academic discipline, the place where its conventions are performed. Lectures are immediate and dynamic texts, staged variously to enact, not merely demonstrate, the discipline's different epistemologies, the different ways in which it can be approached. Importantly, this means that lectures are also embodied texts that can show a tutor's interest for the subject, giving off a sense of personal involvement and passion for its concerns. Despite their orality, lectures are frequently written, often following the structures and conventions of written text. They are situated at the midpoint between speech and writing, occupying a similar genre of language and may thus serve as a bridge between discussions about writing and writing itself (Gee, 2006, p. 154). The tacit assumption behind the centrality of lectures in most degree programmes is that they can be used as a way into the discipline, its ways of speaking, thinking and being.

However, it seems that this assumption may be over-optimistic, since many students, just like the man in *The Trial* who remains outside the Law, are unprepared for the task of 'reading' a lecture, of understanding the invitation to join in contained within it, and this invitation may thus be missed or declined. Our contention is that equipping students — especially in groups — to analyse not just the content but also the form of lectures requires, and generates, an estrangement effect which can shine a light for academics on their own practice, productively rendering explicit their disciplinary writing cultures. That everyone is positioned as alien to the culture by the estrangement effect provoked by lecture analysis is the motivating force behind the method. Students' entering into discussion, not just with staff but also with their peers, over what they experience in a lecture and how they understand and relate to the cultural conventions they have witnessed can, therefore, be illuminating for both staff and students. Whilst lecture analysis may at first be just another alien concept, a technique for entry into a language game that has to be learnt, once assimilated, it can become a powerful lens for scrutinising the discipline.

6.5.   Outsiders Looking in: The Process of Dialogic Lecture Analysis

> If the teacher is able to see how the students are talking about, thinking about, and approaching particular instances of disciplinary practice, and if the students are able to hear how other students are doing this, and how the tutor is doing it, then this (in theory, at least) begins to open up possibilities for new types of understanding. (Haggis, 2006, p. 10)

In 1992, the School of Arts and Humanities at Nottingham Trent University, a large university in central England, set up an academic support service as part of its strategy to support students' academic inclusion and development. This was designed and delivered by Lisa Clughen. It soon became apparent that students required support that went beyond the generic support sessions she was offering and that she needed to know more about the specifics of their modules. How this knowledge was to be generated, however, was the source of an ongoing challenge, and the method of lecture analysis was one strategy she devised to address it. Several writing groups were set up over three years within the School of Arts and Humanities, with the aim of using these groups as a test bed for a model of lecture analysis that had already emerged from one-to-one writing tutorials with students.

When considering how to analyse lectures to assist students with their literacy development, a range of literacy theorists were considered. Emphasising the sociocultural nature of literacy, these argued that writing, as a mode of knowledge construction, is inherently linked to the different epistemologies and practices of the specific disciplines (Ganobscik-Williams, 2006; Lea & Street, 1998; Warren, 2002). Four key assumptions taken from such critics underpin dialogic lecture analysis and are used as ordering principles for its activities. These are as follows:

- Writing, as a process of meaning-making, is linked to clarity in conceptual knowledge.
- Writing demands an awareness of disciplinary epistemologies, practices and discourses.
- Writing is a social act, linked to issues such as power and identity.
- Writing is not only a skill but also a process which involves dialogue with the self and with others.

These principles, which develop an increasing emphasis on the social practice of writing, and on dialogue in particular, emerged as key to the functioning of the writers' groups. The notion of dialogue merits further elaboration, since it is at the heart of academic exchanges.

Drawing on Bhaktin's influential theories, dialogical perspectives on writing and teaching (Dysthe, 2007; Lillis, 2006) seek to mediate between the social and cultural demands on writing in a specific discipline and the personal positions and perspectives of the writers. Accordingly, Lillis places 'dialogues of participation' as fundamental to critical academic writing cultures (2006, p. 33), and the four types of dialogue she outlines provided further guiding influences on the writers' groups' dialogic pedagogy:

- Tutor-directive dialogue aimed at talking the student-writer into essayist literacy practice.
- Tutor-directive dialogue aimed at making language visible.
- Collaborative dialogue aimed at populating the text with the writers' own intentions (…).
- Talkback dialogue aimed at allowing the student-writer to say what she feels about the conventions she is writing within and to explore alternative ways of expressing meaning. (Lillis, 2006, p. 34)

The aim of the groups was to set up a community of writers and, through this, to create a space in which to address some of the Kafkaesque issues of power and identity involved in writing and forging one's own voice in a culture in which, for example, the knowledge one encounters can seem inaccessible or alienating, or where the voices of others can seem so much more persuasive and eloquent than one's own. The groups aimed to create a space in which to respond to such power issues in writing so that students might feel that they *could* participate in academic culture, that they could, as it were, take a step through the door rather than remaining outside. The idea was to erode the sense of being an outsider alienated from the discipline, to foster a sense of belonging so that students could warrant voice within their subject and begin the process of joining a community of their peers aimed at mutual self-help rather than individualistic competition.

The first of these groups was positioned at School level, rather than being embedded within a specific discipline. Whilst fruitful in terms of the discussions that took place, the group did not attract a sizeable membership. Consideration of this suggested that this was because the group did not exploit students' identification with a specific discipline. Also influenced by the emerging literacy agenda of embedding writer support within the disciplines, the decision was made to tailor subsequent groups to the needs of particular disciplines and bespoke pilot groups were set up in the fields of

English and history. Over the three years of these different groups' existence, various experiments in lecture analysis were carried out and gradually a general model for what we have called 'dialogic lecture analysis' emerged. As this process unfolded, it became clear that what began as an attempt to clarify disciplinary requirements for students also clarified them for staff, as an estrangement effect was generated by witnessing students struggle and hearing their questions as they sought to establish what was expected of them. This began to position staff *outside* the discipline in which they were unconsciously competent, aiding them in the process of walking in the students' shoes. Furthermore, this process generated a sense of community for individual students as they saw their peers struggling and began to help each other. Within such a community, receiving the help and support denied to Kafka's supplicants, some students began to know how to reply to the questions asked of them.

A model abstracted from the experiences of these groups is presented schematically in Figure 6.1. The process, which would unfold in a linear fashion on its first adoption, should nevertheless be conceptualised as recursive, since the dialogues occurring in stages 2 and 3 of the process will both feed into each other and also influence decisions about future activities and lectures.

6.6. Using Dialogic Lecture Analysis: A Case Study

This dialogic lecture analysis method was used in a writers' group that was attached to a final-year module on gender and sexuality in the English subject area.

The challenge of clarifying the conventions of writing for this module was met by talking to the subject lecturers, talking to the students to see whether their conceptions of writing for English met with those of the subject staff, analysing student and published texts within the discipline to gain an impression of the expected genre and to identify areas for improvement and, finally, responding to issues arising in the 'talkback space' (Lillis 2006, p. 42). The additional challenge of finding a suitable text to talk students into essayist literacy was met via the lecture analysis method. The group facilitator attended the module lectures and wrote a series of activities which invited students to reflect on the ways in which the tutors were performing academic conventions and then to appropriate them, or not, for their own purposes.

In dialogue with the students, it transpired that producing theorised writing was the aspect of literacy that most vexed them, but it was one they needed in order to write successfully for the course. The following activity

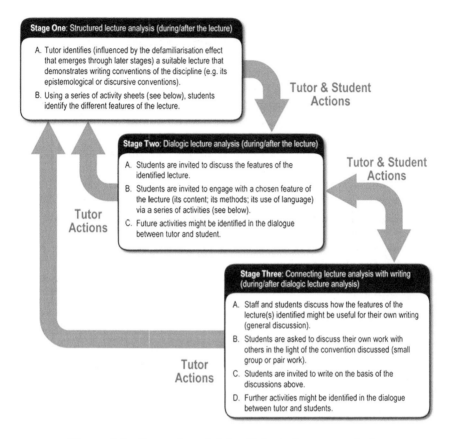

Stage One: Structured lecture analysis (during/after the lecture)

A. Tutor identifies (influenced by the defamiliarisation effect that emerges through later stages) a suitable lecture that demonstrates writing conventions of the discipline (e.g. its epistemological or discursive conventions).

B. Using a series of activity sheets (see below), students identify the different features of the lecture.

Tutor & Student Actions

Stage Two: Dialogic lecture analysis (during/after the lecture)

A. Students are invited to discuss the features of the identified lecture.

B. Students are invited to engage with a chosen feature of the lecture (its content; its methods; its use of language) via a series of activities (see below).

C. Future activities might be identified in the dialogue between tutor and student.

Tutor & Student Actions

Tutor Actions

Stage Three: Connecting lecture analysis with writing (during/after dialogic lecture analysis)

A. Staff and students discuss how the features of the lecture(s) identified might be useful for their own writing (general discussion).

B. Students are asked to discuss their own work with others in the light of the convention discussed (small group or pair work).

C. Students are invited to write on the basis of the discussions above.

D. Further activities might be identified in the dialogue between tutor and students.

Tutor Actions

Figure 6.1: General model for dialogic lecture analysis.

sheets were used to allay fears over the use of theory in writing by demonstrating how the students could analyse the way in which staff were talking about and using theory in their lectures and apply their awareness to their own writing. This task was then used to analyse other lectures so that the students could see the different ways of using theory deployed by the different tutors on the module.

Task 1: How Might You Use Theory in Your Writing? How Do Your Tutors Use Theory?

Think back to the lecture on Ann Bannon's *I am a Woman*. During the lecture, Gregory Woods spoke about Adrienne Rich's classic essay 'Compulsory Heterosexuality and Lesbian Existence' (1980) and then used it in his own arguments as he considered different texts. Consider how he did this by discussing the following questions:

1. When Greg spoke about Rich's theories, how did he do it? What do you notice about the way your tutors weave theory into their lectures? For example: Did he describe her theory at great length? What sort of language did he use to describe the theories he was talking about?
2. Greg then applied the theory to his chosen texts — for example, Dr. Mallory's text (1961). Let's analyse how he did this. What did he do with the theory? In the light of what we were saying about how, to be an English student, you look for the ways in which textual form intersects with ideas, how did Greg approach the texts? What examples did he give of compulsory heterosexuality in the texts he was discussing? How did he look for the ways in which language represented homosexuals in the light of Rich's theories? Did you notice the attention Greg paid to language and the way language use represented gay men or lesbians (i.e. the attention he paid to 'narrative construction'?)

Now we have discussed how, in their lectures, your tutors are demon-strating the writing and argumentation process for you, let's produce a short piece of writing to demonstrate the process of applying theory to a text.

Task 2: Using Theory in Your Own Writing

1. In pairs, discuss how you might finish the following sentence starter*: In her landmark essay 'Compulsory Heterosexuality and Lesbian Existence', Adrienne Rich argues that… (*Note: If you don't want to write about Rich's theory, simply describe briefly any theory you are reading at the moment, or a theory you want to use in your assignment).
2. Now write up your response to question one.
3. In pairs, discuss the following: what do you think of Rich's theory? Are there any ways in which you might critique or extend it?
4. Group discussion of Rich's theories (or other theories chosen).
5. Look at one of the novels from your course and find one example that demonstrates one aspect of Rich's theory (e.g. either (1) her ideas on compulsory sexuality or (2) the ways in which lesbians have been marginalised in discussions of homosexuality).
6. Now write a paragraph, either individually or in pairs, in which you write out your description of the aspect of the theory you have

chosen to discuss and explain how the example you have chosen demonstrates it.

7. Share your paragraph with another group. Do your readers think that the example you have chosen demonstrates your point?

8. Do you have any particular thoughts on using theory in your writing?

6.7.   Analysis of the Case Study: Struggle, Sociality and Solidarity in Writing Development Exercises

This exercise demonstrates one way in which, in Lillis' terms (2006, p. 34), tutors might '(talk) the student-writer into essayist literacy practice' by linking the lecture content and language with the students' own writing. Lillis' call to '(make) language visible' (2006, pp. 34; 38–40) is borne out in the initial lecture analysis task. Student descriptions of theory in their own writing can sometimes be rather convoluted and linguistically dense as they try to mimic theoretical writings in the texts they are reading. This activity can open the possibilities for Lillis' notion of dialogue using talkback spaces (2006, p. 42) to address the difficulties of reading and using theory, and to foster evidenced discussions over how complex the language of theorised writing need be. Tying the language students use in their natural talk about the theories during the pair work activities to their actual writing can make the production of theoretically honed writing more manageable. In other words, it should become less alienating through a co-socialisation that comes through an experience of solidarity.

Crucially, therefore, and with reference to our point that socialisation approaches to literacy development should not be top-down, we want to shift the focus onto the students and value their own contributions to the debates of their subject, as well as encouraging lecturers to use these contributions as lenses through which to regard themselves afresh. In the interests, then, of students' 'populating the text with their own intentions' (see Lillis, 2006, pp. 40–41), the activity must remain open for students to go where they want to go with it and to discuss their own reactions to it. This can be seen in the openness of the activity (they do not have to discuss the theory suggested and can decide for themselves whether they would prefer to write individually or in pairs, for instance) and in the move towards the students finding their own examples to demonstrate the theoretical points under discussion.

To situate this exercise within the Kafka analogy, we might argue that the empathy we are seeking to create by developing writing socially can open the way to an experience of de-estrangement for the student and re-estrangement for the lecturer. As students try together to work out the theories under discussion, they can come to realise that they are not the only ones who struggle with them. The de-estrangement experienced when they see others struggle can be mobilised to generate an air of collegial solidarity so that, rather than viewing it as the duty of others to help them, as in the Kafka quotation, students actually want to collaborate in their writing and learning out of empathy for another who struggles. Student comments on their experience of the writing group seem to indicate that such de-estrangement did indeed occur: 'Sometimes it can be really frustrating when you sit on your own writing an essay. However, the session in which we read each other's work showed me that other students might struggle as well and that I might be able to provide an answer for their questions and vice versa' (level 3 English student). We would argue that it was the social nature of this writing support activity that allowed for the de-estrangement and the subsequent generation of empathy that promoted a sense of involvement in their studies that emerges from a communal admission of struggle. Ultimately, then, sharing this experience of struggle with what it is to read and write within a discipline can operate to turn empathy into solidarity.

The experience at the tutor's end of these activities can also generate a discourse that allows tutors to experience an estrangement effect in relation to their discipline's conventions that, we argue, can bring them closer to the students' perspectives and help them to see that it is not in fact strange that students should struggle with what is asked of them. For tutors, watching the process can bring out realisations such as how difficult producing theorised writing can be for the students, how difficult they can find theoretical language and what a struggle it can be for them to use a theoretical language with which they can become comfortable. Focusing on a specific writing convention, such as the necessity to produce theorised texts, can enhance a tutor's realisation that forms of discourse naturalised for them are still very foreign for the students. This itself can lead the tutors to come up with different ways of talking. For example, they might overlay their discussions of theory with non-specialised and even colloquial ways of saying the same thing. In a dual movement, the tutor may temporarily move away from the insider's relation with the discipline as students move closer to it.

Of course, these intertwining experiences of estrangement (of the tutor) and de-estrangement (of the students) necessarily blur the boundaries of established academic identities, for they urge quite different forms of speaking and being to those to which the academic might be accustomed. Academics are used to demonstrating their competence to each other both linguistically and in their use of disciplinary conventions. If academics are to communicate their material in a variety of registers and use colloquial modes of expression, they might have to give up the feeling that what they are saying sounds less academic, that it is not in keeping with an academic identity or that it is even a shameful process of dumbing down.

6.7.1. Student Feedback on the Writers' Group

We have argued that students can find academic writing conventions confusing, and that we, therefore, need explicit discussion of disciplinary writing conventions. Feedback from the participants in the writers' groups over the years confirmed the usefulness of dialogic lecture analysis for these purposes. In this short section, we present some of this feedback, as it underpins our confidence that these methods can help in the process of 'non-impositional' socialisation.

Throughout the three years of the writers' group, feedback on the group and the activities used was gathered via student questionnaires and via their formal contributions to subject panels. A more informal form of feedback also occurred as students started to email the facilitator, quite spontaneously, about their thoughts and feelings about the group. The following excerpts have been chosen as representative examples of feedback that demonstrate the claims made in this chapter and the students' responses to their experiences of embracing dialogic lecture analysis:

> What I found particularly useful was when you told us to analyse our lectures as the information given is what the lecturers expect from us in our essays. I used to wonder why our lecturers talk very little on the actual book itself in the lectures, however not knowing that they found all the social influences just as important. Like in our lectures you told us to pay attention to how much theory is talked about compared to everything else.

Drawing on sociocultural critics of literacy and literacy development, we have argued that, as writing is an exercise in meaning-making, and because knowledge production is social, cultural and historical, dialogic writing development usefully includes opportunities for students to grapple with the meanings they wish to communicate within a social setting:

- The group is a great chance to discuss ideas, themes, etc. in a very relaxed environment. This I think, allows people to be more open to say and discuss things they think maybe perceived as quite trivial.
- Talking aloud about the point I was trying to make helped me to understand what I was saying.
- I found writing and verbalising the points we were trying to make about texts very useful. When you discuss your ideas within a small group you get other people's perspectives, which can lead you to think of things in a completely different way.

We also argue for the importance of social relations for academic literacy development and for the twofold process of de-estrangement and re-estrangement that we seek to foster. Constructing safe, non-judgmental spaces where participants take on board the complexities inherent in writing in the academy allows students to ask the questions that foster their participation. Moreover, hearing other students ask their questions can generate a willingness to participate as students show solidarity with others, rather than producing a passive expectation of help like that evident in the Kafka example with which we began this chapter:

> Interestingly, it also seems to help me on a psychological level as I see that other students might struggle with their work too and we thus try to help each other.

6.8. Recommendations and Conclusion

Two key points have underpinned this chapter: firstly, we believe that writing in the academy can confuse, intimidate or even alienate students. It is therefore, we argue, the responsibility of the university to structure support for writing into its operations. Such support needs to be open and honest and done in non-judgemental, informal dialogue with students, so that it is accessible and meaningful for them. Writing support materials can be very useful indeed, but are not always enough to deal with the local issues involved in writing. A supportive environment for writing, then, is one that attends to the sociocultural aspects of literacy in its strategy and practice. This takes us to our second argument. Drawing on research from sociocultural approaches to writing, we hold that, if writing is to be supported effectively, it must be seen in its complexity. The ramifications of writing's relationship with the social (that writing is purposeful, that it involves self-positioning and identity construction, that it is saturated with power relationships) and the cultural (that it is performed differently in various arenas which manifest a whole series of different disciplinary and cultural conventions) means that its demands easily exceed the limits of generic writing support. Holding fast to the notion of writing as a skill that can be developed in isolation from the context or without regard to the actual writers themselves leads to insufficient approaches to academic literacy development. Rather, we argue that supportive environments for academic literacy are those that use specific analysis of the experience of disciplinarity in order to produce an estrangement effect for staff and a de-estrangement effect for students. This cannot be generic.

We, therefore, recommend that:

Policymakers/senior management

- Build literacy development into university policies.
- Recognise the limits of technological contact and embrace the importance of face-to-face contact for literacy development.
- Embrace the complexities of writing within their policies on literacy development so that they include opportunities for dialogue around the many different literacy tasks asked of the students.
- Recognise that, whilst overarching principles may indeed unite the disciplines in HE, since literacy is sociocultural, policymakers must register that it is heterogenous and that they should allow room for subjects to develop their own ways of developing it.

Academic staff/literacy development tutors

- Consider and address the ramifications of the sociocultural nature of literacy for their own attempts at literacy development.
- Make room for dialogic approaches to literacy by including opportunities for social interaction and considering the way in which dialogue proceeds such that the omnipresent potential for power within dialogue is disarmed.

Our concluding suggestion is that there is something about the face-to-face encounter in groups that we would like to harness for writing development. Where the Kafka quote bewails the lack of solidarity and a failure of empathy, the face-to-face small group session can work in the other direction, allowing an experience of the struggle of the other that makes the writer feel less alienated. This is the paradoxical conclusion from the estrangement effect — working through it reduces the estrangement that at first is amplified.

Whilst we have here offered a generic approach to academic literacy development in our methods of lecture analysis and face-to-face support, it is important to recognise that writing is different across disciplines, and this is shown by the way our generic model actually ends up being presented through the lens of a particular discipline. Our generic approach aims to modify itself by provoking an awareness and discussion of the heterogeneity of disciplinary conventions, of disciplinary ways of being and thinking. Lecture analysis is an illuminating tool, but the object it illuminates is different each time.

References

Bazerman, C., Elbow, P. Hillocks, G., & Blau, S. (2006). 50 Years of research on writing: What have we learned? In *Voices*, UC Santa Barbara. Retrieved from http://www.youtube.com/watch?v = mrcq3dzt0Uk Accessed on 24 January 2012.

Bhawuk, D. P. S. (1998). The role of culture theory in cross-cultural training: A multimethod study of culture-specific, culture-general, and culture theory-based assimilators. *Journal of Cross-Cultural Psychology*, *29*, 630–655. Retrieved from http://jcc.sagepub.com/content/29/5/630.full.pdf + html Accessed on 13 April 2012.

Bowstead, H. (2009). Teaching English as a foreign language — A personal exploration of language, alienation and academic literacy. *UK Journal of Learning Development in Higher Education*, *1*(February). Retrieved from http://www.aldinhe.ac.uk/ojs/index.php?journal=jldhe&page=article&op=viewFile&path %5B%5D=14&path%5B%5D=10 Accessed on 13 April 2012.

Chanock, K. (Ed.). (2001). *Sources of confusion*. Refereed proceedings of the national language and academic skills conference, La Trobe University, November 27–28, 2000. Published by Language and Academic Skills Units of La Trobe University. Retrieved from http://www.aall.org.au/conferences Accessed on 13 April 2012.

Deane, M., & O'Neill, P. (2011). *Writing in the disciplines*. London: Palgrave Macmillan.

Dysthe, O. (2007). Dialogic postgraduate supervision — Characteristics, constraints and affordances. Symposium on perspectives and limits of dialogism in Mikhail Bakhtin: Applications in psychology, art, education and culture. The University of Crete, Rethymnon, 25–27 May.

Elton, L. (2010). Academic writing and tacit knowledge. *Teaching in Higher Education*, *15*(2), 151–160. Retrieved from http://www.tandfonline.com/doi/full/10.1080/13562511003619979 Accessed on 24 January 2012.

Ganobcsik-Williams, L. (2004). *A report on the teaching of academic writing in UK higher education*. The Royal Literary Fund. Retrieved from http://www.rlf.org.uk/fellowshipscheme/documents/TeachingWritingUKHE.pdf Accessed on 24 January 2012.

Ganobscik-Williams, L. (2006). *Teaching academic writing in UK higher education: Theories, practices and models*. Basingstoke: Palgrave Macmillan.

Gee, J. P. (2006). Oral discourse in a world of literacy. *Research in the Teaching of English*, *41*(2), 153–159. Retrieved from http://www.english.wisc.edu/nystrand/RTE%20Symposium%20Nov06RTE.pdf Accessed on 13 April 2012.

Habermas, J. (1998). *Between facts and norms* (W. Rehg, Trans.). Cambridge MA: MIT Press.

Haggis, T. (2006). Pedagogies for diversity: Retaining critical challenge amidst fears of 'dumbing down'. *Studies in Higher Education*, *31*(5), 521–535. Retrieved from https://dspace.stir.ac.uk/bitstream/1893/457/1/Haggis_Pedagogies_for_diversity_2006.pdf (pp. 1–13). Accessed on 13 April 2012.

Howell, W. S. (1982). *The empathic communicator*. Belmont, CA: Wadsworth.

Kafka, F. (1992). Before the law. In N. N. Glatzer (Ed.), *The complete short stories of Franz Kafka* (pp. 3–4). London: Minerva.

Kafka, F. (1999). *The trial* (W. Muir & E. Muir, Trans.). In *The complete novels* (pp. 11–128). London: Vintage.

Kokkinn, B. (2001). Lifebuoys in a sea of confusion: An integrated learning support program for first year nursing students. In Chanock (pp. 215–223). Retrieved from http://www.aall.org.au/conferences Accessed on 13 April 2012.

Laing, R. D. (1967). *The politics of experience and the bird of paradise.* Harmondsworth: Penguin.

Lea, M., & Stierer, B. (Eds.). (2000). *Student writing in higher education: New contexts.* Buckingham: Open University Press.

Lea, M., & Street, B. (1998). Student writing in higher education: An academic literacies approach. *Studies in Higher Education, 11*(3), 182–199.

Levin, E. (2001). Making expectations explicit. In Chanock (pp. 224–232). Retrieved from http://www.aall.org.au/conferences Accessed on 13 April 2012.

Lillis, T. (2003). Student writing as 'Academic Literacies': Drawing on Bakhtin to move from critique to design. *Language and Education, 17*(3), 192–207. Retrieved from http://www.writing.ucsb.edu/wrconf08/Pdf_Articles/Lillis_Article2.pdf Accessed on 24 January 2012.

Lillis, T. (2006). Moving towards an 'Academic Literacies' pedagogy: Dialogues of participation. In L. Ganobcsik-Williams (Ed.), *Teaching academic writing in UK higher education* (pp. 30–45). Basingstoke: Palgrave Macmillan.

Mallory, R. (1961). *Modern birth control.* New York, NY: Paperback Library.

Mann, S. (2001). Alternative perspectives on the student experience: Alienation and engagement. *Studies in Higher Education, 26*(1), 1–19.

Mitchell, S. (2010). Now you don't see it; now you do: Writing made visible in the university. *Arts and Humanities in Higher Education, 9*, 133–148.

Penrose, A. M. (2002). Academic literacy perceptions and performance: Comparing first-generation and continuing-generation college students. *Research in the Teaching of English, 36*(4), 437–461.

Purcell-Gates, V. (1997). *Other people's words: The cycle of low literacy.* Cambridge, MA: Harvard University Press.

Read, B., Archer, L., & Leathwood, C. (2003). Challenging cultures? Student conceptions of 'Belonging' and 'Isolation' at a post-1992 university. *Studies in Higher Education, 28*(3), 261–277.

Rich, A. (1980). Compulsory heterosexuality and lesbian existence. *Signs, 5*(4), 631–660.

Sperling, M. (1996). Revisiting the writing-speaking connection: Challenges for research on writing and writing instruction. *Review of Educational Research, 66*(1), 53–86. Retrieved from http://www.jstor.org/pss/1170726?searchUrl=%2Faction%2FdoBasicSearch%3FQuery%3DSociocultural%2Bperspectives%2Bon%2Bwriting%26gw%3Djtx%26acc%3Don%26prq%3DTsui%26Search%3DSearch%26hp%3D25%26wc%3Don&Search=yes Accessed on 13 April 2012.

Thomassen, L. (2010). *Habermas: A guide for the perplexed.* London: Continuum.

Warren, D. (2002). Curriculum design in a context of widening participation in higher education. *Arts and Humanities in Higher Education, 1*(1), 85–99.

Willett, J. (Ed., and Trans.). (1964). *Brecht on theatre: The development of an aesthetic.* New York: Hill and Wang.

Chapter 7

Using Story Cards to Facilitate Reflective Thought and Dialogue About Science Writing

Sarah Haas

This chapter introduces story card activities that can be used with writers in the natural sciences at any level of study. The overall purpose is to get students consciously engaged in thinking and talking about writing in the sciences thereby enabling them to participate in their local communities. Specifically, there are three main goals of using the story cards, which are to

1. facilitate reflective thinking in novice research writers, focusing on what it means to write in science;
2. enable dialogue about science writing and its conventions in local contexts; and
3. lead participants to discover some specific knowledge about writing (or to explicitly articulate knowledge that may have before been tacit)

These activities have been successfully used with PhD and post-doctoral students and have been evaluated using criteria derived from the three goals of facilitating reflection, catalysing dialogue and guiding discovery. A fourth criterion considers how useful the story cards were perceived to be by the writers who used them.

The story cards are based on the SPRE textual pattern (Hoey, 1994). SPRE stands for Situation, Problem, Response and Evaluation, a 'minimum structure' (*ibid.*, p. 27) that is applicable to many genres of research writing.

Writing in the Disciplines: Building Supportive Cultures for Student Writing in UK Higher Education
Copyright © 2012 by Emerald Group Publishing Limited
All rights of reproduction in any form reserved
ISBN: 978-1-78052-546-4

This chapter, for example, is minimally structured according to the SPRE pattern: Firstly, I will outline the teaching *situation,* focusing on why it is desirable to have novice writers thinking and talking about writing in their specific contexts. The *problem* facing us is that we need ways *into* this reflective thought and dialogue. My *response* to the problem is to design and implement a story card activity based on the principles of guided discovery and on the SPRE pattern. The procedures of the activities will be described in detail so that readers might replicate this study, or make adjustments to suit different situations. Data were collected in the form of field notes, audio recordings and questionnaires. I will use the data to *evaluate* the story card activities, judging whether or not the goals were met, and determining the how useful the users of the cards perceived the activities to be.

7.1. Why Do We Want Novice Writers Thinking and Talking About Writing?

As Wingate (2006) and Wingate, Andon, and Cogo (2011) point out, generic 'writing skills' that will serve all purposes for all disciplines simply do not exist. Writing differs not only from broad disciplinary distinctions such as 'humanities' or 'science', but study guides with titles such as *How to write in Chemistry* or *How to Write in Biology* (guides are available from the online university writing labs such as Brown, Purdue, Colorado State) indicate that 'writing in science' might also be too broad a category. In *Scientists Must Write*, Barrass (2002) outlines the 'basic requirements in scientific and technical writing [as] explanation, clarity, completeness, impartiality, order, accuracy, objectivity, and simplicity' (p. 35). This statement is hardly arguable. However, *how* these maxims are manifested may well differ from science community to science community. Each discipline, and each smaller community within a discipline, has its own genre, with its own requirements and conventions (Bhatia, 1993). Deane et al. (2008, p. 13) summarise this view of writing as a social activity, saying

> the cognitive skills that writers deploy are socially situated and take place in social contexts that encourage and support particular types of thinking. ... writing is (a) situated in actual contexts of use; (b) improvised, not produced strictly in accord with abstract templates; (c) mediated by social conventions and practices; and (d) acquired as part of being socialized into particular communities of practice.

In order, then, for students to learn to write in their own disciplines, they need an entry into the *specific* discourse community in their own *specific* contexts (Bazerman, 1988; Bazerman & Paradis, 1991; Ding, 2008; Florence & Yore, 2004; Kelly, Chen, & Prothero, 2000; Kostouli, 2009; Sadler, 2009). Wingate et al. (2011) suggest that the most effective way for teaching writing in different disciplines is for the 'insiders' of the discipline, who already know the rules, to teach the writing, and initiate new members into the community (p. 70).

Full entry into a discourse community, however, cannot be a passive endeavour. Scientific writing, in the form of the scientific article, has been around since the 17th century (Gross & Harmon, 1999). The current genre rules of the scientific article are not the same as the rules of 400 years ago (Gross, Harmon, & Reidy, 2002). Since discourse communities and the genre conventions of those communities are in a constant state of (albeit gradual) flux (Bazerman, 1999; Berge, 1994; Taavitsainen, 2001), those who would be initiated must not only be 'taught' what they must do and say in order to adhere to the rules but also take part in constructing the rules (Halliday & Martin, 1993). Lillis (2003) asserts that this role ought to be active, rather than incidental, and calls for 'dialogic' rather than 'monologic' goals of higher education. She summarises 'Bakhtin's notion of dialogue [as] the process by which newer ways to mean, and to be, can come into existence' (p. 199). 'Dialogic' goals of higher education are contrasted with 'monologic':

> the goals of higher education can be described as monologic where the institutional and pedagogic practices are oriented to the reproduction of official discourses of knowledge; in contrast, the goals of higher education can be described as dialogic where pedagogic practices are oriented towards making visible/challenging/playing with official and unofficial discourse. (p. 193)

Applying this dialogic approach to teaching writing in the sciences would mean not only helping new science writers learn and understand the written discourse rules of their specific communities but also to allow them, through dialogue, to play with the official and unofficial discourse, and to possibly contribute to new rules. Thus, for new members to successfully enter into a community, and for the community to be open to new ways of meaning and being, active dialogue among members is essential. Active dialogue among members presupposes active thinking.

The 'Thinking Writing' approach to writing instruction developed at Queen Mary University of London describes its 'overarching aim' as

> the development of students who are engaged with the curriculum, and are reflective, self-aware and organised learners.

[Writing can] help students make connections between areas of
their learning, develop independent thought and reflect on the
processes they are engaged in. (http://www.thinkingwriting.
qmul.ac.uk/reflect.htm)

The qualities of self-awareness, independence and reflective thinking
would most certainly be necessary not only for higher education in general
but also for the active initiation into disciplinary communities — particularly if that initiation involves an active role in forming the norms of the
community. In short, successful entry into specific scientific writing
communities requires active thinking and active dialogue. It was with goals
of promoting thinking and dialogue that the story card exercises were put
into use.

7.2.   The Story Cards: SPRE Text Pattern

The story cards themselves are based on the SPRE pattern, a 'culturally
popular pattern of organisation' (Scott & Thompson, 2001, p. 122) which is so
pervasive in Western culture (Proctor, 1996) that it is referred to by Young,
Becker, and Pike (1970 cited in Hoey, 1994, p. 27) as a 'generalised plot', or as
'the consensus' by Winter (1976, cited in Edge, 1989). The SPRE pattern is
also the minimum global structure of scientific writing (Hoey, 1994; Grimes,
1972, 1975), and is, as Hoey points out, 'worthy of heuristic use' (1994, p. 27).
    The pattern has been used heuristically in EFL (English as a foreign
language) settings for the teaching of both reading (Edge, 1985, 2011; Hughes,
2008; Pereyra, Espinosa, & Tossi, 2011) and writing (Flowerdew, 2000;
Galán & Pérez, 2003; So, 2005; Wharton, 1999). Edge and Wharton (2001),
however, successfully adjusted the pattern to fit academic TESOL (Teaching
English to Speakers of Other Languages) articles, and use the adjustment to
aid native speakers of English in structuring master's degree dissertations and
journal articles in the TESOL discipline. The fact that Edge and Wharton
(*ibid.*) found it necessary to adjust the pattern to suit their own discourse
community in their own setting attests to the earlier claim that even though
there are commonalities in academic writing, each specific community has
its own requirements. The use of the pattern in the current case is not so much
a heuristic for aiding reading or writing, as it is a springboard for writers
to become consciously aware of writing in their own contexts, and as a catalyst
for writers to enter into dialogue about writing in these contexts.
    The current use of the pattern, therefore, is not quite conventional,
neither is the way it is presented. Instead of an explanatory sheet, such as the
one used by Edge and Wharton (2001, p. 282) (which I used to structure this
chapter), the pattern is presented on story cards (Figures 7.1 and 7.2). The

Figure 7.1: Momotaro cards.

Figure 7.2: Tomomi cards.

use of stories and comics is not unprecedented in science education (Ritchie, Tomas, & Tones, 2011; Tomas, 2011). If one would agree with Grobstein (2005) (and I do) that 'science *is* storytelling, and story revising' (p. 6, emphasis added), and that scientists need to know how to write (Gregson, 2005; Yore, Florence, Pearson, & Weaver, 2006; Yore, Hand, & Florence, 2004), the use of stories can be seen as appropriate for science writing classrooms. Even if one takes exception to the claim that science is storytelling, it still stands that 'both the plots of fairy tales and the writings of scientists are built on [the SPRE] pattern' (Grimes, 1975, p. 211). The use of comics can also be justified, even in serious science settings. Chin and Teou (2009) finds that the use of cartoons in the science classroom facilitates 'exploratory talk' in which

> statements and suggestions ... may be challenged and counter-challenged, but challenges are justified and alternative hypotheses are offered ... Reasoning is [also] visible in the talk. (Chin & Teou, 2009, p. 1330)

As it is this kind of reflection and exploration that I aim to promote, the use of manga-type comic pictures does not seem out of place.

7.3.   The Story Cards: Guided Discovery

While students are engaged in the story card activities, the SPRE pattern is neither explained nor handed out on paper; in fact it is not mentioned at all until all the activities are completed, and students have had opportunities for discussions. The intention is not to 'teach' the pattern, but rather to get students thinking and talking about writing. In turn, these thoughts and dialogues about particular writing contexts could lead students to discover some 'general rules' that can apply to most scientific writing, regardless of the particular communities. It is preferable for the students to discover these rules for themselves through dialogue; the teacher's job is to facilitate the discovery (Ruyle & Jacobsen, 2003).

A full discussion on the history and issues surrounding guided discovery learning is beyond the scope of this chapter; for current purposes, guided discovery is assumed to be good science teaching practice (Greitzer, Rice, Eaton, & Perkins, 2005; Hand, Lawrence, & Yore, 1999; Poock, Greenbowe, Burke, & Hand, 2007; Smith et al., 2007; Surlekar, 1998). In this kind of learning, the teacher does not hand anything to students on a plate, but rather nudges them in the right direction to discover for themselves (Brown & Campione, 1994). The teacher does this nudging by creating 'situations where the learner draws on his or her own past experience and existing knowledge to discover facts and relationships and new truths to be learned' (Learning theories knowledge base). The learning 'involves the integration of [these] new [truths, facts, relationships and] ideas into existing knowledge networks such that ideas are connected with each other' (Hand et al., 1999, p. 1029). When students are working in groups, guided discovery learning also opens a space for dialogue (Poock et al., 2007), which is important in science, as it 'more accurately reflect[s] the interactive dialog and construction of knowledge that occurs within the science research community' (Hand, Wallace, & Yang, 2004, p. 136).

7.4. SPRE Story Card Activities

In these story card activities, students draw upon their existing knowledge, particularly their comprehension of fairy tales, and how they are structured. This comprehension is most likely tacit, but it is, nevertheless, existing knowledge that can be used for making connections to new knowledge. I consider the activity successful if students are actively engaged in thinking and talking about what it means to write in their particular contexts. However, it is also my hope that through this dialogue, they will indeed discover new truths, facts, connections, relationships and ideas, and integrate them into their existing knowledge (Hand et al., 1999, p. 1029).

These story cards were developed with Eduardo Shima, the illustrator, 11 years ago; I have used them countless times with various sets of students. The data that are included in this study, however, were collected from nine separate events over the past 3 years. The exercise was used by a total of 85 PhD or post-doctoral writers in the natural sciences at a large university; the writers were participants on a Writer Development course. The data come from field notes, audio recordings and questionnaires.

7.5. Working with the Story Cards

Understanding that good science writing is 'detailed enough to allow others to replicate it exactly' (UNC Writing centre handout on Scientific Reports, n.d.), I will give step-by-step instructions for the story card activities — not so much so that it can be replicated exactly, but more so that readers can make any adjustments they might find necessary. There are 7 different activities to be done with the story cards, but for the sake of clarity and precision, the exercise is broken down into 10 steps, each of which can take from 1 to 20 minutes, depending on the group of writers. For ease of reading, I will include any pertinent data extracts, field note extracts and mini analyses concurrently with the description of each activity.

7.5.1.   Put Writers into Groups of Four or Five Members

This exercise is done in groups in order to increase dialogue, discussion and negotiation of meaning among the writers doing the task. Writers need to be able to discuss local writing contexts, and to make comparisons between them, so if the participants are not already acquainted, introductions are recommended.

7.5.2.   Distribute Story Cards

One set of story cards is given to each group. The sets contain eight cards: four cards having information about a character called Momotaro and four cards containing information about a character called Tomomi (see Figures 7.1 and 7.2).

7.5.3.   Writers Separate the Eight Cards into Groups

After each group has a set of cards, participants are asked to separate the cards in any way they see fit. They are not told any basis for categorisation, nor how many categories there should be; they are simply instructed to categorise the cards. This can cause some confusion at first, particularly if learners are from cultures where teacher-centred instruction, or rote memorisation, are the educational norms.

In each of the nine times data have been collected on this exercise, all groups of students have recognised that 'There's actually a lot of ways these cards [can be divided] up into categories'. Even though all groups (eventually) chose to divide the cards into two categories, Tomomi cards and Momotaro cards, the categorisation has not always been done without discussion:

> A: What if we group it into 'beginnings', 'middles', and 'ends'?
>   We can put B and B in the Beginning group; D, D, A, A in
>   the Middle group, and C,C in the End group.
> B: Or we could just have categories of A, B, C, D. That's also
>   logical. And simple.

These proposed alternatives would make three or four groups instead of two, and would mix the different stories. Although a logical suggestion for categorisation, these ideas were vetoed by other group members:

> C: I can understand your meaning, but I don't ... like it ....
>   We want to ... I like having the two different people in

> separate groups. That's the best grouping, isn't it? Makes
> most sense? I mean ... what would we do with two As two
> Bs two Cs ...?

Some writers were confused as to the point of this exercise (finding it 'too easy and obvious'). Some writers, however, did make the connection to writing. One directly articulated this parallel to science writing:

> It's like working with pages and pages of data. You have to
> decide how to code them and organise them ... and move
> them around and ugh. What a mess.

Another writer told her group that she had

> [done] this with a pile of articles last weekend. I had the whole
> floor covered—had to move furniture. I was like putting them
> in this pile and then that pile ... and then back in this one ...

Her group members pointed out to her that reference managers such as endnote can help with categorising literature, but she insisted she preferred the 'low-tech way—[as she] gets a better feeling for the literature then'.

As the students noted, researchers have to find patterns in the information they gather (articles they read/data they collect); sometimes the patterns may be obvious (as the cards are), but sometimes they will not be, and writers will have to work harder to find categories and patterns. As demonstrated above, even in with seemingly straightforward cases there will always be more than one possibility for groupings. It is up to writers to make conscious choices in their categorisations, leading to better writing.

7.5.4. *Writers Work with the Momotaro Cards*

Writers are next asked to take the four (randomly shuffled) Momotaro cards, and put the cards in the order that they think makes the *best complete* story.

7.5.4.1. Arrange the cards into a story After writers arrange the cards into the order that they think makes the best complete story, they are asked to report their chosen order to the whole group, using the circled letters on top of each story card. Although students are cautioned that there is more than one possible answer, invariably, the order that writers choose is ⓑ, ⓓ, ⓐ, ⓒ

7.5.4.2.   Writers explain *why* they have chosen this order   Although it is quite easy for groups to put the Momotaro cards into the ⓑ, ⓓ, ⓐ, ⓒ order, when asked to explain *why* this is the best possible story, there is normally a bit more trouble. Vague answers such as 'it's logical' or 'that's the story' are most common. When pressed, however, in most cases the writers, working together and talking with each other, can come up with some reasons for this being the 'right' order. There are chronological clues, lexical clues and rhetorical structure clues.

Chronological clues   There is an evident chronology (supported by the illustrations) that Momotaro was found as a baby (earliest time-event in the story) by old man and woman, then was raised by them until he *grew up* (time must have passed). Chronologically, it would also be necessary for the Oni to first come to the village to steal the treasure before Momotaro and his friends would need to go retrieve it.

Lexical clues   There are also lexical clues, particularly in the organisation concepts of 'given' and 'new' information: 'the ***given*** part [of a text] represents the part which is already familiar to the [reader] ... while the ***new*** part represents a [new] contribution' (Trask, 1999, p. 106). As one student explained it

> there are some stuff introduced in one card, then mentioned in the next card ... like the old man and old woman and Momotaro are introduced in card B, and then they come again [in card D] ... and then it's **an** old man and woman in the first card, and **the** old man and woman in the next card. And then I have the Oni come in one card, and then go fight the Oni in the next. So it builds on what was in the card before it. There are new characters or information in every card with some stuff I already know.

Rhetorical structure   Along with the lexical clues, some groups were able to identify the SPRE pattern present in stories (although they did not call it that yet), and even made explicit connections to scientific writing:

> A: well, you have the introduction to the character right? And then there's some kind of conflict, yeah? And they go and resolve the conflict, and then there has to be the happy ending.
> B: Yeah, okay. Yeah. It's just ... even ... it's like the structure of a paper, isn't it
> A: Oh. Yeah. Right.

B: We have to introduce our research and ... well, I don't
know what the 'conflict' is, but we ... we have to say what
we do ... the experiment, and then we have to say it is all
brilliant solution.

Although pinpointing *why* the B, D, A, C order is the 'right' order can
be a difficult, and somewhat frustrating exercise for some writers, the
important point to make is that writers *need* to make *conscious* choices
about the order in which to present their information to readers. They also
need to make *conscious* choices about presenting it in the *best* way for ease of
reading — which includes not only the order they choose to present isolated
bits of information but also the way they link the bits together lexically.

7.5.5.   *Writers Work with Tomomi Cards in the Same Way*

After writers have identified the best structure for the Momotaro story, and
have satisfactorily explained why this is the best order, they next do the same
exercise with the Tomomi cards: first putting the cards in order that makes
the best story, then justifying their decisions. Writers are reminded that there
is no one 'right' answer, but they must be able to clearly explain *why* they
chose the order they did.

This exercise brings forth more discussion and disagreement in and
among the groups, regarding what should go where, and the 'best' order for
the cards. The Tomomi cards have no chronological clues, either lexical or
visual (Tomomi looks the same age in all the cards); nor are there any other
lexical clues suggesting a correct order. Even so, the most common order
offered by group members was ⓑ, ⓓ, ⓐ, ⓒ. Although it is the most common
order, unlike the Momotaro cards, the decision was not always unanimous.
The most common alternative order offered was ⓑ, ⓒ, ⓓ, ⓐ.

Given the absence of the other clues. Writers more often looked to the
rhetorical structure for reasoning their chosen order.

A: Well, you have to introduce the main character. So that's this
[ⓑ and ⓒ] and she'll probably dream about travelling ... or go
travelling as a ... result of her dreaming .... So, yeah. She
dreams to travel and then goes to travel. So it's ⓑ, ⓒ, ⓓ, ⓐ
B: Yeah. Yeah okay.
C: Hmmmm
A: What?
C: But what about ... where is the conclusion?
A: She goes travelling.

> B: yeah. She's out there seeing the world. That's the result.
>
> C: Yeah, but I want ... that's .... You need an ending ... a beginning, a middle and an end.
>
> D: You want her to live happily ever after? You're so ... such a romantic. So, what? (8 sec) ⓑ, ⓓ, ⓐ, ⓒ?
>
> C: Yeah. That's it ... that's better.
>
> D: Are you happy now?
>
> C: Yes, I'm very happy.
>
> A: Yeah, okay.

The group above had first decided on the b, c, d, a order, and then through negotiation with each other and by using their existing knowledge of fairy tales, opted instead for the SPRE pattern of b, d, a, c. Most groups produced the b, d, a, c order, although they took on average three minutes longer to come to that conclusion than they did with the Momotaro story. A few groups maintained the b, c, d, a order, but in telling the story out loud, added the 'ending' onto it:

> Tomomi lived in a nice house on a hill with a beautiful view of the ocean. She was very satisfied with her life. Even so, Tomomi's dream was to travel, so she travelled around the world and saw many things. So she was living her dream.

7.5.6. Each Group Writes Out the Story of Tomomi (in Their Chosen Order)

After the group members agree on the order of Tomomi's story, they are asked to write out a narrative, using the cards as an outline and connect the pieces of information together so that it is easy for a reader to process. This exercise leads to more interaction among the group members, deciding how the events lead to one another and how to link them together. Some groups were minimalist in their linking, producing stories such as

> A girl called Tomomi lived happily in a nice house on a hill with a beautiful view of the ocean. However, she had a dream to travel. So she travelled around the world and saw many things. As a result, Tomomi was very satisfied with her life.

Although the group who produced the story above claimed that it was 'boring', they still maintained, and rightly so, that it is a complete story, and the ideas are linked together in a way that makes the story easy for a reader to read and process.

Other groups made more elaborate stories containing more details, though still maintaining the order of information as the minimalist story:

> Once upon a time there was a young woman of an unknown age called Tomomi. She lived in a nice house on a hill with a beautiful view of the ocean. But Tomomi was not satisfied with her life, because the ocean view made her dream. Her dream was to travel. 'Where to go?' Tomomi wondered. What to bring? She grabbed her camera, put it in a sack, tied it on a hobo stick … . Time to go! Pyramids, Eiffel Tower … so much to see, so little time … so small a sack. But go she must. She travelled all around the world and saw many things. After many months of traveling, Tomomi returned home, many experiences wiser. *Now,* as she lay on the hill overlooking the ocean, chewing on grass, she realised that she was very satisfied with her life.

Interestingly, and Hoey (1994) might say predictably, most of the groups who had chosen an order differing from the ⓑ, ⓓ, ⓐ, ⓒ (SPRE) order adjusted their stories so they eventually maintained the order. The most common alternative order ⓑ, ⓒ, ⓓ, ⓐ used the C statement as an expansion of the situation at the beginning of the story, and then repeated it as an evaluation at the end of the story, in order to complete the pattern:

> Tomomi was a girl who lived in a nice house on a hill with a beautiful view of the ocean. She was very satisfied with her life, but her dream was to travel. So she travelled around the world and saw many things. Indeed, in the end, she was very satisfied with her life.

Some groups, however, left the evaluation non-explicit, ending with Tomomi travelling around the world:

> Tomomi lived in a nice house on a hill with a beautiful view of the ocean. She was very satisfied with her life, but her dream was to travel. So she travelled around the world and saw many things.

When questioned about how things turned out for Tomomi, this group replied that readers can assume that Tomomi is happy because she is following her dream, thus leaving the evaluation implied rather than stated.

7.5.7.   Groups Randomly Shuffle the Cards, and Make the Jumbled Story Make Sense

We want to impress upon writers that, even though some rhetorical structures might be more intuitive, it is *possible* to make a story make sense to readers even if there is an unconventional or counter-intuitive order of information. Regardless of the order of information, it is the writer's job to connect the ideas in a way that makes it easy for readers to read and process. This is to reinforce the idea that writers need to make conscious decisions about the order in which they present information, and they need to make conscious decisions about how they link that information together for the sake of easy reading.

To get writers focused on this concept of consciously producing text that is easy to read, groups were asked to randomly shuffle the Tomomi cards, and, regardless of the order of information that resulted from the shuffle, to link the ideas together in order to produce a story that would make sense and that would be easy to read. This exercise led to more dialogue among group members as to how to make the pieces fit together, and how to lexically link the ideas together. The conversation below, which was written down in field notes and later checked by the participants for accuracy, exemplifies this negotiation. The order of cards that the group was working with was c, a, b, d (Tomomi was very satisfied with her life; Tomomi travelled around the world and saw many things; Tomomi lived in a nice house on a hill with a beautiful view of the ocean; Tomomi's dream was to travel)

> SA: Oh. This doesn't make sense. We start with the ending ...
> SB: Then her dream and her realising her dream are split up by her introduction ...
> SA: How does she get from here (pointing to a) to here (pointing to b) and back to here (pointing at d)?
> SD: The first two kind of make sense. We start out with Tomomi satisfied because she had travelled around the world. Maybe she is daydreaming? Or remembering?
> SA: Lying on the hill daydreaming about travelling? So she doesn't really travel?
> SC: So she daydreams about travelling and wakes up and realises she lives in a nice house on a hill ...
> SB: But then why is she satisfied at the beginning?
> SC: She's satisfied until she has her dream.
> SD: Is this a dream dream when she's sleeping? Or a daydream?

> SC: It must be a dream dream. If it's a daydream she already has the dream to travel. And if we want her to wake up with a new desire when before she was satisfied ...
>
> SD: Okay, so she's satisfied, then she has a dream dream, then she wakes up to realise that she is still in her house
>
> SB: Or *by* her house
>
> SD: By her house. And then she thinks that she really does have a daydream to travel.
>
> SA: How does it end then? With her being unsatisfied? Because she wants to travel?
>
> SD: Let's just write it down.

The excerpt above, particularly student A asking 'how does she get from here to here' shows that the writers are quite aware of the need to connect the thoughts in a way that would make the story make sense. Although it took a little time, groups had very little trouble making meaning out of the jumbled cards. They had less success, however, in writing out the story.

7.5.8. Groups Write Out the Story

To demonstrate to writers that it is much easier to make a story make sense in their own heads than to make a story make sense to a reader, the groups are next told to write out the complete story they have constructed out of the jumbled cards. Some groups are more successful than others. The story the group above eventually wrote was

> Tomomi was a girl who was very satisfied with her life. She lay on a hill smiling, chewing grass and thinking about how great her life is. Eventually, she fell asleep and started to dream. In her dream, she was travelling around the world and seeing many things. She woke up to realise that she wasn't travelling, but lying by her nice house on a hill, that had a beautiful view of the ocean. After that, Tomomi started to daydream a lot about travelling.

Although this story does somewhat leave the reader hanging with what could be considered a newly introduced problem right at the end, the group was successful in pulling the seemingly unorganised bits of information into a coherent story. When groups read each others' work (the next-to-last step in the story card suite of activities), the story above was criticised somewhat for not having a final evaluation; however, all readers agreed that the story was easy to read, despite the slight cliffhanger ending.

Some groups, however, while making perfect sense out of the story while they were *talking* about it, failed to produce coherent text. An example of this is a group who had randomly selected the same order as the group above. While they were talking, they discussed Tomomi becoming bored of lying around on beautiful hillsides, and so then going around the world to see things. She came back to her nice house for a while, but then started dreaming again. The story in their conversation made sense, but the text they produced (these were native speakers of English and PhD students) did not:

> Tomomi was very satisfied with her life, therefore she travelled around the world and saw many things (Chin & Teou, 2009). She lived in a nice house on a hill with a beautiful view of the ocean, but her dream was to travel (Chin & Teou, 2009).

It may have been that the writers were too tired, or perceived the task as too easy to be worth any effort in writing down the story. However, the gap between a writer's thoughts and the quality of the text s/he produces is something that cannot be ignored, unless we want to perpetuate bad writing by good scientists. Groups having perfectly good ideas while talking, but producing unacceptable text was not as unusual as I would have liked. It was after I was surprised at the low-quality text that I introduced the next step: critique of the stories. So that students could make use of the SPRE pattern in giving critiques, it is introduced to students before starting the next step.

7.5.9.   Groups Read and Critique Each Others' Stories

Next, the groups circulate, or exchange stories, and read each others' work. They evaluate the stories based on two simple criteria: (1) 'Is this a complete story?' and (2) 'Is this story easy to read?'.

There are two reasons for keeping the critique limited to these two questions. Firstly, the creativity of the group is not under fire: 'boring' stories like the one cited in Section 6 will be accepted as meeting the criteria put forth for the writing task. Secondly, students are also asked to say explicitly *why* the story might be incomplete, or difficult to read. Being able to give good critiques on others' work is an important part of improving one's own writing (Aitchison, 2009, 2010). However, as the students found out, it is much easier to criticise writing than to say exactly what needs to be done to fix it. By limiting to these two questions, the students can use the SPRE pattern to judge the completeness, and to some extent, the readability of others' work.

Although students often struggled with critiquing, and saying *why* a piece of writing is 'not quite right', statements about readability, explained in terms of the problem/solution pattern, could be heard during the critique time. The second story in Section 8 was criticised thus

> Hmmm ... there is something not so good .... I don't see how your problem connects logically to your situation .... You say, 'Tomomi was satisfied with her life, therefore she dreamed of travelling' ... this doesn't really work for me. And then you jump from her travelling to living in a nice house on a hill ... that's a crap story.

When faced with this criticism, the group explained, perfectly clearly, the story they had produced while talking about the jumbled cards. The fact that they had not clearly written what they had talked about became apparent to the group through the critique.

The other jumbled story (the first story in Section 8), which was quite well written, was nevertheless criticised for not having a 'proper ending':

> I really like how you connected the satisfied with life and the dream and then the living on a nice hill ... but then after she goes travelling, it just stops. There's not a proper ending. A ... what did Sarah call it?... an *evaluation* of her going off to travel.

One participant explicitly commented on how difficult he found judging even a very short story, but that doing so helped him with his own writing:

> It's really hard, you know ... saying what's wrong with that story. Harder than I thought it would be, actually. You know there's *something* but you can't say ... think what. I think though, after we've done this, I can see that my abstract is missing the S-factor. I don't have a 'situation'.

The final step is to have a general discussion.

7.5.10. *Introduce the SPRE Pattern, and Have a General Debrief (Whole-Group Discussion)*

After all the activities and lively discussions, we have a general whole-class debrief starting with the question 'what did you learn?' In one particularly pleasing exchange, a group of scientists who were on the course together,

and all had the same supervisor, discussed what their supervisor expected
from them:

> L: [Our supervisor] is always telling us, 'you have to write the
> story, you have to write the story'. Now I finally see what
> she means ... . She would love these story cards.
> Lo: but do you *have* to write it this way? I mean, what if
> I wanted to do it differently, like we did with the cards?
> C: She wouldn't let you do that.
> Lo: Yeah, but if it was written really well ...
> L: Why don't you ask her?

At this juncture, Lo emailed their supervisor asking whether or not a
non-conventional story structure would be acceptable. The reply, he
reported later, was

> ... as long as I don't have to read crap, I don't care what you
> do. If you give me a good story, you can write it any way you
> want. If your story is crap, then I'm going to tell you how to
> write it.

This exchange was, I thought, a nice snapshot of novice writers being
initiated into a discourse community.

The debriefing at the end also brought forth discussions of what different
discourse communities might call the different elements of the SPRE pattern.
For one participant, for example, the 'R' element would be changed to
'materials and methods'; another participant said she preferred 'context' as
opposed to 'situation'. This is, of course, exactly the kind of dialogue I had
hoped for: rather than seeing the SPRE pattern as a model to adhere to, most
of the time the participants saw the pattern (and the activities that preceded it)
as opportunities to think and talk about writing in their own contexts.

Particularly pleasing in the debrief sessions were some of the things
students said they had learned about writing. By going through this series of
exercises, from simple categorisation, to writing a simple story, to critiquing
the stories, it seems that they did indeed incorporate existing knowledge to
new thoughts and make connections. From the notes I took during the nine
debrief discussions, I was able to consolidate and summarise seven points
that were mentioned by students as being 'learned' or 'realised':

1. There is more than one way to categorise information that must be
   presented in a piece of scientific writing (this is true for categorising
   literature for a review, for working with data or for presenting information in a paper).

2. The usual rhetorical structure of scientific writing is similar to that of a fairy tale, and writers already know this structure.
3. Writers need to be aware of the structure they are imposing on a piece of writing (this is my paraphrase, not a quote from students); they need to make conscious choices, and be aware of *reasoning* behind the choices.
4. Deciding on an easily-followed order of information is only the first step; a writer must then explicitly tie the concepts together so that the reader can follow.
5. It is possible to present information in almost any order, but the responsibility lies with the writer to make the structure and meaning clear for the reader (and it will be more work for the writer to make unconventional structures readable).
6. *Thinking* about links and relationships between concepts, and making them make sense in your mind, is a lot easier than *writing* text that clearly reproduces these links.
7. It is easier to say that a piece of writing is 'not quite right' than it is to pinpoint what exactly is wrong with it, but being able to identify what exactly is wrong will not only help other writers but will also help oneself as well.

The students, for the most part, picked up on all the points I had hoped to make through working with the cards. It must be noted that the above are a consolidation notes taken from all group discussions. Not every group came up with every 'discovery', and none of the groups came up with all seven.

7.6. Evaluation

In accordance with the SPRE pattern, I will now evaluate the story card activities against the goals I had in mind when I started using them in the Writer Development courses. The two main goals of using the cards were to get writers thinking and talking about writing. As it is impossible to quantify the thinking that participants were doing, I will assume that the quality of the dialogue produced around the story cards is reflective of the thought processes going on in the participants. The data that is presented in the sections above are representative of discussions that have gone on every time I have presented the story cards. Writers have been unquestionably engaged in the discussions, talking about their own writing in their own contexts, coming up with ideas or reasons or connections or simply talking about scientific writing in general. It seems safe to conclude that the thinking/talking goals of the story cards were met quite well. The down side of participants talking so much is that the audio recordings I tried to collect were, except for the whole-group discussions, completely useless; there was such a din that any coherent conversations could not be distinguished.

The secondary goal of guiding the students to 'discoveries' about writing was somewhat successful. Although I did not keep records of which of the seven 'discoveries' listed above were discovered in which sessions, I do have records of each of the seven items being mentioned at least once by at least one of the nine groups. No group has produced all of them, and some groups produced only one of them (that they already tacitly knew the structure of a fairy tale). If this goal were to at some point take a higher priority, careful thought about how to present the materials would be necessary.

The final criterion for evaluating the activities is based on questionnaires given to participants at the end of the Writer Development course. The questionnaires had both Likert-type scale and open-ended questions. As the story card exercise was done as only one part of an entire course, the questionnaires contained items unrelated to this present study. The two questions that will be used from the questionnaire are the Likert-type scale question: 'How useful did you find the SPRE exercises with the story cards?' The possible responses were very useful, useful, neutral, not very useful, useless. Responses are shown in Table 7.1. The open-ended question that yielded data about the story cards was 'Was there anything in particular you liked about the course?' Responses are recorded in Table 7.2.

Given 48 responses of 'very useful', 35 responses of 'useful', only 2 neutral responses, and no negative responses at all, we can easily conclude that the students perceived the story card exercise to be useful. These responses do not reveal, however, what, specifically, students found the value of the exercise to be. Minimal insight into this was gained through the open-ended responses. Because the question that brought forth these data was about the course in general, it yielded only six responses that are explicitly about the story cards. I cannot claim, therefore, to have solid answers, but rather inklings that spark enough interest to warrant further investigation. As the data is manageable in-text, each response will be reproduced in full in Table 7.2, and the discussion will follow.

Although there is not enough data to claim any 'themes', three of the responses mention that the exercises were 'easy' but at the same time 'challenging', and that they led to a clearer understanding of how to

Table 7.1: The responses to the Likert-type scale question.

Very useful	Useful	Neutral	Not very useful	Useless
48	35	2	0	0

Table 7.2: Responses to open-ended question.

Response	Data (verbatim)
1	*Very good techniques for writing were presented. Especially I liked the way you used cards to introduce writing/SPRE/using stories. By using and making up easy stories, it was difficult but easier to understand how to write.*
2	*I liked the card activity, and I would like to practice it more in the class. I find it easy, but challenging and useful to help me understand what I [need] to do.*
3	*I found it [a] very enjoyable [course], where surprisingly (for me) I came away learning quite a bit that I know will help going forward. The card/story technique you used resulted in demonstrating clearly how to approach construction and why; the result was being that both explanation and understanding were simultaneously delivered — a big (and very clever) achievement.*
4	*I ... appreciate the easy exercise about the story line with which I always have troubles. They made some things so clear. I was able to get rid of the initial fear of actually starting and feel like I am ready to continue with the actual writing up of the story of my thesis. The importance of writing a story to understand and to make story of my thoughts ... has been a very valuable experience.*
5	*I loved the story cards. It made it so clear to me that even scientific writing has to be (can be!) a story. And it gave me a good idea how to make a good story from my work.*
6	*Your story cards are great. They seem really easy, but when you look at it closer, it's not that easy. You have to really get your brain into it and think. It makes me a little bit nervous about writing a whole thesis when I see a little story is so difficult ... but at the same time I have an idea of how to approach the thesis. At least I think I do.*

approach scientific writing — as a story. None of the participants mentioned anything about the story cards being a good starting point for talking about writing; the value that was seen by participants was the teaching/learning value rather than the dialogue value. This is not surprising: It was *my* goal to get them talking; they were on a course, and had come to *learn* something, to get something they could take home with them.

It was interesting to me that one participant observed that using the story cards meant that 'explanation and understanding were simultaneously delivered'. While I was pleased that he thought it was a 'very clever achievement' I wanted to point out to him that I actually had not 'explained' anything; it was he and his classmates who had discovered it.

It seems safe to say that the story card exercise is successful: they get people thinking; they get people talking; they lead students to discover some things about writing. There is, however, a lot more to find out.

7.7.   Further Study

If science can be seen as writing and rewriting stories (Grobstein, 2005, p. 6), this chapter is only a very beginning of a story. This simple evaluation of the story card activities is only a tentative first step. I had originally used the cards with undergraduate EFL learners in Japan (thus the Japanese characters in the story cards). I was somewhat dubious about using the cards with much more experienced, native or native-level English speakers, but decided to try them anyway as a medium for starting discussion. It became clear after the first time I used them that the participants enjoyed the activity, and got something out of it. It was then that I started taking notes. More notes will need to be taken, and more data collected, with more focused intent; this study has raised more interesting questions than it has answered — questions that call for a deeper look into what is going on with student writers when they use the story cards.

Firstly, I need to obtain more detailed information about *what* writers perceive the usefulness of the story cards to be. A specific open-ended question on the questionnaire followed up by interviews or group discussions could give a better idea of what writers find useful about the activities.

Secondly, a text analysis comparison of academic text (an abstract, perhaps) written before and after doing this activity would give us an idea of whether the usefulness perceived by writers translates into outcomes of higher quality text. Given that some of the student writers seemed to understand the necessity of linking ideas, and did so while discussing orally, but failed to do so when writing, we cannot assume that writers' understanding of the ideas we are trying to get across will necessarily be internalised enough to show up in text.

It would also be of use to study the difference between what writers *talk* about in step 7 (making sense of jumbled story cards) and the stories they *write* in step 8. Audio recordings of the groups as they negotiate the jumbled story cards could be compared to the stories that are produced. If there are consistent patterns across groups regarding where written stories break down, or if we are able to pinpoint where the gaps in the writing are (whereas there were no gaps in the dialogue), this could aid in further instruction.

Next, audio recording the writers as they critique each others' stories could give us an idea of how to help writers better critique each others' work, and can give us an idea of whether or not the SPRE pattern is a possible tool for improving critique as well as for improving reading and writing skills.

Finally, audio recordings could give us a better look at the dialogue that is being produced around the story cards. Are the cards just a starting point for talk in general? Or could they, if presented to a group whose members were of the same writing community, for example, actually bring to the foreground the rules of that community? If the rules were brought to the foreground, would the discussion then turn to how the rules could, or ought to be, be changed?

If we want higher education to move more towards inclusive and dialogic goals; if we want novice writers to not only adhere to but also to play with the rules of their particular genres; if we want students to use existing knowledge to make connections to new knowledge; if we want newer ways to mean and to be to come into existence ... then we need to promote reflective thinking, and we need ways into dialogue. The story cards presented in this chapter, as whimsical as they might appear, are a successful way into dialogue. According to the users of the cards, they are also enjoyable. Enjoyment in education, and especially in science writing—which can be a "daunting task" (Shah, Shah, & Peitrobon, 2009, p. 511)—is a good place to start.

References

Aitchison, C. (2009). Writing groups for doctoral education. *Studies in Higher Education, 34*(8), 905–916.

Aitchison, C. (2010). Learning together to publish: Writing group pedagogies for doctoral publishing. In C. Aitchison, A. Lee & B. Kamler (Eds.), *Publishing pedagogies for the doctorate and beyond.* London: Routledge.

Barrass, R. (2002). *Scientists must write: A guide to better writing for scientists, engineers and students.* London: RoutledgeFalmer.

Bazerman, C. (1988). *Shaping written knowledge: The genre and activity of the experimental article in science.* Madison, WI: University of Wisconsin Press.

Bazerman, C. (1999). Changing regularities of genre. *IEEE Transactions on Professional Communication, 42*(1), 1–2.

Bazerman, C., & Paradis, J. G. (1991). *Textual dynamics of the professions: Historical and contemporary studies of writing in professional communities.* Madison, WI: University of Wisconsin Press.

Berge, K. L. (1994). The diachrony of textual norms; or, why do genres change? A presentation of a theory illustrated by its relevance for the teaching of writing. *Changing English, 1*(1), 217–228. doi:10.1080/1358684940010116

Bhatia, V. (1993). *Analysing genre: Language use in professional settings*. London: Longman.

Brown, A. L., & Campione, J. (1994). Guided discovery in a community of learners. In K. McGilly (Ed.), *Classroom lessons: Integrating cognitive theory and classroom practice* (pp. 229–270). Cambridge, MA: MIT Press.

Chin, C., & Teou, L. (2009). Using concept cartoons in formative assessment: Scaffolding students' argumentation. *International Journal of Science Education*, *31*(10), 1307–1332.

Deane, P., Odendahl, N., Quinlan, T., Fowles, M., Welsh, C., & Bivens-Tatum, J. (2008). *Cognitive models of writing: Writing proficiency as a complex integrated skill*. ETS Research Report No. RR-08-55, ETS, Princeton, NJ.

Ding, H. (2008). The use of cognitive and social apprenticeship to teach a disciplinary genre: Initiation of graduate students into NIH grant writing. *Written Communication*, *25*(1), 3–52.

Discovery Learning (Bruner). (n.d.). Retrieved from http://www.learning-theories. com/discovery-learning-bruner.html

Edge, J. (1985). Do TEFL articles solve problems? *ELT Journal*, *39*(3), 153–157.

Edge, J. (1989). Ablocutionary value: On the application of language teaching to linguistics1. *Applied Linguistics*, *10*(4), 407 417.

Edge, J. (2011). In search of the hybrid: Discourse analysis, TESOL methodology and cultural politics. *BAAL language learning and teaching SIG conference*, Aston University, Birmingham, UK.

Edge, J., & Wharton, S. (2001). Patterns of text in teacher education. In M. Scott & G. Thompson (Eds.), *The patterns of text* (pp. 255–286). Amsterdam: John Benjamins.

Florence, M. K., & Yore, L. D. (2004). Learning to write like a scientist: Coauthoring as an enculturation task. *Journal of Research in Science Teaching*, *41*(6), 637–668.

Flowerdew, L. (2000). Using a genre-based framework to teach organizational structure in academic writing. *ELT Journal*, *54*(4), 369–378.

Galán, A. D., & Pérez, M. C. F. (2003). *The problem-solution pattern: A tool for the teaching of writing?* Barcelona: Les Publications de la Universitat de Barcelona.

Gregson, R. (2005). *Improving student writing in science: A help or hindrance*. Association for Active Educational Researchers. 2005 conference proceedings. http://www.aare.edu.au/05pap/abs05.htm#G

Greitzer, F. L., Rice, D. M., Eaton, S. L., & Perkins, M. C. (2005). Learning to pull the thread: Application of guided discovery principles to the inquiry process. In *Interservice/industry training, simulation, and education conference (I/ITSEC)*, November 28–December 1, 2005, 11pp. National Training Systems Association (NTSA), Arlington, VA.

Grimes, J. E. (1972). *The thread of discourse*. Technical Report no. 1. National Science Foundation, Washington, DC.

Grimes, J. E. (1975). *The thread of discourse*. The Hague, Netherlands: Mouton De Gruyter.

Grobstein, P. (2005). Revisiting science in culture: Science as story telling and story revising. *Journal of Research Practice*, *1*(1)Article-M1.

Gross, A., & Harmon, J. E. (1999). What's right about scientific writing. *The Scientist, 13*(24), 6.

Gross, A. G., Harmon, J. E., & Reidy, M. S. (2002). *Communicating science: The scientific article from the 17th century to the present.* Oxford, UK: Oxford University Press.

Halliday, M. A. K., & Martin, J. R. (1993). *Writing science: Literacy and discursive power.* Washington, DC: The Falmer Press.

Hand, B., Lawrence, C., & Yore, L. D. (1999). A writing in science framework designed to enhance science literacy. *International Journal of Science Education, 21*(10), 1021–1035.

Hand, B., Wallace, C. W., & Yang, E. M. (2004). Using a science writing heuristic to enhance learning outcomes from laboratory activities in seventh-grade science: Quantitative and qualitative aspects. *International Journal of Science Education, 26*(2), 131–149.

Hoey, M. (1994). Signalling in discourse. In M. Coulthard (Ed.), *Advances in written text analysis* (pp. 26–45). London: Routledge.

Hughes, G. (2008). Text organisation features in an FCE reading gapped sentence task. *Cambridge ESOL: Research Notes, 31*, 26–31.

Kelly, G. J., Chen, C., & Prothero, W. (2000). The epistemological framing of a discipline: Writing science in university oceanography. *Journal of Research in Science Teaching, 37*(7), 691–718.

Kostouli, T. (2009). A sociocultural framework: Writing as social practice. In R. Beard, D. Myhill, J. Riley & M. Nystrand (Eds.), *The handbook of writing development* (pp. 98–116). Sage.

Lillis, T. (2003). Student writing as 'academic literacies': Drawing on Bakhtin to move from critique to design. *Language and Education, 17*(3), 192–207.

Pereyra, A. P., Espinosa, B. A., & Tossi, C. (2011). Exploring patterns: How to teach when the signals seem to be missing. *The Especialist, 29*(2), 205–231.

Poock, T. J., Greenbowe, T. J., Burke, K. A., & Hand, B. M. (2007). Using the science writing heuristic in the general chemistry laboratory to improve students' academic performance. *Journal of Chemical Education, 84*(8), 1371.

Proctor, M. (1996). What marks language as discourse — From prose to poetry. In *Solving language problems: From general to applied linguistics* (pp. 132–168). Exeter, Devon, UK: University of Exeter Press.

Ritchie, S. M., Tomas, L., & Tones, M. (2011). Writing stories to enhance scientific literacy. *International Journal of Science Education, 33*(5), 685–707.

Ruyle, K., & Jacobsen, P. (2003, February 3). Guided discovery teaching methods and reusable learning objects. *The ELearning Developers Journal,* 1–10.

Sadler, T. D. (2009). Situated learning in science education: Socio-scientific issues as contexts for practice. *Studies in Science Education, 45*(1), 1–42. doi:10.1080/03057260802681839

Scientific Reports. (n.d.). *Scientific reports.* Retrieved from http://writingcenter.unc.edu/resources/handouts-

Scott, M., & Thompson, G. (2001). *Patterns of text in honour of Michael Hoey.* Amsterdam: John Benjamins Publishing Co.

Shah, J., Shah, A., & Pietrobon, R. (2009). Scientific writing of novice researchers: What difficulties and encouragements do they encounter? *Academic Medicine, 84*(4), 511.

Smith, M., Desimone, M., Zeidner, L., Dunn, C., Bhatt, M., & Rumyantseva, L. (2007). Inquiry-oriented instruction in science: Who teaches that way? *Educational Evaluation and Policy Analysis, 29*(3), 169–199. doi:10.3102/0162373707306025

So, B. P. C. (2005a). From analysis to pedagogic applications: Using newspaper genres to write school genres. *Journal of English for Academic Purposes, 4*(1), 67–82.

Surlekar, S. (1998). Teaching biochemistry in a "guided discovery curriculum". *Biochemical Education, 26*(3), 218–222.

Taavitsainen, I. (2001). Changing conventions of writing: The dynamics of genres, text types, and text traditions. *European Journal of English Studies, 5*(2), 139–150.

Tomas, L. (2011). Merging fact with fiction: Developing students' scientific literacy through story writing on a socioscientific issue. *Curriculum Leadership, 9*(5).

Trask, R. L. (1999). *Key concepts in language and linguistics.* Psychology Press.

Wharton, S. M. (1999). *From postgraduate student to published writer: Discourse variation and development in TESOL.* Unpublished PhD thesis, Aston University, Birmingham, UK.

Wingate, U. (2006). Doing away with 'study skills'. *Teaching in Higher Education, 11*(4), 457–469.

Wingate, U., Andon, N., & Cogo, A. (2011). Embedding academic writing instruction into subject teaching: A case study. *Active Learning in Higher Education, 12*(1), 69–81. doi:10.1177/1469787410387814

Winter, E. O. (1976). *Fundamentals of information structure: Pilot manual for further development according to student need.* Unpublished manual, Hatfield Polytechnic.

Yore, L. D., Florence, M. K., Pearson, T. W., & Weaver, A. J. (2006). Written discourse in scientific communities: A conversation with two scientists about their views of science, use of language, role of writing in doing science, and compatibility between their epistemic views and language. *International Journal of Science Education, 28*(2-3), 109–141.

Yore, L. D., Hand, B. M., & Florence, M. K. (2004). Scientists' views of science, models of writing, and science writing practices. *Journal of Research in Science Teaching, 41*(4), 338–369.

Young, R. E., Becker, A. L., & Pike, K. L. (1970). *Rhetoric: Discovery and change.* New York, NY: Harcourt, Brace & World.

Chapter 8

Writing Differently in Art and Design: Innovative Approaches to Writing Tasks

Erik Borg

Writing in art[1] and design education is different from writing in most other areas of university education. Art and design have their own forms of meaning-making, expressed through their creations. Writing is usually subsidiary to the creative output, supporting it but frequently to its side rather than central to the process. There are historical reasons for a role of writing in art and design education, and writing in art and design can contribute significantly to learning in these fields. However, writing differently draws on the strengths of art and design. The methods that teachers and students have developed to encourage writing when students have chosen to express themselves in other ways — and often have chosen against writing — may offer suggestions for writing in other areas.

8.1. Introduction

Paraphrasing Brian Eno, art and artists operate as a cultural observatory, projecting future developments and enacting them within society

---

1. Throughout this chapter, *art* refers to an area of study sometimes called Fine Art Practice, which involves the creation of artefacts or experiences set in the context of art, rather than, for example the study of the history of art.

Writing in the Disciplines: Building Supportive Cultures for Student Writing in UK Higher Education
ISBN: 978-1-78052-546-4

(Graham-Dixon, 2005). Their sensitivity to cultural changes allows them to intuit shifts that later are embraced by the wider society, and to critique current practices. One result of this is that writing in art and design education is frequently more innovative than writing in other disciplines. For example, the advent of writing on computers and the easy ability to integrate graphic elements with text has changed the nature of writing in almost every area. Images, graphic representations of data and new forms of page design are now part of 'written texts' in most disciplines, and writing is widely understood to be a multimodal activity (Bezemer & Kress, 2008; Kress, 2003). Nevertheless, writing in art and design has moved forward faster than writing in other areas in integrating multimodal content into written texts, as well as developing innovative approaches to writing for assessment purposes. Another area of innovation is intertextuality, in which art and design have developed approaches that allow for new configurations of meaning-making while respecting intellectual property rights as these are understood at universities.

Art and design are practical fields that produce artefacts or outcomes that are based on practice. They can be compared with other practical disciplines that are now taught at university such as nursing. As in art and design and many other new or emergent areas, conflicts arise because of the demands of academic study that are quite different from those of traditional experiential learning, conflicts that must be mediated in the written texts submitted for university assessment (Baynham, 2000). In nursing, the critical output is appropriate nursing care, which writing underpins and structures with evidence. Nurses must read and interpret evidence (as well as use writing for records and instruction), but unless nurses move into education, writing itself is secondary. However, because the evidence for best practice is communicated through writing, writing has an important role in nursing education. In contrast, the best evidence for a successful creative work or design is the work itself, not its interpretation through words. Nevertheless, writing has an important role in art and design education: it facilitates reflection and it can provide a context or, in the case of a design brief, the starting point for creative work. However, writing is substantially more ancillary to the process of art and design education than in most other fields of study.

This chapter will discuss the historical development of the role of writing in art and design education. It will then discuss some of the ways that writing is used for learning and for assessment in these fields, and some of the innovative practices that are used in art and design education.

8.2.   Theory and Writing in Art and Design Education

As described in Borg (2007), art education and design education followed very different trajectories, but in neither field was writing a crucial element.

Before the Renaissance (and, in most cases, long after), learning how to make art required an apprenticeship to an artist, during which the apprentice learned the materials and practices of art making. Beginning in the 17th century, art education might also include studying in a school, but the focus of this education was drawing, perspective and the absorption of the vision of masters. Only in the 20th century did the pattern of art education begin to change, and only late in the century did writing become a significant component of this education. On the other hand, design as a separate practice is largely an outgrowth of 18th- and 19th-century industrialisation. With the recognition that there was a need to improve the quality of industrial design, an institution for design education was established as the first form of publicly supported education in Britain. Initially patterned on art education, it too did not include writing until late in the 20th century.

Formal education in art and design had dual goals: it was not only intended to improve practice but also to raise the status of artists and designers from the level of craftworkers to that of those in society who worked with theories and ideas, particularly natural science which had gradually separated itself from alchemy (Gieryn, 1983). The inclusion of writing in the 20th century as part of artists' education continued this process.

Artists in Western societies were educated through apprenticeships until the later part of the Renaissance, and the art historian Ernst Gombrich compares the status of artists before Giotto with that of 'a good cabinet-maker or tailor' (Gombrich, 1995, p. 202), as being a person of purely local renown. Artists were craftworkers, respected in their society for their skill but not honoured. They trained and worked through guilds, which also qualified them as masters in their field, capable of teaching apprentices as well as fulfilling the expectations of an artist. During the Renaissance, however, this began to change. According to Nikolaus Pevsner, in his ground-breaking social history of art education,

> humanists ... began to praise individual works of art and individual artists to an extent incompatible with the medieval tradition of paint and sculpture as crafts in no way above others ... . Thus, already during the Quattrocento, *the bonds which held the artist in his class were loosened here and there.*
> (emphasis added; Pevsner, 1940/1967, p. 32)

As artists studied classical sources, they recognised that they provided a theoretical grounding, and that these theories could enhance their social status. Both Leonardo da Vinci (1452–1519) and Michelangelo Buonarroti (1475–1564), like other artists of their time, were apprenticed and trained in artists' workshops, where they received training in the crafts and skills of an artist, which Gombrich summarised as foundry-work for sculpture, life drawing and perspective, and the use of colours. However, as artists studied classical texts and theories, and their status increased in the artistic ferment of Renaissance Florence and Rome, some began to call for artists to receive education in theory as well as craft skills. Gombrich and Pevsner argue that both Leonardo and Michelangelo were committed to the creation of schools for artists in which students would learn theory as well as the practical skills of an artist.

The first of these schools, the *Accademia del Disegno*, was founded in 1562 by Georgio Vasari under the sponsorship of Cosimo di Medici. Vasari's plan was

> to do away entirely with the medieval system of guilds for artists. An artist, [Vasari] felt, should not be in a dependent position, in the same way as a common craftsman. To make him a member of an academy instead would demonstrate that his social rank was just as high as that of a scientist or another scholar. (Pevsner, 1940/1967, p. 54)

The Accademia was followed by academies in France and Britain, sponsored by the monarch and serving to enhance the prestige of the nations by contributing to the development of great artists. In these academies, young artists learned how to draw, first by copying drawings, then by sketching plaster copies of classical sculpture and finally drawing from life models. (In France, the academy had a monopoly on life drawing.) Students also learned geometry, perspective and anatomy. The programme of study taught the artist not simply how to accurately represent the world, but how to create an ideal, a vision of 'nature corrected' (Goldstein, 1996) which was essentially an idealisation of nature. The education of artists in this manner continued through the 19th century and was a major component of art schools into the 20th century.

Beginning in the 17th and 18th centuries, industrialisation and the mass manufacture of goods led to decreased opportunities for skilled craftworkers and a perceived lowering of standards of design. In Britain, the first publicly funded educational institution (Bird, 2000), the Normal School of Design, was established in 1837 to improve the quality of design. This school, and others founded subsequently followed the pattern of art education, with a focus on conveying the vision of nature improved through training in drawing, perspective, geometry and anatomy. Students were not trained in industrial processes, and as a result, manufacturers tended not to hire them, limiting the success of design education. The Arts and Crafts movement in the latter part of the century, led by William Morris, reinvigorated design through a rediscovery of 'the organic inter-relation between material, working process, purpose and aesthetic form' (Pevsner, 1940/1967, p. 259).

The Arts and Crafts movement in turn inspired the founders of the Bauhaus in the period after the First World War. They established a school to educate artists that approached art analytically. Students learned the elements that comprised a work of art: point, line, geometric shape and the spectrum. In addition, they received practical training in handling materials (e.g. stone, wood, metal, glass and pigment), as well as classes in geometry, art history, science and design. This programme of art education was widely influential, teaching as it did a modernist approach to art creation that replaced the goal of teaching artists how to idealise nature.

In the period after the Second World War, art education in Britain moved from independent art schools supported by local councils into the polytechnics, which in 1992 were granted university status. The change in the site of art education was accompanied by two changes that transformed the nature of this education. Over the course of the 20th century, there was a shift towards art practices being increasingly driven by explicit theory, rather than the implicit theory of representation and improvement in nature. While at the beginning of the century, artists issued explicit theoretical manifestos (e.g. Futurism), later critics and philosophers filled this role. Arthur Danto described the new role for theory in art: 'To see something as art requires something the eye cannot descry — an atmosphere of artistic theory, a knowledge of the history of art: an artworld' (Danto, 1964, p. 580). This shift towards theory-laden artwork meant that literacy was increasingly central to art education and artists. The art critic, Harold Rosenberg, pointed out that 'only one of ten leading artists of the generation of Pollock [1912–1956] and de Kooning [1904–1997] had a degree' while the majority of artists shown in the exhibition 'Young America 1965' had undergraduate degrees (Rosenberg, 1972, p. 39, artists' dates added).

The other change was the creation of a qualification for art and design students, the Diploma in Art and Design (DipAD), that would be equivalent to a BA degree and would be awarded by art schools. Evans and Le Grice (2001) describe the implications of the previous practical training in fine arts or design:

> In Britain, an education as an engineer and in other fields of practical or applied knowledge had a lower status than an education in the theoretical, historical and philosophical subjects of the university. This powerful and class-based division in education only reflected the lower status of these professions in Britain. (p. 106)

A committee under the Ministry of Education, the National Advisory Committee on Art Education (NACAE), was formed to look at the state of art education. Known as the Coldstream committee after its chairman,

William Coldstream, it recommended the creation of the DipAD. Pevsner had a prominent role in the committee, and used his study of art education to argue for changes that would improve the status of artists and designers. As set out in the committee's report, 'the aim [of the Diploma in Art and Design] should be to produce courses conceived as a liberal education in art' (Ministry of Education, 1960, p. 4). In order to do this, the committee included as one of their recommendations that students study both art history and contextual studies, and that these should be assessed and comprise about fifteen per cent of the total course. In a subsequent report by the NACAE, Pevsner argued that the reservation of fifteen per cent in the art and design curriculum for contextual studies was 'a dire necessity. It is clarity of thought and expression, it is unbiased recognition of problems, it is the capacity for discussion and it is ultimately understanding they must achieve' (Department of Education and Science, 1970).

This recommendation was accepted and contextual studies became a required component of the DipAD. The DipAD did not continue but was transformed into an honours degree in 1974, but, as art schools were assimilated into polytechnics, this element, which required a grounding in theory and written texts, continued. In 1992, the polytechnics became universities, and today most post-secondary art education is carried on in universities, rather than in specialist art schools. The shift in the site of art education inevitably changed the nature of art education. Describing the changes brought on by formalising art education within a structure equivalent to a first degree, Firth and Horn wrote (1987, p. 42), 'Coldstream [the NACAE] represented an academic takeover of an education previously based on more intangible qualities. Romantic ideology came up against a new bureaucratic barrier'. Art education took on many of the characteristics of university education in other areas — universities favour commensurability across the qualifications that they issue — and, in a survey of art education universities in Britain, written communication skills were required by the overwhelming majority of universities that taught art (Brind, 2004).

Christopher Frayling, the Rector of the Royal College of Art, used a distinction first proposed by Herbert Read between teaching *to* art and teaching *through* art. Teaching to art meant teaching the skills and attitudes of how to become an artist, while teaching through art meant teaching an adaptive frame of mind through the practice of art: skills such as 'problem-solving, resourcefulness, independence of mind, flexible thinking, preparation for an unpredictable world' (Frayling, 2004, p. 39). Read, Frayling wrote, felt both were necessary, but that achieving the balance was difficult. Pevsner, for example, believed in what might now be called transferable skills that 'the purpose [of writing] is to make the student think and argue on a subject in which his interest has been roused and which is not art ...' (Harries, 2011, p. 618). Finding the appropriate balance between art and design practice on the one hand and the ability to articulate and argue ideas orally and in writing on the other is a continuing issue in art education, one which Frayling said 'makes the subject-area almost uniquely divided against itself' (Frayling, 2004, p. 40).

A number of art theorists have spoken out against 'linguistic imperialism', the idea that 'without a written commentary and analysis, the work that we do as artists cannot be accessed, given academic weight or properly evaluated' (Thompson, 2005, p. 224). Writers holding this position argue that art practice provides a meaningful, mature mode of expression that can be recognised by practitioners, and a text is not necessary to explain the work. Currently, arguments about the need for writing in art education centre on the practice-based PhD in art and design, in which a candidate submits both a body of work and a text that contextualises it. Discussing this, Candlin (2000) argues forcefully that the requirement for a written text privileges theory over the artwork, and that the requirement misunderstands writing. In a passage that most writing instructors would agree with, she argues that, like art, writing is a practice, one which is embedded in particular contexts. Those who require a text to explain art perceive writing 'as so naturalised that it is not recognised as having a form. Nevertheless, there is a particular style to academic writing .... In a similar way to studying oil painting or drawing, academic writing has to be learnt and practised' (Candlin, 2000, p. 99). For reasons similar to those put forward by Candlin and Thompson, while undergraduate art education almost always includes a requirement for a written component, in some master's courses there may be no required written text (Hockey, 1999).

This survey of the inclusion of a written element in art and design education suggests that, from the time of the Renaissance to recent developments, theory and writing were included at least in part to elevate the status of artists, and that there are theoretically grounded arguments for not requiring writing as part of art education. Art and design students, while not necessarily having a developed critique of the requirement for writing, often resist it. Many identify themselves with their creative practice and see writing in opposition to that practice. They find it constraining and difficult; it is a 'secondary activity, which at best takes time away from making and at worst is painful in itself' (Hockey, 1999, p. 41). Interviewed about her writing, one PhD candidate in fine art practice I spoke with said

> I've been thinking I'm not good at expressing myself in words, that's why I chose art, and I wonder sometimes, 'Why am I doing, doing this?' to write up, you know, a big chunk of essay to get the PhD. I like painting, I like painting, that's what I've been trained for, I don't know, it's more natural doing my practice than reading and writing, umm ...

Many students and art tutors resist writing and worry that it may displace their practice. One result of this conflict between writing and practice is the development of innovative approaches to writing tasks. The resistance to writing that art and design students often feel is replicated in other disciplines, and the innovations that lecturers in the subject area have developed may well be valuable to lecturers using writing in other areas.

8.3.   Writing Tasks in Art and Design

8.3.1.   Writing Different Genres

Though a recent study of writing at university (Nesi & Gardner, 2006) identified up to 22 different types of academic writing, coursework assignments tend to be dominated by 'the essay'. However, in some disciplines, particularly emergent or practical disciplines, there is greater variation than in disciplines that have a longer history of university study. Art and design are among the disciplines in which students create a wide range of types of text or genres. *Genre* identifies the purposes (or ostensible purposes) of texts, and, from that, suggests their structure and goals. Although Nesi and Gardner identified a large number of genres, the number can be reduced to a set of 'elemental' or basic genres (Coffin, Donohue, & North, 2009, p. 273):

- personal recount
- narrative
- taxonomic report (classifying and describing phenomena)
- procedure
- explanation
- discussion or argument.

As Coffin, Donohue and North note, precise classification of a text requires finer discrimination such as that done by Nesi and Gardner (2006). In contexts in which texts are important such as academia, genres are increasingly specialised and are frequently combined in more complex texts. However, for the purposes of this chapter, the broad categories can be informative. The essay falls in the category of discussion or argument and is characterised by a thesis or position and arguments for and against an issue. It depends on an array of evidence, and is usually supported by references and a bibliography. Art and design students frequently find essay writing challenging; Swift argues that 'the conventional, academic essay form, which appears to encourage simplification and authoritativeness can be seen as part of a hierarchical education system set up to disempower rather than empower students' (1999, p. 282).

Instead of setting tasks in the discussion genre, lecturers in art and design frequently choose other genres, such as the personal recount (reflective writing), taxonomic reports (classification and description) and procedures (the stages of a process). Reflective writing is extremely important and will be treated separately, but both the taxonomic report and the procedure offer significant advantages for students writing in art and design. Many students find them easier to write than discussion texts, as they can be based on students' experience rather than on the synthesis of others' research, and they allow students to create multimodal texts using images and drawings as well as words. Texts in these genres are often structured chronologically or by the steps of the procedure, so organising the paper is simpler than the discussion genre. They can also be directly related to students' professional practice, leading to greater engagement with the writing task. For example, at one institution second-year students in fashion design were asked to choose a clothing store and document its layout and allocation of space in relation to stock and target customers. The essence of the task was a taxonomic report, in which students had to analyse customers, merchandise, store, and implicitly its competition. This complex analytic task, though, was arranged so that students had to pay close attention to the design of the store in order to make sketches and layout plans, as well as to think through the marketing of the clothing that the store stocked. The combination of multimodal presentation and descriptive writing facilitated the development of the students' analytic skills far better than essay assignments that try to instil analytic skills more directly. Writing in the genre of procedures can involve students explaining the steps of a craft or skill, or other staged process. In describing procedures, often procedures that they are quite familiar with, students have to analyse and make explicit tacit knowledge. Through tasks such as these, students' writing ability is improved along with their transferable skills.

8.3.2. *Reflective Writing*

Reflective writing, which is part of the elemental genre of personal recount, is one of the most important types of writing that art and design students engage in. Many applied subjects such as nursing use reflective writing to encourage students to be self-critical and self-aware. It is a particularly well-theorised area. Donald Schön, who wrote one of the seminal books in the area (Schön, 1983), identified the importance of reflection *in* and *on* action as a response to the positivist tradition that dominated universities from the late 19th century. He sought to revalue the ability of practitioners to act and to reflect on tacit knowledge, arguing that 'practitioners may become reflective researchers in situations of uncertainty, instability, uniqueness, and conflict ... Here the exchange between research and practice is immediate, and reflection-in-action is its own implementation' (Schön, 1983, pp. 308–309). This is strikingly similar to Frayling's characterisation of the skills gained through the practice of art. Schön's thinking underpins many of the writing assignments in art and design, as dealing with uncertainty, instability, uniqueness and conflict are both characteristic of artistic creation and outcomes that modern art frequently tries to encompass.

In their approach to reflective writing, art and design differ from many other practical or applied disciplines, such as nursing. In other disciplines, reflective writing tasks are often highly structured, using frameworks such as Gibb's reflective cycle (Gibbs, 1988). Because art and design often try to generate instability, they draw on more playful approaches to reflective writing. Reflective texts in art and design need to be open to the variety of experiences, visual and verbal, that may influence students, and this would not be enhanced by a highly structured form. One area that tutors and writing instructors in art and design draw on is writing development, adapting strategies that are used to overcome writer's block and other inhibitions to writing. As noted by Candlin (2000), writing is a practice, one that is different from artistic practices but with which *as a process* it shares similarities. Some of the methods used to engage students with writing tasks are derived from writing studies, while others advance from these ideas, often by using materials other than pen and paper or computer. All are intended to encourage reflection and writing in stages.

An art student spoke for many student writers when she realised 'Oh I can do bits?! – Oh I can do that' (quoted in Francis, 2009, p. 29). In order to encourage students to write more fluently, writing instructors encourage students to write frequently, but in smaller amounts, and to keep a notebook in which to write ideas and insights. Notebooks and journals can be written in a more informal style than is normal in academic writing, which reduces students' apprehension and delay. Once ideas have been committed to paper, they can be polished to make them conform to a more formal academic style. In order to reduce the marking load and to improve the quality of the work, tutors can get students to summarise their thinking or to use the journal as a data source for a commentary on the process of creation.

Journals encourage reflection; in fact, in some cases students do not need to be required to keep a journal. Medway (2002) described how architecture students kept sketchbooks that were not read by lecturers or even by other students, except in glimpses over the shoulder. When Medway looked at some of these sketchbooks, he realised that they contributed not simply to the process of learning the knowledge of an architect but also to the process of self-identification as an architect. The development of a disciplinary identity is one of the goals of assignment writing in every discipline. Tutors in art and design often require students to keep sketchbooks, notebooks or journals in order to foster their identification as artists and designers.

I observed art students at master's level who were required to keep a journal, which formed the basis for discussions with their tutor (Borg, 2004). In the journal, students kept a record of literacy events (readings and thoughts on readings, seminar and tutorial discussions), as well as reactions to artworks. The goal laid out for the course and carried forward through the journal was 'profound self-reflection [that] can be matched to the expanded field of methodological, critical and theoretical options' available in fine arts practice. The journal and discussions with the tutor surrounding the entries contributed to the student's final paper, required for the contextual practice element of the course. For the students I observed, the journal was maintained as a computer file that was printed out and kept in a loose-leaf notebook. In the journal, besides text there were sketches and doodles that were added to the printed page, as well as notes by the tutor and written comments by the student. On the pages of the journal, I could trace a multi-sided discussion between tutor, student and her reading and observation. This ongoing conversation, which she referred back to throughout the course, fed directly into her final paper, as well as facilitating a high level of self-reflection about her artistic practice.

Francis (2009) suggests an alternative way of organising the journal to foster a reflective dialogue. Because students value aesthetic qualities, the form of the journal is important, and students may prefer an attractive book that allows them to combine sketches and text immediately, rather than adding them to computer printouts. Medway (2002) noted that the sketch-books kept by the architectural students were similar: black, with small neat writing. If students use a handwritten notebook to keep their journal, Francis suggests that they might write current reflections only on the left- or right-hand page, while saving the opposite page for later annotation and rethinking. Francis calls this a double-entry journal and points out the opportunity provided by this arrangement for writers to reread and reflect on their earlier thoughts. She also suggests that, if the journal is to be assessed, it may be better (and more practical) for tutors to get students to summarise what they have written, which also encourages both analysis and reflection.

In the MA course mentioned above (Borg, 2004), students were required to submit a 5000-word essay that complemented their final exhibition. The aim of the essay was

> to transform [students'] intellectual deliberations (a set of ideas of unique personal interest) into a fully referenced and well-argued essay ... [By writing this essay,] an opportunity is thus created for the articulation of ideas that do not easily find expression in the process of producing and exhibiting artworks.

In other words, students were being asked to shift genres, to move from the elemental genre of personal recount to that of discussion or argument. The criteria for the visual work that the students made were creativity, inventiveness and originality. These ambitions influenced the choice of topics for the essay. Because the topic was to be 'a set of ideas of unique personal interest', the range of areas addressed varied widely, from an autoethnography of a personal journey from Japan to Britain that referenced Courbet and Hokusai and the ideas of Gaston Bachelard, to dream writing, and *Alice in Wonderland*.

For other courses and programmes, the approach to the final essay or dissertation may be quite different, but the issues that tutors try to address through the written texts are often similar: to establish through writing a relationship between students' practice and their values and interests. One example from the WritingPAD website (Lydiat, 2004) described the aims of the dissertation for students:

- write their own experiences
- to be personally reflexive, reflecting upon the ways in which their own values, experiences, interests, beliefs, political commitments and wider aims in life and social identities have shaped their research
- to be aware of other knowledges and to understand and evaluate their own place within those knowledges both practically and theoretically.

The movement from the genre of personal recount to the genre of discussion is also a movement from reflective writing to the more academically familiar genre of the essay, even if, in this context, it includes distinctive features. In the programme that Lydiat describes, students begin writing about their personal experiences, reflecting on these, and move to the genre of discussion, in which ideas are evidenced, acknowledged and evaluated. One element of the movement towards the more conventional essay form is the use of evidence and the acknowledgment of that evidence (citation and referencing), though this may take forms that are unfamiliar in other parts of the university. Turner and Hocking describe the use of collage in student writing, citing Lucy Lippard's view that 'collage is the prevalent aesthetic of feminism' (2004, p. 155). They note that students are encouraged to draw on contemporary critical theory. Students in the programme they discuss build on their interests and subjectivities, which may result in writing that uses collage or sampling. This approach to intertextuality tries to build on students' independence and originality while encouraging them to explicitly acknowledge sources.

In addition to the reflective journal, art and design students are frequently asked to write personal statements. Artist's statements are part of artists' practice, the text with which artists contextualise (or refuse to contextualise) an exhibition or presentation of their work. In exhibitions, these texts stand alongside the art creation, in some cases guiding the gallery goer to an understanding of the creation, in other cases perhaps misdirecting her and in others refusing to say more than the artist's name and the date of the work. Writing a personal statement forces the art or design student to reflect on their work and consider how they wish to position it. Students often find this difficult, a moment in which they have to put themselves forward, rather than letting their practice speak for them, and in student exhibitions it is common for the personal statement that accompanies the work to have only a minimum of information. As an assessed piece, though, students can be asked to locate their work, not historically, as though they were only the sum of previous artists' work that they had seen, but rather intellectually.

Artists' statements may also do more than guide viewers in understanding the artefact. Although less fashionable now, artists' statements have expressed political views or views about art. *The Futurist Manifesto* (Flint, 1972) from the early 20th century is a particularly vivid example of this, while at other times artworks have required insight into the theoretical underpinnings of the creation in order to interpret them (Danto, 1964). Finally, some artists have subverted both the text and the viewing experience in museum practice, in which viewers experience of the explanatory texts recontextualise objects that are already included in museums, or they smuggle their own objects into the museum, along with texts that reframe the experience of museum going (Dorsett, 2007).

8.3.3. *Expressive Approaches to Writing*

Art and design frequently use innovative ways to present texts, ways in which texts are combined with artefacts so that the unified creative object works synergistically. Many tutors encourage students to create visual essays that bring together in different ways texts and objects. Swift (1999) found herself teaching fine art in context to a group of second-year mature art students. She replaced the requirement for a conventional essay with a visual essay that would combine words and objects to illuminate their practices. Among the aims of the visual essay were

- To integrate and relate the processes of making and writing
- To create an awareness of theoretical structures and their relevance to making/writing/thinking
- To become aware of personal working/thinking patterns (Swift, 1999, p. 283)

Swift encouraged students to find expressive forms for their writing. One student took a block of wood, roughly the shape of a railroad tie 80 cm long.

She sawed the wood part way along its length and slipped the pages of her text in the slits. Initially the text printed on acetate could be moved within the slits, suggesting the freeing of words locked in. As the green wood dried and shrank, the text became trapped, a metaphor for writer's block.

The WritingPAD website (Writing Purposefully in Art and Design; http://www.writing-pad.ac.uk) has examples of delightful responses to writing tasks that call for an integration of words and artefacts. These responses are intended to be singular; they are individual answers to a common task, though one that may be expressed in different ways, a task that asks students 'to integrate and relate the processes of making and writing'. For a dissertation at York St. John's University, Alexandra Hutchinson wrote her paper, and, to relieve stress, as she wrote, she folded the printouts into the shape of small stars, which she used to fill a jar. A note she put on the jar asked, 'I am worried the structure is too fragmentary. Do you think there's time to change it ...?'

One approach to getting students to write, whatever their discipline, is to get them to put ideas down on paper and then to rearrange them into a structure that is communicative and appropriate for the audience. The cut and paste facility of word processors has made this easier for writers who write with some assurance and who recognise the problem in their text. Students, however, often 'begin at the beginning, go on to the end', and hand in the assignment when they have reached the word limit. Francis (2009) reminds us that writing is a physical process, one that relatively recently migrated from materials such as baked clay, papyrus, bark and parchment to manufactured paper. She suggests a variety of techniques to encourage art and design students to write in small, manageable increments. Postcards, scraps of paper, fabric and package labels can all be used as writing surfaces. A few words written with charcoal on a scrap from a drawing pad may have more meaning for a student than a neater note. These bits of writing have an advantage over an outline on a full sheet of paper of being able to be moved around freely, so that thoughts can be put in new arrangements, and students can see the contingency of writing in the materiality of bits of text.

Another way to work with the strengths that students bring to writing is to get them to create visual representations of their texts. Mind maps and shapes that show the flow of ideas within the text can help students plan their assignments and also encourage them to step back and analyse the structure of an assignment in progress. Setting out the organisation of a text in visual form can make it easier for students to understand not only what they need to do but also what they have done so far. Sharples (1999, pp. 82–83) gives examples of a 'notes network' for an essay and a template that can be used to understand the structure of an essay, while Francis (2009) provides examples of a variety of sketches, using blobs, silhouettes and clumps, that can be used to clarify the organisation of an assignment. Many students, not just art and design students, find visual forms more approachable for the inchoate ideas they have about a topic rather than outlines or lists, which seem to commit writers to a structure and hierarchy before their ideas have taken form.

One approach to writing that can take different forms is patchwork writing. This approach is not unique to art and design; a special issue of (Ovens, 2003) had articles on the use of patchwork texts to teach social work, nursing and science among other areas. Patchwork writing in art and design could include an assignment to write in different styles on a single topic (Francis, 2009, p. 195). In response to an exhibition, students might be asked to write from the point of view of a newspaper reviewer, the artist and to create a description of the layout of the exhibition. They might also be asked to write an academic response to the exhibition, placing the artworks in historical context, as well as other possibilities. All of these different texts would then be submitted. Students would gain experience in writing for different audiences, and each text can be relatively short, with the whole accumulating to an assignment of appropriate size for the module or course.

As noted earlier, some writers feel that collage is a particularly apposite form of creation for the modern moment. Texts can be physically assembled into an overarching text. One student, Asuka Kawabata, at Central St Martin's was described on the WritingPAD website as having investigated the construct of 'authorship'. She created a 6000 word assignment by cutting each individual letter of her text from a variety of printed documents. Without the tremendous labour of assembling a text by pasting each letter, students may be asked to create a text by bringing together sources that are photocopied or printed out from the Internet. In the next stage of the task, students could be asked to make explicit the relationships between the sources, first by drawing these relationships and later by writing passages that clarify similarities and contradictions among them. By physically assembling the texts into a patchwork, students can be brought to see the ownership of the original texts and the links that can be drawn among them.

To close this section, it may be worthwhile to revisit the strengths of the traditional essay, with its references and bibliography. Assigned topics may ask students to write about techniques, artists or designers who influenced them, set cultural phenomena in a context or, to give the task a clearer sense of audience and purpose, they may be asked to write an introduction to a catalogue to accompany an imaginary exhibition that they must plan. Traditional essays are familiar if perhaps unloved, and students, who for a variety of reasons might not feel confident about writing, can find comfort in the structure of tasks such as these. In interviews that I carried out with students on a PhD programme in fine arts, one student offered as a reason for following a traditional model was that writing in an innovative and creative manner might engage the practitioner in him, and he already had an art practice that he was following, while an international student said, 'I have never thought about that, because, you know, writing in English is itself is really hard. I don't want to, dare to, do something very strange and creative. I think it will be a disaster'. Both students, for different reasons, found the familiarity and constraints of traditional essays easier to work with than more innovative tasks. Another student reported that an essay that she had written in the past now looked much easier now that she understood how to write in an academic style: 'what I have been learning is basically the obedience to a certain style and academic writing. You follow through that. That's a lot of it. In that sense it's quite liberating' (Hudson, 2009, p. 124).

8.4. Conclusion

There is much that those who support writing in other disciplines can learn from art and design. Art and design approach writing from a different perspective than many other disciplines, though, like many other areas of the university, they have significant numbers of students who find writing challenging. Tutors in art and design have extended tasks and approaches that are used in many areas of writing support to encourage students to engage with writing, such as writing in genres other than the academic essay and connecting their writing closely with their professional goals. These tasks help students understand how writing can support their art and design practice. Tutors in art and design frequently assign tasks that get students to write small amounts of text, but to write them more frequently. These tasks are often not directly assessed, but instead they contribute to assignments that gather up the small bits of writing into a larger, coherent whole. This reduces the marking load on the tutor, while making the writing task more manageable for students.

Multimodal texts are used in many disciplines, as images, graphs and charts provide clearer and more concise ways to present information than writing. Art and design tutors also ask their students to combine visual content with written, but they also prompt students to go beyond these forms of information design to investigate the support that texts are written on and the ways that texts might be presented. Drawing on the inherent strengths that students bring to the study of art and design, these tasks elicit in some instances strikingly innovative responses.

References

Baynham, M. (2000). Academic writing in new and emergent discipline areas. In M. R. Lea & B. Stierer (Eds.), *Student writing in higher education: New contexts* (pp. 17–31). Buckingham, UK: SRHE.

Bezemer, J., & Kress, G. (2008). Writing in multimodal texts: A social semiotic account of designs for learning. *Written Communication, 25*(2), 166–195. doi:10.1177/0741088307313177

Bird, E. (2000). *Art and design education: Historical overview.* Working Papers in Art and Design, 1. Retrieved from http://www.herts.ac.uk/artdes1/research/papers/wpades/vol1/bird2full.html

Borg, E. (2004). Internally persuasive writing in fine arts practice. *Art, Design and Communication in Higher Education, 3*(3), 193–210.

Borg, E. (2007). Writing in fine arts and design education in context. *Journal of Writing in Creative Practice, 1*(1), 83–99.

Brind, S. (2004). A curriculum for artists. In P. Bonaventura & S. Farthing (Eds.), *A curriculum for artists* (pp. 10–19). Oxford: University of Oxford.

Candlin, F. (2000). Practice-based doctorates and questions of academic legitimacy. *Journal of Art and Design Education, 19*(1), 96–101.

Coffin, C., Donohue, J., & North, S. (2009). *Exploring English grammar: From formal to functional.* London: Routledge.

Danto, A. C. (1964). The artworld. *Journal of Philosophy, 61*(19), 571–584.

Department of Education and Science. (1970). *The structure of art and design education in the further education sector* (pp. viii + 63). London: Her Majesty's Stationer's Office.

Dorsett, C. (2007). Exhibitions and their prerequisites. In J. Rugg & M. Sedgwick (Eds.), *Issues in curating contemporary art and performance* (pp. 77–87). Bristol, UK: Intellect Books.

Evans, S., & Le Grice, M. (2001). The state of the art: Research in the practical arts doctorates — autonomous methodologies. *European Journal of Arts Education, 3*(2-3), 105–113.

Firth, S., & Horne, H. (1987). *Art into pop.* London: Methuen.

Flint, R. W. (Ed.) (1972). *Marinetti: Selected writings.* New York, NY: Farrar, Straus & Giroux.

Francis, P. (2009). *Inspiring writing in art and design: Taking a line for a write.* Bristol, UK: Intellect Books.

Frayling, C. (2004). *To* art and *through* art. In P. Bonaventura & S. Farthing (Eds.), *A curriculum for artists* (pp. 38–41). Oxford: The University of Oxford.

Gibbs, G. (1988). *Learning by doing: A guide to teaching and learning methods.* London: Further Education Unit.

Gieryn, T. F. (1983). Boundary-work and the demarcation of science from non-science: Strains and interests in professional ideologies of scientists. *American Sociological Review, 48*(6), 781–795.

Goldstein, C. (1996). *Teaching art: Academies and schools from Vasari to Albers.* Cambridge: Cambridge University Press.

Gombrich, E. H. (1995). *The story of art* (16th ed). London: Phaidon.

Graham-Dixon, A. (2005, 2 March). *Lecture — Is the art school dead?* Retrieved from http://www.thersa.org/acrobat/eno_020305.pdf. Accessed on 29 March 2005.

Harries, S. (2011). *Nikolaus Pevsner: The life.* London: Chatto & Windus.

Hockey, J. (1999). Writing and making: Problems encountered by practice-based research degree students. *Point, 7,* 38–43.

Hudson, C. (2009). *Art from the heart: The perceptions of students from widening participation backgrounds of progression to and through HE Art and Design.* London: National Arts Learning Network.

Kress, G. (2003). *Literacy in the new media age.* London: Routledge.

Lydiat, A. (2004). *Case study: Writing as practice-practice as writing.* Retrieved from http://writing-pad.ac.uk. Accessed on 30 August 2011.

Medway, P. (2002). Fuzzy genres and community identities: The case of architecture students' sketchbooks. In R. M. Coe, L. Lingard & T. Teslenko (Eds.), *The rhetoric and ideology of genre* (pp. 123–154). Cresskill, NJ: Hampton Press.

Ministry of Education. (1960). *First report of the national advisory council on art education.* London: Her Majesty's Stationer's Office.

Nesi, H., & Gardner, S. (2006). Variation in disciplinary culture: University tutors' views on assessed writing tasks. In R. Kiely, P. Rea-Dickins, H. Woodfield & G. Clibbon (Eds.), *Language, culture and identity in applied linguistics* (pp. 99–117). London: Equinox.

Ovens, P. (Ed.) (2003). Editorial. *Innovations in Education and Teaching International, 40*(2), 109–111. doi:10.1080/1470329031000088969

Pevsner, N. (1940/1967). *Academies of art past and present* (Reprint edition of 1967 by University Microfilms, Ann Arbor, MI, ed.). London: Cambridge University Press.

Rosenberg, H. (1972). Educating artists. In H. Rosenberg (Ed.), *The de-definition of art: Action art to pop to earthworks* (pp. 39–48). London: Secker & Warburg.

Schön, D. A. (1983). *The reflective practitioner: How professionals think in action.* New York, NY: Basic Books.

Sharples, M. (1999). *How we write: Writing as creative design.* London: Routledge.

Swift, J. (1999). Proper listening, proper heeding: A midwifery of thought. *Journal of Art and Design Education, 18*(3), 281–292.

Thompson, J. (2005). Art education: From Coldstream to QAA. *Critical Quarterly, 47*(1-2), 215–225. doi:10.1111/j.0011-1562.2005.00641.x

Turner, J., & Hocking, D. (2004). Synergy in art and language: Positioning the language specialist in contemporary fine art study. *Art Design & Communication in Higher Education, 3*(3), 149–162. doi:10.1386/adch.3.3.149/1

Chapter 9

Social Writing

Rowena Murray

9.1. Introduction

> I need to be ignored, by the world, so that there are no other
> possible things I could be doing. I read in the paper today that
> a student from Oxford was presumed to be missing, and his
> friend undertook a search online, only to have him turn up
> three weeks later with a thesis. I can relate.

For this student writing is a solitary activity — an activity that demands
solitude — and many students and academics relate to this concept, but it is
not the only way to write. It is not the only way to produce writing or
develop academic literacy. Writing is inherently social because it involves
communicating with others, but it can be social in the sense that talking
about writing becomes part of the process:

> ... you don't feel alone in your misery of writing, especially at
> the start. So I think it is very useful to know that everyone is in
> the same boat ... everyone has the same problems with
> writing, i.e. structuring or disciplining or just getting through
> putting words on paper, so that was very useful. I think,
> because you are in a group you actually work harder. (writer
> quoted in MacLeod, Steckley, & Murray, 2011, p. 8)

**Writing in the Disciplines: Building Supportive Cultures for Student Writing
in UK Higher Education**
Copyright © 2012 by Emerald Group Publishing Limited
ISBN: 978-1-78052-546-4

At the very least, writing with other people can counteract that sense of being 'alone in your misery of writing', but it can have other benefits. It can set up a series of reactions: comforting recognition that others not only see academic writing as a challenge but also experience the challenge of writing in similar ways — 'everyone has the same problems with writing' — constructive discussion of these problems — 'structuring or disciplining or just getting through putting words on paper' — and this, in turn, can stimulate thinking about solutions to writing 'problems'.

However, students — and many academics — do not generally talk about their writing in these terms. Where there is no routine discussion of developing academic literacy, the social practices of literacy need to be learned and nurtured. However, there may be resistance to this from academics — and students — who define literacy in terms of skills that are more closely linked to writing in the disciplines, but social writing is one way to develop disciplinary skills. It also provides opportunities to develop understanding of students' writing, and students can develop their understanding of writing in the disciplines. How we think about academic literacy — whether we see it as solitary, social or both — will shape how we support students' literacy development.

Social writing is when students talk about writing. This is one way of practising literacy. They identify concepts and practices, describe their own writing experiences in their own terms, compare them with others' and develop their understanding of writing. These insights into students' understanding and practice of writing create contexts for our literacy work with them. These insights can — and should — shape how we do literacy work with students.

In this chapter I draw on my work with students and academics to explain why I think social writing is critical for literacy development, what it involves and what I think it achieves (Murray & Newton, 2009; Murray, Steckley, & MacLeod, 2011; Murray, Thow, Moore, & Murphy, 2008). I use quotes from interviews and informal discussions with writers from different disciplines not only to illustrate these points but also to show the range of reactions students can have to the idea and the experience of social writing. My approaches have been influenced by Elbow's (1973) work on student writing (and more recently on faculty writing), by the Rhetoric and Composition literature (Fahnestock & Secor, 2003) and by collaboration with colleagues in other disciplines (MacLeod et al., 2011) who bring new theoretical perspectives to the business of learning how to write well.

Elbow (1973) argued that short writing tasks that are not part of formal assessment help students develop fluency in their writing. He prioritised the production of words on paper and learning to be better at generating words, over focusing on generating better words. He found that this led to benefits in writers' self-management and in their ability to resolve confusion in the writing process. It does this by helping writers to clarify what is involved in writing and to become better at judging writing. The key to this approach is the 'teacherless' writing group:

> ... in proposing the teacherless writing class I am trying to deny something – something that is often assumed: *the necessary connection between learning and teaching.* The teacherless writing class is a place where there is learning but no teaching. It is possible to learn something and not be taught. It is possible to be a student and not have a teacher. If the student's function is to learn and the teacher's to teach, then the student can function without a teacher, but the teacher cannot function without a student. (Elbow, 1973, p. ix)

In my work and in this chapter I have adopted Elbow's principles and developed writing activities that set out to achieve some of these aims. Above all, I have kept to the principle of combining short writing activities with writers' discussions. These activities provide audiences for writers:

> The teacherless class comes as close as possible to taking you out of the dark about how your words are experienced, and thus making it easier to produce meaningful words on paper ... . You eventually learn that it's not even very useful to learn someone's judgement of your words compared to learning his perceptions and experiences of them. (Elbow, 1973, pp. 125–126)

Writers learn from these discussions with audiences to make their own decisions about writing, which can be a complex, even overwhelming, process.

The Rhetoric and Composition movement, as represented by Fahnestock and Secor (2003), emphasises learning the skills of argument. A crucial early phase in constructing argument is definition: how key terms are defined, the different techniques of definition and the linkage of definition with other parts of the argument are all taught and learned in writing courses across the United States. Again, I have adapted some of this work in the activities I use with students and academics. I have kept to the principle of defining rhetorical skills — the skills of constructing texts.

The third component of the approach described in this chapter is theoretical: with colleagues in the discipline of Social Work I use containment theory to explore how the combination of writing activities and regular discussions works to enhance the experience of writing and increase productivity (MacLeod et al., 2011). Containment theory helps to explain how social writing works to address some of the challenges that writing poses for students and academics. Containment theory provides a theoretical underpinning for social writing.

This chapter makes the case that social writing is a way for students and academics to make writing their own, so that they not only reduce the 'misery' of writing but also reap the benefits of writing for their learning and practice. This is not to say that there will be no more solitary writing, but that writing can be both solitary and social, as the need and opportunity arise. In fact, discussing experiences of solitary and social writing — and sharing ideas about what can be achieved in each mode — is itself a valuable activity. It exposes deep-seated assumptions about the 'best' way to write, reveals experiences of what works and what does not, surfaces emotions and interrogates myths about writing in the disciplines.

This chapter provides both conceptual and practical frameworks for the process of academic writing. With these frameworks, students and staff can develop their understandings of writing and can own their writing. In due course, the frameworks can be stripped down, and their components can be put back together again in a range of ways for different student groups. The writing activities proposed here can be adapted to bring them closer to writing in the disciplines, for example, but in the form outlined here they will help students progress in their literacy development.

9.2. Primary and Secondary Socialisation

> I do a lot of my writing with [others] and find this the ideal way to keep motivated through regular discussion about ideas and also in terms of meeting deadlines.

Socialisation in writing usually means learning to write in a discipline. This usually refers to the rhetorical modes, types of argument and style of referencing that are expected in writing for a specific discipline. However, for the purposes of this chapter, socialisation refers to the process of writing in the company of others. This is because the social groupings that I work with do not routinely differentiate the writing practices required for disciplinary contexts (Murray & Newton, 2009). Instead, people talk across disciplinary boundaries. They share and compare experiences of the writing process. Their writing experiences do not seem to be differentiated solely by their disciplines of study or research. When they talk about the different requirements of different disciplines, this in itself can be interesting and helpful: discussing them, and how to implement them, is one way of working out what these requirements mean.

It might therefore be useful to think in terms of primary socialisation — learning about the requirements of writing in a discipline — and secondary socialisation — learning about the writing process. Primary socialisation could be defined as learning rhetorical and conceptual frameworks and comes from reading and writing in the discipline; secondary socialisation could be defined in terms of writing practices and comes from writing with others.

Writing is a social process, where the writer operates in discourse communities, and social writing exposes the processes of producing writing and stimulates exploration of those processes. In social writing, writers can play a range of roles:

> I have two study buddies for accountability – writing as a social process.
> I share my techniques, successes and failures – writing as a social process.

Writing with others brings social processes to writing. Writing in solitude is not wrong, but it can obscure the workings of writing. Writing in groups, where everyone in the group not only writes but also discusses writing-in-progress, reveals writing processes, and writers report that this makes writing seem more manageable.

Discussing writing exposes concepts and practices. Duff (2010) argues that socialisation is a 'dynamic, socially situated process' (p. 169), with the 'social positioning by oneself and others' (p. 169) at work — but how can the individual student manage this 'dynamic'? Social writing reveals a writer's 'positioning' and, even if students do not, at first, use this term, social writing makes thinking and deciding about it part of the writing process. Social writing is not, therefore, simply about providing a supportive environment for writing; it is a way for students to learn about writing and about themselves as writers.

9.3. Forms of Social Writing

> My writing time sometimes feels lonely and isolated, which is why retreats work so well for me because there's this immediate community of people all tackling similar challenges and usually willing to share their struggles, which I always find a huge help.

Many forms of social writing have been created to provide academic writing development: writing retreats, writer's groups, writing courses with group writing sessions and discussion of writing-in-progress and one-to-one writing consultations (Murray, 2008; Murray & Moore, 2006; Murray et al.,

2008). These can be led by a facilitator or tutor, or participants can run them. These forms of social writing are all different, but they share the component of discussion: discussion of writing-in-progress. While some or all of these modes might be new to some or most academics, these activities are easy to run. They also create time, while students are writing, for academics to do a little of their own writing.

Since students — and academics — often have inhibitions about showing their writing to others or talking about it with others, these discussions can be challenging initially. Talking about writing-in-progress is not the norm; most discussions of writing focus on finished products — the student project or the academic publication. There may be several different kinds of barrier to talking about writing, and the following sections are written with that in mind, sensitive to the difficulty of talking about writing for the first time and the challenge of managing such discussions for the first time.

9.3.1. Activities That Get Students Writing and Talking About Writing

This section is not just about 'things I can do with students'. It shows how social writing is fundamental to academic literacy development. The writing activity described in this section will seem, to some, far too simple for developing undergraduate writing skills, but it has been used with a range of undergraduate groups and doctoral students (Murray, 1992). For under-graduates and postgraduates alike, it stimulates discussion of writing skills and prompts critique of their own writing habits, the concepts underpinning them and the writing demands of the disciplines. Given the complexity of this exploration, it is appropriate that the writing activity is short, focused and, apparently, simple. In fact, while it may seem simple, it combines Elbow's (1973) principle of prioritising the production of text and Fahnestock and Secor's (2003) principle of learning about the role of definition in the construction of arguments.

Writing Activity

The topic for this writing is 'last week' — i.e. events that happened last week.
The purpose of this writing is to make the point that last week was a 'good' week.
In order to do this, stick to the main point and be specific.
Write in sentences for 10 minutes.

When introducing this activity, it helps to reassure students that it is designed to develop their writing and is not for assessment purposes. They may ask for additional explanation:

Students' Questions About the Activity

What do you mean by the 'main point'?
The main point is that last week was 'good', and everything you write should be about that. Jot down a list of possible topics to write about before you start.
What does 'specific' mean?
It means giving examples of your definition of 'good' — when you write 'for example' and give names, dates, times and places to illustrate your point.
How is this relevant to essay/report/dissertation writing in my subject area?
This is a different kind of writing than you normally do for your courses. However, the skill of sticking to the point relates to developing a line of argument for an essay, and being specific relates to using evidence and citations to support an argument. These are two key skills in academic writing. We will discuss them once you have tried this activity. Bear with me and try it. We will come back to the question of relevance to your courses in our discussion, but focus on the topic of last week for the moment.

It helps to ask the students to 'Bear with me' or 'Try it and see', knowing that there will be time to discuss the task after they have had tried the activity for themselves.

Alternatively, if students have no questions, or seem mystified or intimidated or both, you can ask them to discuss the task with each other for two or three minutes, listen in to their discussions, as appropriate, and then invite questions or comments. This may make it easier for them to ask questions, when they see that others are unclear about what they have to do or why, which is one of the benefits of this social process.

Generally, initially, students find this writing activity strange but straightforward. They do not have to read before they write. All they have to do is write about one week, and they can draw on their own experiences for content. Usually, they have to be prompted to stop writing after 10 minutes, which suggests that once they start they do get into it and certainly have enough to write about.

Once they have stopped writing, the next step is for them to scrutinise their own writing: specifically, to underline references to the *main point* — that last week was a good week — and to circle or use bold for *specifics*. Alternatively, they can swap and do this on each other's writings. There is likely to be discussion of what 'main' and 'specific' mean in practice, in writing. They now test their understanding of what these terms mean, as they read their own and/or each other's writing. This social writing lets them see and hear different definitions and specifics from their own.

The advantage of using students' lives as subject matter for writing is that they can focus on the two key skills. This activity means that all the students have something to write about — they all know about the past week in their lives — and they can focus on the two key skills of academic writing, both in writing and reading.

The next step is for students to evaluate the writing. Again, this is for learning, not assessment. Allocating points for these criteria is different from how their writing is usually assessed, and there may be discussion of these criteria, as students prepare to allocate points. The purpose of using points here is to make their judgements concrete, rather than to formalise their evaluations.

Criteria

1. If the first sentence includes the word key word 'good' ... 2 points
2. If it is defined — 'good' in what sense? ...   2 points
3. If the examples illustrate that definition ...   2 points
4. If the writing comes back to the main point at the end ... 2 points
5. If it's all about the main point — nothing irrelevant ... 2 points

TOTAL   10 points

They then give themselves or each other a mark out of 10. This gets them looking for the key skills of sticking to the point and being specific and debating whether or not these are present in their and other students' writing. At this stage, they can exchange writings and read three or four pieces by others, seeing, potentially, three or four different ways of performing the writing task and three or four evaluations.

The next step is discussion:

- From the writing you did or read, what would you say is a good example of a 'good week'?
- Did you find anything irrelevant in any of the writings, including you own?
- How specific are the examples — could they be more specific?
- Are there examples of 'good' that do not match the definition provided in the writing?
- What are the pros and cons of defining the key term?
- What are the pros and cons of defining it at the start and end of the writing?

- Are link words used between or within sentences — if so, which ones; if not, should they be?

This is an opportunity to prompt thinking and introduce information about paragraph structure, including topic sentences, what should go in them and how difficult it can be to make sense of writing that does not have the key term in the topic sentence. Ways of linking sentences — transitions, conjunctions, repetition of the key term and punctuation (e.g. colon and semi-colon) — can be defined, and students can practise adding them to their texts, trying out different sentence structures, combining long and short sentences — for a purpose — and maintaining the focus on their main points, as they have defined them.

There is often an interesting discussion about 'relevance': is it relevant to talk about bad things that happened last week that turned out well in the end, so as to use the contrast to make the point that it was a good week? This can be opened up for discussion — what do the students think? Some will see it as relevant, since the information is used to make the main point — 'good week'. Others will see it as irrelevant, since some of the information included is not about the 'good' subject.

When writers discuss illustrations of 'good' in great detail, they can lose sight of the main point. Sometimes a student will ask, 'But how is that relevant to the main point?' This is a fantastic moment. It is exactly the right question. Again, the students will generate answers: 'it's not relevant, it is related', 'it's only relevant if you say that it is, and that means you need to say how it is relevant'. These are excellent answers, and students see — or can be prompted to think about — how these points might be relevant to their academic writing.

Switching from this task to consider how this question — and their various answers — might apply to their academic writing, they can consider the pros and cons of using different examples to support a point, of including several examples without weighing their relative relevance and of making connections between ideas and examples that, as one PhD student put it, lead to 'wandering off' the main point. Many students talk about how easy it is to do this and how difficult it can be to stick to the point. We also talk about referring to the main point throughout the piece, returning to the keyword and mentioning it at the end of the writing. Students often see this as repetition, which many have learned is a weakness in writing, rather than a unifying device.

This phase in the activity might seem to run counter to Elbow's (1973) principle of generating text — as in freewriting — since it involves definition and structure at an early stage. This is why it is probably important to remove considerations of sentence and paragraph structure, coherence and relevance and disciplinary contexts from the initial briefing for this writing and keep them for this second phase of social writing. This will seem odd to students and academics at first, since it seems to invite unstructured writing, but Elbow has established that there are benefits to the writer's development in doing exactly that.

These discussions make visible the process of selecting a focus, developing an idea, selecting evidence, choosing words and constructing sentences to convey the idea. They show how a piece of writing is developed, how important it is to simply generate text and how they can use discussion to develop their ideas and their writing. The interactions show options and differences of opinion and interpretation. While a textbook or website on writing will give students most of this information, social writing means that the process of acting on the information is made visible, comprehensible and manageable. This is not to say that this activity will address all their issues and every challenge that academic writing presents, but it does get at many components of academic literacy:

- deciding what the main point of a piece of writing is;
- using definition in making the point;
- deciding on the role and nature of examples to illustrate the main point;
- matching examples to the definition;
- selecting what's relevant and weeding out what's not;
- distinguishing what is related to the main point from what is relevant;
- spelling out how examples make the point;
- repeating a key term to create coherence;
- returning to the main point at the end of the piece to elaborate.

These components of academic literacy are made visible and manageable in this task. The two key skills of sticking to the point and being specific can be discussed in different terms, using examples from essays or articles, or other forms of writing in the discipline. However, the writing activity itself defines the key skills for students in ways that an explanation from a tutor does not. They get the point about the relevance of these skills to their writing and the work of performing them in their writing and revising. They see that there are many ways of doing this, that there are many interpretations of their writing and that they have to decide what to write. The next step is to repeat the task, with one change:

Writing Activity

The topic is 'last week' — i.e. the events that happened last week.
The purpose is to make the point that last week was a 'bad' week.
Again, stick to the point and be specific.
Write in sentences for 10 minutes.

This means the writers draw on the same body of material — their memories of the week before — but make a different selection of those events, or describe the same events in different terms. If the first writing activity seemed strange, this may seem even stranger, or it may seem simpler, because they now know what's required. Usually, some students start writing immediately. They may see — though it may be worth pointing out — that this is a chance to put into practice what they learned from the first writing task, from the evaluation and from the discussion that followed.

Since the subject of students' writing is personal, and since some of them might have had some dreadful experiences in the previous week, or some wonderful private ones, there is no requirement for students to show each other their writings, and it can help to prompt them to steer away from the truly awful, rather than to delve into it in their writing in this setting. This might not be the best environment for them to do that. Writing about intense highs or lows in their weeks might distract from the purpose of the task — to practise sticking to the point and being specific — or it might prevent them from discussing their writing in detail and benefiting from the discussion. However, as I spell all this out, I make it clear that what they write about is their decision.

After 10 minutes, once they have stopped writing, they mark up the 'main point' references and specific examples, as before. Again, they award themselves or each other a mark out of 10, and there is discussion. There is often another debate about what constitutes 'relevance to the main point' and 'specific' illustrations of the main point, as defined by the writer. There are often comparisons of the first and second tasks: was the second one easier or more difficult?; was this because the task was more familiar?; was it because the material they had — i.e. what actually happened in the previous week — was easier or more difficult to write about as 'bad'?

In discussion, there are often accounts of what students 'normally' do when they write, when and where they feel they write best, what they feel they have to do before they write — such that this task was a huge, or bearable, imposition on their usual practices. All of these are important talking points, and many of these topics do not routinely come up in discussions of completed writing assignments.

It may be sufficient that students describe and externalise what they do, that they compare how they write with others, that they identify problems with focusing, for example, and think about how they can begin to address writing problems. They can critically reflect on what they think about writing and how they do it. They can normalise some of these problems — to see that the process of finding a focus for writing and then sticking to it just is hard work. They can think about what they can do to maintain focus in their writing, what is feasible in the composing stage and what they must look for when they revise. This often raises the question of time: Do they usually leave enough time to revise? What constitutes 'enough time', and what exactly do they do — or should they do — in that time? If this is an intended change in their writing process, how will they manage that? What other factors may impinge on their writing and planning? Can they support each other as they make these changes?

These two writing activities raise issues about discipline-specific writing and writing processes or practices, but it is the discussion, the social aspect that makes this happen. If students were simply to read this chapter, to read about the activities and do them in solitude, with no discussion, what would they learn? It is difficult to say, but it is likely that they would think less deeply about the writing process, about the relevance of the task to their academic writing. They might not see its relevance — and the only comparators would be those they imagine for themselves. They might have questions, but would not benefit from discussing them. Moreover, solitary writing, by its very nature, cannot provide all the features of the supportive writing environment provided in these social writing activities.

Social writing means opening writing up to discussion of content, process and evaluation. The short writing tasks described in this section do, to some extent, make similar demands on students as writing in the disciplines does. These tasks socialise writing in two ways: they open up writing for discussion and they bring social interaction into writing. This develops academic literacy.

9.3.2.   Snack Writing

I have written about this many times (Murray, 2008, 2009, 2011a, 2011b), but have not yet fully developed the argument in terms of social writing. Moreover, some still do not see how they can use snack writing, but for those who do try it, while it is a radical change in their writing process, it appears to be so helpful that it should be incorporated into the social writing model. It is one way to write in groups, and it challenges and extends writing habits and concepts. My approach again draws on Elbow's (1973) free-writing, but adapts it by using discussions of time to prompt thinking about the nature, scale and scope of stages in the writing process. In addition, discussions of 'time' generally reveal a range of issues and potential barriers to writing, and it is important that these are addressed.

Many students and academics, who in many cases have been doing academic writing for many years, believe that they only do their best writing in large chunks of time, such as five-, six- or seven-hour blocks, a day or two every week and a week or two over the summer. If large blocks of time are available for writing, this will work. However, if large blocks of time are not available (as is the case in many settings and schedules), this 'binge' writing model will fail, and an alternative model is needed — the 'snack' writing model: for example, writing in shorter time increments, such as 90 minutes or even as little as 15 or 30 minutes. Ideally, in theory, we should be able to do both 'snack' and 'binge' writing, as and when we can, in order to make best use of the time we have. For some, this is a huge conceptual shift, and even for those who like the idea it is significant behavioural change.

This change is easier to achieve in social writing settings, where writers are all working towards putting this model into practice. The social factor sustains the intended change. The critical factor is, again, discussions that writers have about how they do/did 'snack' writing. This is not just about creating a support group; it is about growing understanding of ways to write and using discussion to keep writing going.

'Snack' writing is about being able to dip in and out of a writing task, learning to leave writing aside for a period and becoming a regular writer. This seems to raise anxieties about a number of issues: the quality of the writing, writers' ability to return to the project after a break from it, to carry on from where they left it and their ability to make time for the next writing tasks, given competing demands on time (MacLeod et al., 2011). Social writing is a way of both privileging writing — making it the primary task for a fixed period — and of sustaining writing, because writers support each other's efforts to write. This does not mean neglecting other tasks, but managing them and leaving them in a state that makes returning to them straightforward.

This is not about developing technical writing skills, but developing social writing skills, perhaps the least developed aspect of writing:

> I actually really struggle with 'getting down to writing' and work best if I am working collaboratively, so that someone else needs me to complete my efforts. Then I sit up all night if necessary – I find it hard to do this for myself.

This relational aspect of writing is not only available in co-authoring but also available in social writing settings, where writers develop the writing self in relation to others.

9.3.3. The 'Typing Pool' Model for Dissertation Writers

The term 'typing pool' describes a social form of writing retreat, where participants write in the same room, as opposed to the 'solitary confinement' model, where everyone writes in solitude (Murray, 2008). This is one of the best ways of developing social writing. It combines generation of text (Elbow, 1973) and consideration of rhetorical strategies (Fahnestock & Secor, 2003).

A key developmental stage in academic literacy is writing a dissertation. Many students find the prospect exciting, but some are intimidated by the scale of the writing task. They are not sure how they will write so many words, find it difficult to get started and procrastinate, which increases anxiety. A key stage in students' writing development can be a writing day — a mini-retreat — a day dedicated to writing. The main purpose is to start writing for their dissertations. This may sound like a very modest goal, but it is the most important — if they cannot start writing, they cannot start to focus and develop their ideas.

Starting to write (for) a dissertation may involve a range of processes: outlining, thinking about stages in a dissertation argument, planning sections, practising critiquing the literature and drafting sections of the dissertation. However, the key components of the day are writing time, strategies for starting writing and discussing writing-in-progress. The mini-retreat programme should include time for all of these.

Dissertation Writing Day

9–9.30	Introduction: purpose of the day, approaches to writing (including freewriting and generative writing), Q & A.
9.30–10	Freewriting about dissertations + discussion.
10–10.30	Generative writing about dissertation topic and/or literature + discussion.
BREAK	
11–12	Writing.
LUNCH	
1–1.30	Overview of dissertation structure, outlining activity, writing to prompts and writing goals + discussion.
1.30–2.30	Writing.
BREAK	
3–4.30	Writing.
4.30–5	Feedback, taking stock, setting new goals, arranging writing times.

This is a flexible framework that can be adjusted to meet students' needs. For example, for students who are just starting to think about their topics, the above programme emphasises strategies for getting started. Once they have started their research, and are using these strategies, there can be more time for writing in the programme. Later, a mini-retreat programme could include short presentations on work-in-progress and peer review of writing.

This kind of activity, and these claims for its potential, often raises — for both academics and students — the 'quality' question: namely, it is all very well getting students to start writing, but what about the quality of their writing? — it is the quality of the writing, not the quantity, that counts. Many academics will assert that it is not enough to simply sit and write, or to write more or more often; it is important to write well, to have a knowledge of grammar and to demonstrate independent thought, critical thinking and/or a programme of focused reading.

The answer is that social writing develops writing skills and produces 'quality' writing, but that it is unrealistic to expect 'quality' writing in rough drafts or in these pre-rough draft stages. For those who remain unconvinced, the test is to try it with students. The key to social writing is discussion: when students talk about their ideas for their research, about how they want to go about the work, when they write it down, give and receive feedback, think about how their projects and the writing will be managed in the time they have — i.e. when they produce 'quality' writing.

Once students have experienced this programme, once they see that they can write, that writing can be useful in developing their ideas and once they start to discuss their writing, they can run writing days or half-days themselves. As they progress with their research projects, and as they find other topics to write about, they can dedicate more time in the programme to writing. Once they have learned a range of strategies — freewriting (Elbow, 1973), generative writing (Boice, 1990), writing to prompts (Murray, 2009), using outlines to structure writing (Murray, 2009) — they can fit them into the programme as activities for warming up, focusing or clarifying, as the need arises. As long as there is time in the programme for discussion — to externalise writing goals (Murray, 2011a), articulate writing processes and take stock of the extent to which goals are achieved — this will socialise dissertation writing.

Reviewing completed dissertations can be part of this social framework (Thow & Murray, 2001). Students can develop their understanding of dissertation structure. They explore in discussion the different kinds of research in each dissertation, the different methods used and the different ways of writing about them. They share their perceptions of each project and each type of writing. They develop understanding of the perennially challenging demands of dissertation writing:

- What does 'critique' the literature mean? — students review and discuss examples from completed dissertations in their discipline.
- How much do you need to say about the methods? — students compare answers to this question in completed dissertations and consider how these might relate to the methods used, and they see the correct system for referencing, which also seems to be a constant challenge.

Practising social writing with dissertation students not only creates a supportive environment for a demanding writing task but also helps them understand the task and see how writing in different ways helps them to achieve it. Social writing has an added benefit for dissertation supervisors — seeing students in groups saves tutors and supervisors time.

9.4. Writing to Prompts

This section introduces one of the most useful strategies for developing academic writing, writing to prompts, which means writing in response to a question or fragment (Murray, 2009). This is a further adaptation of Elbow's (1973) freewriting, in the sense that it involves students writing what they think, without constraints of academic style and structure, but it is different in the sense that the prompts are topics for academic writing. Writing to prompts may work as a bridge between freewriting and structured academic writing.

For example, one of the best ways of getting students to talk and think about their writing is to make it the subject of their writing:

Prompt to Write About Writing

What writing (for your dissertation/paper/report) have you done and what do you want to do (in the long, medium and short term)?

- 5 minutes' writing
- in sentences
- private writing — no one will read it
- to be discussed in pairs/groups

It is not just this writing activity, but the discussion that follows that leads to comparisons, reflections and clarifications of writing ideas, purposes and goals. Writing is therefore the subject of both the writing and the discussion. The specific writing project that students are working on is subject to discussion and analysis: what are they planning to do, what is their topic, what are their ideas, what problems do they anticipate having with their writing, why are they interested in this subject?

Again, this may seem strange. Getting students to write about their writing — and students may find it strange, at first. Why write about writing, when we all know what we have to do? But students and academics regularly report that writing about writing is different from thinking about it: it forces them to clarify their thinking and to choose between a number of different options for their research and/or their writing.

At the very least, this activity is an excellent warm up for writing. It prompts students to start writing. It gives them a starting point in their writing. It eases the frequently laboured transition to from not-writing to writing and prevents procrastination. It gives everyone something to talk about; even if they are not sure about their topic or how to write about it, they can write and talk about that. It normalises that uncertainty, while allowing for expression of the writer's interests, in spite of the uncertainty. This might seem like a recipe for disaster — surely students will go into a spiral of despair as they list writing problems? What generally happens is that everyone starts writing, and this in itself is reassuring for students. They are often surprised and relieved that they can write between 150 and 250 words in 5 minutes. They begin to think about how to manage their writing in real time.

How academics and students manage these discussions is important for making this activity purposeful, keeping it productive and making it effective in terms of learning about writing. This is why the discussion should be fairly structured: after the 5-minute writing task, students talk in pairs for 10 minutes; for the first 5 minutes, one person does the talking while the other person listens; for the second 5 minutes, they change roles. The purpose of imposing this structure on the discussion is to ensure that writers talk about each person's writing project separately, rather than exploring the background to the topic or project or their individual or shared interests. This discussion focuses on each project and the writer's ideas for working on it. There is then an important discussion about this activity: what did the students think of it; what did they write; what did they talk about; what do they think about this combination of writing and talking; do they do this kind of thing already, or not?

In this discussion, students may show that they understand that the activity made it easy for them to start writing quickly. They may see its potential for helping them to stop procrastinating with writing. Some will enjoy writing in this way. Others will have reservations, and the 'quality question' may be raised again here:

- What is the point of doing bad writing or freewriting?
- What is the point of writing about writing?
- Why can they not just do writing for their assignments/dissertations?

There should be some discussion at this point about the value of writing to develop ideas, and perhaps to develop understanding of the writing task, rather than only writing for assessment. That there is value in doing non-assessed writing will seem like a relief to some, but others will see it as a waste of time. This is not to say that trying a new writing activity once will persuade all students that it will help with their writing, it is worth repeating and it is worth continuing this debate with students.

While this warm up prompt can be used at the start of any writing session, in order for students to benefit from the discussion element, they have to be writing with others, and this too may be strange. Students who see writing as a solitary activity will not immediately see the value of writing with others. If these activities are regularly built into their courses, however, they will have more opportunities to weigh the pros and cons of each type of activity covered in this chapter, and can develop their own adaptations. For example, there are other forms of prompt. While the prompt for the activity described above involved writing about writing, other prompts can focus on the subject of the writing:

Prompts to Make the Main Point of the Writing Clear

- The main point of this discussion is ...
- The main point of this essay is ...
- The main point of this section is ...
- The aims of this dissertation are ...

Using these as prompts for writing and discussing what students write to these or other prompts are topics for discussion either before or after writing — or both. Specific features of academic writing, such as debate, can be prompts for writing.

Prompts for Writing About Debates on the Topic

- Some have argued that ...
- One interpretation has been/could be ...
- However, this could also be seen as ...
- This is not to say that ...
- Possible interpretations are ...
- Debate on this subject has focused on ...

Alternative prompts of this type are numerous, and lecturers can identify key academic writing skills they want students to develop, and this will help to explain their relevance as writing and talking points.

Students may see assessment criteria as appropriate prompts for writing — they can make explicit in their writing where they meet the course criteria. More importantly, they can use this combination of short writing activity followed by discussion, and perhaps further writing, to develop their understanding of what the criteria mean for their writing. If this discussion is then opened up across the whole course group, there are opportunities to explore different ways to meet the criteria in their writing.

Another option is using verbs as prompts. Again, while this is an extension of the prompts technique, it is also relevant to the development of academic literacy: deciding on the purpose of a piece of writing is central to focus and clarity in thinking and writing, and since purposes can be defined in verbs, students usually see the value of reviewing a repertoire of potential purposes for their writing:

Using Verbs as Prompts for Writing

Informs, reviews, argues, states, synthesises, claims, answers, explains, reconsiders, provides, maintains, outlines, supports, compares, lists, acknowledges, confirms, analyses, disputes, concludes, reveals, implies, reminds, refutes, assembles, shows, adds, clarifies, identifies (Ballenger, 2009).

This can provoke an interesting discussion: there are many possible definitions of each of these purposes for academic writing. It is probably crucial that students engage with these words not only as the language of assessment but also as purposes for their writing, some with specific requirements, in terms of form or structure, perhaps also scale or scope, and others more open to variation.

Some of these verbs can be combined in particular ways. This is not to say that this list is exhaustive, and everyone — students included — will have other prompts for academic writing to suggest and, perhaps, to add to this list. This discussion will help students to develop the skill of defining purpose in writing, discussing purpose(s) with potential audiences — tutors and supervisors — and developing their understanding of the meanings of these terms. Discipline-specific purposes for writing can be introduced to this discussion. Selecting a purpose for a piece of writing is an important stage in the writing process to practice:

Writing Activity: Using Verbs as Prompts

- Write one sentence on the main purpose of your dissertation, essay or report.
- Use a verb in this sentence.
- If you are not sure which verb to use, try using two or three different verbs, in two or three sentences.
- Write verbs for sections of your dissertation/essay/report.

The discussion that follows this activity can be exploratory, as students begin to use terms they have not yet fully defined — or perhaps not yet fully understood — in relation to their writing, or confirming, as students recognise that a particular verb helps to define what they need to do and how to structure their writing to do it. For some, this will prevent them from deferring an important decision till they feel 'sure' about what they want to write. Since this is another non-assessed writing activity, they are free to develop alternatives and discuss their pros and cons. In discussion, this gives them space to express their emerging understandings and check them with each other and with tutors or lecturers. Potentially, they can be learning about academic writing — including discipline-specific writing — in this activity and the discussion that follows it.

As with other writing activities in this section, this one is worth repeating, as students develop their writing projects and as they produce drafts. Studying the verbs — or purposes — in their writing, and in each other's writing, is one way of checking the coherence of a piece of writing, and this can help students to develop their skills for analysing writing. They can comment on each other's stated purposes, think about how these are defined and analyse how these are followed through in writing.

Prompts and the sentences that they generate — and it does seem important to perform these activities in sentences, rather than bullet points or notes — are not just separate components of writing; they can also be used in series. This technique can stimulate students to think about the structure of their writing. Writing a series of prompts helps them to develop the whole 'story' of their writing, and this can help them to check the coherence of their argument, to outline chapters or sections and to establish that there is a 'story' or argument in their writing:

Writing Prompts in Series

This research needed to be done/was worth doing because ...
The aims of my study were ...
What I did was ...
How I did that was ...
What happened when I did that was ...
I worked out what that meant by ...
I did what I set out to do to the extent that ...
The main finding is ...
The implications of my research are ...
What still needs to be done is ...

While other writing-and-talking activities in this section are short 5-minute writings, followed by 10-minute discussions, this activity needs more time — between 20 and 30 minutes is usually enough to write to this series of prompts, with 20 minutes for discussion in pairs (10 minutes on each person's writing).

Using word limits signals the scale and scope of writing required, but it also forces students to select key points only. There is no room or time to develop or elaborate. For some, this seems like a pointless constraint — why not develop your ideas and get them down while they are in your mind? For others, it is a benefit — because they have no room to manoeuvre, they have to decide on their main point and not 'wander off'.

The discussion that follows this activity can go into more depth about the content of students' writing. They can also discuss the strategy of using prompts in series. They may have ideas for alternative prompts, and these may be more relevant to their projects, or may provide more detail, or be problematic, deviating from what might be seen as a 'standard' structure required in their writing. Either way, discussing their writing is a chance to consolidate their writing intentions and/or revise them.

Discussing writing-in-progress is a way of making sense of writing. Engaging students in these discussions of their writing is a way of giving them tools for developing their understanding of writing. Talking about writing goals, content and activities, sharing references, discussing readings, exchanging hints and tips — this is how students recognise that they are all in the same boat, and this can build confidence, reduce anxiety and develop understanding of the problems that writing presents. They also see that it is not that the writer has 'problems'; it is that these are the demands writing makes on writers. Once writing problems are defined as writing problems — rather than solely as individual deficiencies — and once students have learned strategies for writing 'problems', they can write for learning and assessment.

For some, this may be a major shift — from using writing mainly or only for assessment to using it for learning. For some academics, who have not used this type of writing activity in their teaching before, have not experienced this type of writing activity themselves and perhaps do not initially see the value of doing so, this will seem strange. However, once students are talking about writing, it will become obvious that they have plenty to say about it, that they can interrogate the writing that university courses require them to do, that they can deconstruct academic writing, in their own terms, and that they can learn about writing by doing so. Research tells us that this is an important part of academic literacy development. For tutors, listening to students talking about writing is one way of finding out what they know and how they are adding to what they know in the course of these writing–talking–writing activities.

9.5. Containment

One way of theorising the practices of social writing described in this chapter is as containment (MacLeod et al., 2011; Ruch, 2007). In the context of academic writing, containment theory helps to explain how these social writing activities work. Containment theory (Bion, 1962) explains the processes that enable people to manage (contain) what seem to be unmanageable (uncontainable) thoughts, feelings and experiences. It is relevant to academic writing because being in a state of containment means that the individual can think clearly and manage experience and emotions. Ruch's (2007) model of 'holistic containment' is a framework for understanding the components of containment. Holistic containment has three components: (1) emotional containment — making unthinkable or unmanageable feelings thinkable and manageable; (2) organisational containment — where policies, procedures and organisational practices contribute to organisational, professional and managerial clarity and (3) epistemological containment — enabling members of the organisation to make sense of complex issues in their work. Holistic containment is, therefore, a systemic approach to understanding the interdependence of the individual and the collective context.

Containment enables clear thinking. Writing is difficult, if not impossible, without clear thinking, and it is difficult to think clearly about writing when (a) there is no forum regularly to do so (as is often the case in universities), (b) there are no regular activities for doing so and (c) there is no social grouping to legitimise thinking and talking about writing. In the context of academic writing, where containment is present, writing is the primary task, anti-task behaviours stop and writing-related anxiety is contained and thereby reduced. The social writing activities in this chapter are containing environments:

> [Academic writing] involves thinking, formulating, experimenting, drafting, reflecting, reading, synthesising, generating ideas, pulling together a lot of information, drawing out key themes, articulating complex ideas, adopting positions, generating explanations, reaching conclusions etc. I guess the point is that academic writing requires so many different competencies and skills that you need, metaphorically, to clear your desk … . I do know that some people seem to be able to write in a way that sits very comfortably with their other work responsibilities — but for me, while I can do some writing in a somewhat disjointed way — I always need at least some time for a total switch off from other activities in order to feel I'm making substantial progress, and in order to 'nail' certain aspects of the writing. So, during the course of my daily work for example, I may be able to sketch out an outline and generate some ideas — but in order really to get my teeth into it, I usually have to find some smart way of disengaging.

That this disengagement from other activities in order to make writing the primary task does not routinely occur is an argument for regular writing days (as described above). For academics, a containing environment means that they are able to manage competing tasks and 'push other issues to the margins'. This environment means they can legitimise writing and give it equal status to other tasks — 'I'd love to feel able to legitimately send my apologies to meetings on account of needing to spend time writing'. This means legitimising the writing process, not just the written outputs that are legitimised in the academic system and institutions. For students, a containing environment means that they are able to think clearly about writing in a social and relational — not just individual — process.

Creating containing environments, where students can think clearly about their writing is therefore a key role for those who teach in higher education. This involves constructing settings that contain anxieties related to writing, prevent anti-tasking and make writing the primary task. This is not just about providing social support and/or interaction; it is about making space for writing in environments that require outputs but do not contain processes. This suggests that there should be mechanisms to support students, and perhaps academics (Murray et al., 2011), in defining and achieving the primary task, managing task-related anxiety, identifying anti-task tendencies and managing competing primary tasks. If this support is not available, those with writing to do need to take the initiative in arranging activities that allow them to experience these processes and their benefits. Once containment has been experienced at a mini-retreat or writing day, for example, it is more likely to be experienced outside those settings.

9.6. Conclusion: A Paradox

Social writing is about not having to be 'ignored, by the world' in order to write. It is about learning about writing by doing writing and talking about writing with others who write. When writers do this, they seem to move from thinking about writing as a formal, impersonal or institutional practice to a personal process, a process they can shape for themselves, as they assess their own strengths, weaknesses and preferences and develop their own solutions to the challenges that writing presents.

Paradoxically, therefore, through social writing comes personal writing — in the sense that there is a shift from the 'writing I am required to do' to 'my writing'. This shift gives students the chance to take charge of their writing, rather than seeing it is a 'misery' imposed on them that they must endure. They can take responsibility for their own writing by writing with others, and by writing and talking about writing they are likely to find out much more about their own writing and about writing in their disciplines than if they did all their writing in solitude.

References

Ballenger, B. (2009). *The curious researcher: A guide to writing research papers* (6th ed.). New York, NY: Pearson Longman.

Bion, W. R. (1962). *Learning from experience*. London: Karnac.

Boice, R. (1990). *Professors as writers: A self-help guide to productive writing*. Stillwater, OK: New Forums.

Duff, P. A. (2010). Language socialization into academic discourse communities. *Annual Review of Applied Linguistics*, *30*, 169–192. doi:10.1017/S0267190510000048

Elbow, P. (1973). *Writing without teachers*. Oxford: Oxford University Press.

Fahnestock, J., & Secor, M. (2003). *A rhetoric of argument* (3rd ed.). New York, NY: McGraw-Hill.

MacLeod, I., Steckley, L., & Murray, R. (2011). Time is not enough: Promoting strategic engagement with writing for publication. *Studies in Higher Education*, *37*, 5. doi:10.1080/03075079.2010.527934

Murray, R. (1992). *Introduction to writing skills*. Glasgow, UK: University of Glasgow.

Murray, R. (2008). Innovations, activities and principles for supporting academics' writing. In S. Moore (Ed.), *Supporting academic writing among students and academics*. London: Staff and Educational Development Association. [SEDA Special 24]

Murray, R. (2009). *Writing for academic journals* (2nd ed.). Maidenhead, UK: Open University Press.

Murray, R. (2011a). *How to write a thesis* (3rd ed.). Maidenhead, UK: Open University Press.

Murray, R. (2011b, April). Developing a community of research practice. *British Educational Research Journal*. doi:10.1080/01411926.2011.583635.

Murray, R., & Moore, S. (2006). *The handbook of academic writing: A fresh approach*. Maidenhead, UK: Open University Press.

Murray, R., & Newton, M. (2009). Writing retreat as structured intervention: Margin or mainstream. *Higher Education Research and Development*, *28*(5), 527–539.

Murray, R., Steckley, L., & MacLeod, I. (2011). Research leadership in writing for publication: A theoretical framework. *British Educational Research Journal*. doi:10.1080/01411926.2011.580049.

Murray, R., Thow, M., Moore, S., & Murphy, M. (2008). The writing consultation: Developing academic writing practices. *Journal of Further and Higher Education*, *32*(2), 119–128.

Ruch, G. (2007). Reflective practice in contemporary child-care social work: The role of containment. *British Journal of Social Work*, *37*, 659–680.

Thow, M., & Murray, R. (2001). Enabling student writing for undergraduate projects: A practical approach. *Physiotherapy*, *87*(3), 134–139.

About the Contributors

Erik Borg is a senior lecturer at Coventry University's Centre for Academic Writing, where he teaches undergraduate and Master's level modules on writing and research. His research focuses on intertextuality and multimodal communication, particularly in fine arts and design, and it might be characterised as research into the nature of writing in a rapidly changing communication environment. He has published widely, including recent articles in *Assessment and Evaluation in Higher Education, The Journal of Writing in Creative Practice* and *Teaching in Higher Education.*

Helen Boulton is reader in technology enhanced learning and teaching, Nottingham Trent University. Helen's research is focussed on using new technologies in learning and teaching. Her current research interests are in the application of new technologies to learning and teaching; the use of Web 2.0 technologies to support the development of reflective practice and building communities of practice; assessment and feedback currently focussing on the transition into undergraduate and postgraduate study and student engagement. Helen has co-authored several books focussing on learning and teaching. She is a committee member of the Association for Information Technology in Teacher Education and reviews for a variety of journals and conferences. She has worked in the FE, secondary and HE sectors. Helen's work is published nationally and internationally.

Lisa Clughen studied at Oxford, Sunderland and Newcastle universities. She has taught at Northumbria and Sunderland universities and is currently a principal lecturer in Spanish in the School of Arts and Humanities at Nottingham Trent University, where she is also learning, teaching and academic support co-ordinator. She has worked in literacy development in a variety of settings for over 20 years and runs the School's Academic Support Service. She has published and presented numerous papers on academic literacies, especially academic writing development, García Lorca and eating disorders. Alongside her work on literacies, her research interests range from feminist philosophies to cultural and critical theories.

Matt Connell is subject leader of the social theory team in the School of Arts and Humanities at Nottingham Trent University. He lectures on programmes in communications, media and philosophy. As well as working on theories of pedagogy and writing development, his research has various other foci: psychoanalysis, critical theory, DJing and intergenerational community arts work.

Lisa Ganobcsik-Williams is Head of the Centre for Academic Writing, Coventry University, UK. She has taught and tutored writing in both UK and US universities, and has published in journals including *Rhetorica*, *The Writing Center Journal* and *Computers in Composition*. She has also published an edited book, *Teaching Academic Writing in UK Higher Education: Theories, Practices and Models* (Palgrave Macmillan, 2006). From 2009–2011 she served as chair of the European Association for the Teaching of Academic Writing (EATAW), and, since Autumn 2011, has been the editor of EATAW's journal, the *Journal of Academic Writing*. She has also served on the executive boards of the European Writing Centers Association (EWCA) and the International Writing Centers Association (IWCA), and is an active member of the UK-based Writing Development in Higher Education (WDHE) research and discussion network.

Sarah Haas is a teaching fellow at the University of Ghent, Belgium. She also runs courses, retreats, and groups for writers from the United Kingdom, the United States, Europe, and Japan. Her research interests lie in the area of writer support and writer development. She is interested in finding ways to help writers gain confidence and self-efficacy, thereby developing into self-directed writers. She is also interested in writers' understanding and control of their own writing processes, and in what makes writers' groups work (or not). Sarah spends a lot of time designing teaching materials that will facilitate writer development.

Christine Hardy is a principal lecturer in the School of Art and Design, Nottingham Trent University. She has a PhD from Nottingham University in adult reading, which was published in 2008 — *To Read or Not to Read: Adult Reading Habits and Motivations*. Christine's recent teaching is focused on research methods and academic writing with postgraduate students. She also works across the academy leading pedagogic research and student induction. Her current research interest, and the subject of national and international publications, is student engagement. This includes transitions, academic writing and internationalisation, taking a student perspective. She is co-founder of the international network RAISE (researching, advancing and inspiring student engagement) who are currently organising their second international conference. She is a fellow of the Higher Education Academy.

Alison Hramiak is a senior lecturer in education at Sheffield Hallam University, working primarily with ICT Teachers and in Teach First where she is the Regional ICT Subject Lead for Yorkshire and Humberside. She also teaches on the masters and doctoral courses at Sheffield Hallam. Her research interests include, assessment and feedback, pedagogy and ICT — particularly

Web 2.0 technologies and digital literacy. She has published books and papers on these topics, nationally and internationally and presented her work at national and international conferences. She has co-written and edited a number of books on education and is a member of the national committee for information technology in teacher education and a fellow of the HEA.

Rowena Murray has an MA from Glasgow University and a PhD from Pennsylvania State University. She is fellow of the Royal Society of Arts and Higher Education Academy. She is Reader in the Humanities and Social Sciences Faculty at Strathclyde University. She is adjunct professor at Swinburne University, Melbourne. Her teaching and research focus on academic writing, the subject of her journal articles and books, including *How to Write a Thesis*, *Writing for Academic Journals* and *The Handbook of Academic Writing* (co-authored with Sarah Moore). Her research has been funded by the Nuffield Foundation and the British Academy.

Hilary Nesi is professor in English language in the Department of English and Languages at Coventry University. She was principal investigator for the project to create the BASE corpus of British Academic Spoken English (2001–2005), and for the project to create the BAWE corpus: 'An Investigation of Genres of Assessed Writing in British Higher Education' (2004–2007). She is interested in the design and use of dictionaries and reference tools for academic contexts, and in the teaching and learning of English for academic purposes. She was chief academic advisor for the EASE series of multimedia EAP speaking and listening materials, and is currently leading an ESRC-funded project to produce online academic writing materials for the British Council 'Learn English' website.

Patrick O'Connor is a lecturer in philosophy at Nottingham Trent University. He received his PhD from NUI Galway in 2005. He has taught at the Manchester Metropolitan University and the Open University. His teaching interests are 20th century European philosophy, 20th century French philosophy, ethics, and philosophy of religion. His research interests are mainly European philosophy, phenomenology, 20th century French philosophy and the philosophy of education. He has written on Derrida, Agamben, Husserl, Badiou and Lucretius and on various pedagogical issues. He has published in the *Journal of the British Society for Phenomenology*, *Journal of Cultural Research*, *Southern Journal of Philosophy*, *Discourse: Learning and Teaching in Philosophical and Religious Studies* and *Irish Studies Review*. His book 'Derrida: Profanations' was released in 2010 with Continuum Press.

Melanie Petch is a senior lecturer in writing development at De Montfort University, and has also taught undergraduate modules on poetry and society in the Department of English and Creative Writing. She has recently published a chapter on the mid-Atlantic imagination in 'The Cambridge Companion to Twentieth-Century British and Irish Women's Poetry' (2011). Her current research explores the value of writing groups on the research student journey, and is also looking at how creative writing practices can offer a playful entry into language for art and design students.

Index